Grand Schemes
and
Nitty-Gritty Details

GRAND SCHEMES
and
NITTY-GRITTY DETAILS
Library PR That Works

ANN MONTGOMERY TUGGLE
and
DAWN HANSEN HELLER

1987

LIBRARIES UNLIMITED
Littleton, Colorado

Printed in the United States of America

LIBRARIES UNLIMITED, INC.
P.O. Box 263
Littleton, Colorado 80160-0263

Library of Congress Cataloging-in-Publication Data

Tuggle, Ann Montgomery.
Grand schemes and nitty-gritty details : library PR that works /
Ann Montgomery Tuggle and Dawn Hansen Heller.
xvi, 237 p. 22x28 cm.
Includes bibliographies and index.
ISBN 0-87287-565-2 : $19.50
1. Public relations--Libraries. I. Heller, Dawn Hansen.
II. Title.
Z716.3.T83 1987
021.7--dc19 87-21171
CIP

Libraries Unlimited books are bound with Type II nonwoven material that meets and exceeds National Association of State Textbook Administrators' Type II nonwoven material specifications Class A through E.

Contents

First Things First
Introduction

Every library, of every type, has a public relations program. Granted, it may be an unplanned one. It may even be a "bad" one. But in every library situation, an impression is continually made on patrons, staff, policy makers, and local media. That's why we are firmly convinced that effective public relations can't be left to chance.

If the old adage "nothing succeeds like success" is true, then those who don't want to leave anything to chance—those who are looking for ways to create successful public relations programs for their libraries—should examine, extract from, and emulate the efforts of those libraries that have award-winning public relations plans. To us, such adapting seems eminently logical and practical.

ABOUT GRAND SCHEMES

Since 1978, we have annually reviewed the winning entries in the John Cotton Dana Library Public Relations contest (see figure A). We have scanned the winners' scrapbooks, which document the range of approaches, the techniques, and the results of their library public relations campaigns. We have reported on the winners each year in our newsletter, *Library Insights, Promotion, and Programs* (*LIPP*).

Rather than starting with theoretical "models" and then inductively offering guidelines to be followed, we have concentrated on looking at numerous programs with "winning ways," discovering the principles and elements which are obvious in these efforts. As a result of our analyses we have identified nine "grand schemes" which we believe are at the heart of successful and winning library public relations programs.

Chapters in part I concentrate on these nine grand schemes or public relations principles that have worked in real public relations programs in actual libraries of all types. Each principle is explained and illustrated by selected examples from the award winners. The appendix lists all winners cited in each chapter. We regret that it was not possible to include every Dana winner.

John Cotton Dana and the Dana Awards

John Cotton Dana was a librarian noted as a pioneer in librarianship. Born in 1856, he was graduated from Dartmouth in 1878, studied law for two years, and served as a surveyor in Colorado in 1880-1881. Admitted to the New York Bar in 1883, he returned to Colorado as a civil engineer in 1886-1887.

It was in Colorado that he began his third career, librarianship, serving as the librarian of the Denver Public Library from 1889 to 1897. During his tenure at Denver, he opened the first children's department and was the first to open all bookshelves to readers. During this period, he was also elected to the presidency of the American Library Association (1895-1896), the eleventh to hold that office.

The City Library of Springfield, Massachusetts, was Dana's next professional library post (1898-1902). This was followed by his long tenure at the Free Public Library of Newark, New Jersey, which was under his leadership from 1902 until his death in 1929. While at Newark he opened the first branch library for the business community.

Dana founded the Special Library Association in 1909. Throughout his career he was known as a change agent, a gadfly, and a thorn in the side of conservative elements in the library profession. Always he promoted library service to patrons through outreach techniques that were revolutionary for his time.

Because of his important role in librarianship, the premier award for library public relations has been named for John Cotton Dana. Established in 1946, these awards are made to libraries or library organizations of all types that submit materials representing their public relations programs.

The John Cotton Dana awards are jointly sponsored by the Public Relations Section (PRS) of the Library Administration and Management Association (LAMA), American Library Association, and the H. W. Wilson Company. A judging committee from PRS meets each spring to review all entries, and winners are presented with citations during the summer ALA annual conference. Winning entries are on display during the conference and are also available on interlibrary loan from the ALA Headquarters Library.

Fig. A.

ABOUT NITTY-GRITTY

Part II tackles the nitty-gritty details. These chapters provide practical tips for designing and judging programs, successful public speaking, working with printed pieces such as newsletters and annual reports, and communicating via slide shows and videotapes.

Part II offers very specific suggestions on how to proceed, with hints from voices of experience to help readers avoid common pitfalls and outright disasters. These chapters are intended as a foundation upon which to build. They are not, nor could they be, the one source, an instant training manual which all of us might seek. However, we believe they will help the reader know which questions to ask when starting in a new direction which requires additional personal and professional skills. We have included significant detail to provide a sense of what is involved, for example, in preparing a slide show or an annual report. Finally, we present an overview of the processes usually followed to enable intelligent discussion of a project with others.

Examples from library programs are used, where appropriate, to illustrate the nitty-gritty details, but there is a greater emphasis on offering a useful how-to-do-it guide and reference section.

HOW TO START

We suggest that readers start with the chapters in part I to gain insight into what the library award winners have done. The nine grand schemes—the general principles—should be related to each library's individual situation and present public relations efforts. Which ones are currently being used? Which are most neglected? Which ones seem to offer the most promise in accomplishing current goals and objectives?

The reader is then ready to consider part II, particularly chapter 9, "How to Design and Judge a PR Program," especially if the library does not now have a plan in place, or if the current plan needs revamping and strengthening.

Once that key element, the public relations plan, has been designed or improved, the reader can return to specific chapters in part I for insight and inspiration, and can also refer to the other nitty-gritty chapters in part II as needed—when he or she is involved in specific activities such as developing a video production, designing a newsletter, or drafting a speech.

One other way to access the information we have gathered is through the index. For example, the index can be consulted for citations to specific efforts related to a fund-raising campaign or a library dedication. Similarly, ideas for other types of public relations efforts such as statewide library awareness campaigns or library anniversary celebrations can also be found through the index. All libraries whose public relations programs have been cited are also listed in the index; all states where these libraries are located are also indexed. This, too, should prove useful since other libraries of similar types or close geographic location often face similar obstacles and problems.

IN CONCLUSION

Good ideas are not dated. They certainly are often adaptable to other settings. In fact, if an idea has been successful in one place, there is a good bet that it can be transferred successfully to another.

One of the recent John Cotton Dana winners used "Not alone—but together," as a theme for a year-long campaign for all the libraries in a library system (Illinois Valley Library System, Pekin, Illinois). We applaud that concept.

We believe that by sharing ideas we are all enriched. And improved library public relations will mean stronger support for library service, better informed patrons, and a greater sense of worth for library staff.

So, onward—to grand schemes and nitty-gritty details.

Part I

❋❋❋

GRAND SCHEMES

1
Winners Develop a Wide Variety of Approaches

What makes a winner? Each year, the judges of the John Cotton Dana Library Public Relations contest must determine the answer to this question. The John Cotton Dana Library awards, presented annually by the American Library Association and the H. W. Wilson Company since 1946, recognize outstanding achievement in the promotion of library service to the community. When the countless scrapbooks, videotapes, slide presentations, and other documentation of effort arrive in New York City for the week-long evaluation session, the members of the committee must be prepared to weigh the efforts of the library entrants and judge the success of their public relations (PR) programs. There are two different categories in the Dana contest. "Special awards" recognize outstanding efforts for individual projects. The other category, "national winners," acknowledges exemplary comprehensive public relations programs.

Are there certain qualities that characterize the public relations campaigns of the award-winning libraries? After an analysis of winning entries in the last decade, we identified nine qualities that are apparent in their PR campaigns. These are the basis for the chapters in part I of this book.

CAMPAIGN QUALITIES

"Campaign" is a particularly apt descriptor for successful public relations programs, for they incorporate many of the qualities that are inherent in military campaigns. For example, there are long-range planning; strategy, timing, analysis, and deployment of resources; and assessment of gains or losses, in preparation for future "battles." Throughout the ages, military historians have analyzed the great campaigns. They have studied the battle plans, looked at the impact of strategies and ploys, and drawn lessons which future leaders can learn and apply to their own encounters.

So, "What makes a winner in library public relations?"

The Winner's Circle

Like military historians, we have gone to the actual campaigns – to the successful "battles" fought and won and to the winner's circle – to determine what makes a winner in library PR. In looking at those libraries which earned prestigious *comprehensive* Dana awards for outstanding PR campaigns, we have identified nine important qualities inherent in these public relations efforts. Because we believe these qualities are significant and that other libraries can benefit from a study of them, the chapters of part I have been structured around these nine "grand schemes." Winners:

- develop a wide variety of approaches
- form partnerships with other groups
- offer strong programs featuring services and resources
- capture attention with imaginative, creative ideas
- spotlight special events
- use eye-catching graphics
- demonstrate a concern for people, both patrons and staff
- create an appealing, "we care" environment
- find ideas to adapt creatively.

Winning libraries have been able to offer ongoing and sustained public relations programs because their boards, directors, and staff members understand the importance of these qualities. It is true that not every campaign may include all nine grand schemes, just as successful military campaigns will vary because of unique topography or local conditions. But, in general, a majority of these nine are incorporated in the various winning entries.

The first grand scheme is of overriding importance: *library winners develop a wide variety of approaches in their campaigns.* They do not rely on a single strategy to inform, to change attitudes, to urge participation, and to promote action. They know that there are times for subtle diplomacy and times for a blitzkrieg, and sometimes there is a need for both. Therefore, in this discussion of tactics available to libraries in their public relations campaigns, we provide a brief summary of the individual grand schemes that we have identified as hallmarks of library PR winners. In succeeding chapters an in-depth analysis of these principles is delineated, along with representative examples of each grand scheme as used by libraries, as well as tips for incorporating each scheme in library PR strategies. Since winners develop a wide variety of approaches in their campaigns, it is important to illustrate what some of the various combinations can be.

Profitable Partnerships

First, *winning libraries form partnerships with other groups.* Military leaders understand the importance of allies. Comrades-in-arms strengthen the fighting force, increase the available resources, and thus offer greatly enhanced chances for success.

This concept of allies is also true for libraries. It may be the business community, a service organization, or an interest club with which the library joins efforts. In chapter 2, an in-depth study of how winning libraries form partnerships with other groups is offered. In terms of developing a wide variety of approaches, these partnerships are often an important part of an overall PR campaign, for they offer the same kinds of advantages—strengthened numbers, more resources, increased media attention, etc.

Programming Priorities

The second grand scheme which characterizes PR strategies of winning libraries is *they offer strong programs featuring their services and their resources.* In military affairs, commanders draw up battle plans and marshall their arguments to support the strategies that offer the best opportunity to use their strengths—in personnel, supplies, and equipment. Smart generals build upon the solid core of men and materials that they command.

Smart library PR operatives also design programming that is focused on the strong segments of the library's collections, including those that are new as well as those that are long established, and the library's services, both traditional and unique. Chapter 3 illustrates that programming is a significant approach used in virtually all of the campaigns conducted by library national winners.

Using the Unique

Winning libraries capture attention with bold, creative imaginative ideas. Their efforts are filled with sparkling ideas and clever, catchy slogans. In military history, the general who surprises opponents and comes up with the unorthodox, wins the day. Napoleon said, "Surprise is the essence of tactics," and it is these brilliant strategies that capture the attention of military scholars.

Similarly, our attention is captured by the creative and even the unorthodox ideas that the library award winners have used. Certainly, these national winners recognize the value of that which is unusual and eyecatching (not just flashy) and appropriate for the library's purposes. Creativity is high on the list of strategies that winners include in their public relations, and is an important element in overall campaigns. We examine them in detail in chapter 4.

Spotlighting Special Events

In any military history, there are high points, turning points, and focal points which were pivotal to the outcome. Occasionally these are happenstance, occurring by accident or coincidence. But more frequently these turning points are a result of precise planning and diligent application of effort—surprising to others but not to those who precisely planned and diligently labored.

The inclusion of special events in winning comprehensive library PR programs is the result of advance planning and hard work by library staffs. Certainly, those libraries which include them in the PR repertoire have found that *special events put the library in the spotlight.*

In chapter 5 we present a variety of these library stars whose performances in special events merit enthusiastic applause. We also look at how these special events can serve as a focal point for broader PR campaigns.

Great Graphics

It is essential that libraries *use eye-catching graphics to enhance the library's image.* Because contemporary advertisers spend hundreds of thousands of dollars to produce 30-second television spots or create magazine ads, the public has become a highly sophisticated audience.

Notice how military enlistments are sought by the use of highly polished visual campaigns, from appealing television ads to colorful brochures and recruitment posters. Remember: "The Marines: all we need is a few good men," and "Be all that you can be, join the Army."

For these reasons, library managers whose libraries win John Cotton Dana awards find it essential to use appealing graphics to enhance the library's image. They know because they are competing for attention with all of the other media messages being produced today, an important grand scheme in their public relations plan is a professional approach to graphics.

Chapter 6 illustrates the variety of approaches that library winners employ to develop noteworthy graphics. We also consider methods that can be used to produce affordable and attractive items, even when the budget appears to be austere and staff artistic talent limited.

"People" People and Places

Another grand scheme centers on the significance of people in all successful PR campaigns. *Winning libraries demonstrate a concern for people, both patrons and staff.*

The best battlefield commanders have always inspired deep, abiding loyalty in their officers and the troops they command. The very heart of successful library public relations is also an abiding and demonstrated concern for people, both patrons and staff.

In chapter 7 the variety of ways in which winners make evident their concern for people is examined. These libraries are easy to recognize because they have staff members who wouldn't work anywhere else. Often these libraries succeed in securing community support and funding, while surrounded by libraries that are struggling to exist.

Can a library's appearance convey a "we care" atmosphere to patrons? Our library winners often demonstrate that it can for they believe it important *to create an appealing, "we care" environment.* This is another of the grand schemes, and in the final part of chapter 7, we provide suggestions on the variety of ways that a warm and caring ambiance can be cultivated.

Profitable Pirating

Another quality often found in the PR campaigns of library winners is that there is adaptation of ideas from other fields of endeavor into workable solutions for that library. In other words, they continually monitor what is happening in business and industry; the newest trends in advertising; in the print and electronic media; in education; and in government and social services, not just to provide information to patrons but to seek out workable solutions to the challenges facing the library.

These library managers recognize that no one has a corner on the market of good ideas, and they understand the concept of creative adapting – taking an idea from one setting and modifying it to suit theirs. *They find ideas in the real world to adapt creatively*, which is the last of the grand schemes. It might be the adaptation of an evaluation form for guests at a popular motel chain, which with a bit of restructuring and rewording, can serve as a library patron satisfaction questionnaire. Or perhaps the library is able to copy a local department store's clever use of inexpensive items to create an unusual window display. National advertising campaigns with catchy slogans have also proven to be fertile ground for libraries which creatively adapt them to promote their own services.

The use of creative adapting is certainly evident in our winner's circle. In chapter 8 we document a number of fascinating examples of creative adapting at work in libraries of all types.

Nine to Count On

These are the nine grand schemes that are often employed by library PR champions. This brings us back to the first principle or grand scheme involved in the creation of successful comprehensive PR programs – *winners develop a wide variety of approaches in their PR plans*, making use of any or all of the tactics we have briefly described. They may not use all of them in a single plan, although we suspect that they frequently do. Certainly, some elements will stand out as more significant than others in a particular program. But the central concept is that a comprehensive library PR program will be based on a carefully developed plan that incorporates specific objectives related directly to the overall goals and objectives of the library.

Part of the entry form for the Dana contest asks for a list of the objectives of the PR efforts undertaken. It is understood that successful PR doesn't just happen. Public relations must be planned and designed to suit the objectives of the library.

NEEDS AND STRATEGIES

Once the library staff has identified what they want their PR program to accomplish, they must decide on the strategies they will employ. In other words, first they determine priorities such as: "We want our teachers to incorporate reference skills in the curriculum," "We want to establish visibility for our new hot line information service," "We want to increase attendance at preschool story hours," or "We want to educate local officials about the library's long-range financial needs." Then they are ready to consider the variety of possibilities for doing so.

Certainly, this process will include the identification of the specific groups of patrons they are trying to reach. Who are likely candidates to use the new hot line? Which groups of preschool children are currently not enrolled in the story hours? What civic officials are most in need of accurate information and which ones have the power to assist the library in its quest for additional funding?

Once library staff members know which specific groups they are trying to reach, they are ready to consider the various ways or methods they can use to inform and influence each of the "publics" that have been identified and targeted. This is why a library with a well-executed and comprehensive public relations program will incorporate a variety of approaches in that program.

The saying that a plan is based on "different strokes for different folks" is common among PR types. In other words, different target groups or publics must be approached in different ways. The method that will be effective in reaching and influencing civic officials will probably not be the best method to reach the mothers of preschool children. Therefore, the first grand scheme is the importance of a variety of approaches in the design of a PR plan.

Arizona Approach

A number of comprehensive library PR programs examined in this book illustrate this point, including the winning effort developed and executed by the Tucson Public Library. Attractive print items incorporating the library logo were a high priority for Tucson, and they were designed so they could be used for a number of different target audiences and a variety of purposes. One attractive folder was used primarily for flyers accompanying new library cards. However, the fold-up design of the folder allowed other types of pamphlets for other audiences to be inserted. The folder's versatility encouraged the library staff to assemble packets for all types of outreach to other groups.

Appealing flyers were prepared in Tucson to promote the wide variety of programming for which the library is famous. In order to appeal to all sorts of audiences in the Tucson area, program topics run the gamut: taxes, inflation, self-expression, crafts of all types, and how teenagers could get a summer job. These are just a few examples of the kinds of programming that is an ongoing effort in this library.

The Tucson Library actively seeks special grants and builds library public awareness through these special focus programs. Often they come up with clever schemes that attract local media attention. As a concluding activity for the third year of a National Humanities grant on the Sonoran Heritage Project (see figure 1.1), for example, they asked community members to contribute to "100 bright ideas on ways to make our region a better place to live." Submitted items could be far out or down to earth. This program attracted media attention since it had a natural appeal for the community at large. In addition, the library included the top 100 ideas submitted in a packet of materials that was distributed as a final part of the humanities project.

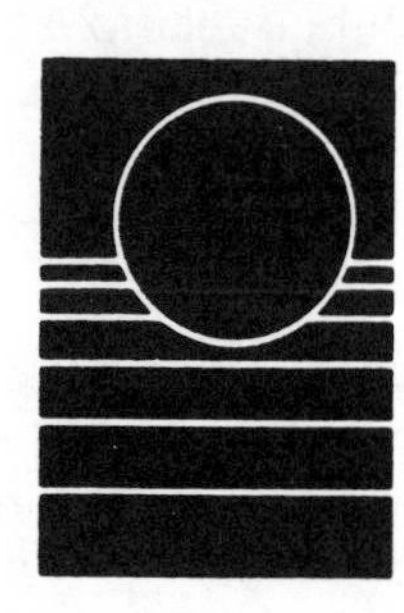

Fig. 1.1. Sonoran Heritage Project logo. Reprinted with permission of Tucson Public Library, Tucson, Arizona.

In another successful grant program, the Tucson Public Library sought and received a Library Services and Construction Act grant and used the services of a professional advertising agency to prepare materials for a campaign to stimulate public awareness of the need to read to and with children. The Plant the Seed: Read program used a wide variety of approaches including an attractive logo which was developed and incorporated on all kinds of items such as billboards, T-shirts, book bags, and bumper stickers. Other tactics included the Friends' group participating in the campaign by selling many of these items, and radio and television interviews highlighting the campaign.

Sometimes a new service needs a special promotional effort. In Tucson it was a new information hot line at the main library. A special press conference/reception proved effective in gaining media attention for the I Thought You'd Never Ask campaign. In fact, the library reported that the telephones started to ring immediately.

Publications, specialized programming, community input, specialized grants focusing on particular audiences, use of all kinds of media from television to billboards, press receptions, and an active Friends' group are a representative sampling of the Tucson PR program.

And They Understand in Utah

Specialized programming and unique printed pieces have been the hallmarks of the Salt Lake City Public Library's wide-ranging PR efforts. Here, too, the planners have understood the importance of a wide variety of approaches in their efforts.

To encourage interest in a Friends' used book sale, Salt Lake City sponsored a combination Book Sale and Collectors' Fair and Exhibit. Local collections of all sorts of items, from matchbooks to buttons, autographs to dolls, were included. This was a successful special event for the library as library receipts were over $8,500.

Since teenagers and their parents were identified as an important target audience, the library's Young Adult (YA) department sponsored a valuable back-to-school workshop for parents and teens. Featured were programs on school learning problems and on teen health issues. It worked and they drew excellent crowds.

Handsome posters are a hallmark of the Salt Lake City approach to advertising their special programs. Especially worthy was one on white water rafting, as well as another for a foreign film series cosponsored by the local chapter of Alliance Française. This program included discussions in French after each evening's French movie classic.

Building in New York

Building campaigns and tax referenda, although special purpose PR efforts, require the same variety of approaches in order to reach the various constituencies involved.

What happened in Somers, New York, when the public library began its new building initiative is an excellent example of a comprehensive PR program in action. The campaign relied heavily on advance planning, volunteer effort, and community involvement. Seven different subcommittees were established, each with specific assignments to meet.

The campaign organization used a number of ways to reach out to involve others and to influence public opinion.

1. The publicity and community relations committee was responsible for brochures, mailings, flyers, news releases, ads, posters, and radio spots. They established a liaison with a local printer and with a professional graphics designer. They also selected and ordered promotional devices such as buttons, pens, and shopping bags.

2. A door-to-door campaign committee involved the library's trustees as cochairs. They recruited and trained volunteers, who called on residents ahead of the referendum date. Also they organized an election-day phone campaign to get out the vote.

3. A speaker's bureau worked hard to get prolibrary speakers on the agendas of clubs and organizations in town.

4. Several mailings were planned and coordinated by a special mailings committee.

5. Realizing that school children and their parents were natural allies, there was a school and youth committee to provide information at school functions, and speakers for classrooms and faculty meetings.

6. A special event, designed to focus attention on the library's proposed new building, was held in connection with the Lions County Fair, a popular annual event in the community.

Notice how many of the grand schemes were employed by these planners. The chronicle of the campaign earned a national Dana award. The hard work at Somers also resulted in the passing of the referendum and a new building for the public library.

Statewide Efforts

Coordinated statewide efforts to increase library awareness and library use have also required that their planners identify their target audiences and then plan the types of approaches to use in their campaign. In Florida, for example, the Council for Florida Libraries adopted as its slogan "We're your public library: IT'S OK TO GET SMART WITH US" (see figure 1.2). A multimedia approach was undertaken tapping all possible avenues of communication, including promotion gimmicks such as buttons, stickers and key chains; radio and television public service announcements; newspaper articles and graphics; posters; flyers; and even billboards.

Fig. 1.2. "Get Smart" campaign. Reprinted with permission of Council for Florida Libraries, Fort Lauderdale, Florida.

A grid was created identifying major newspapers and the types of library services/programs receiving coverage. The grid was then filled in with the dates the articles were published showing at a quick glance which papers were giving coverage of which services.

A fascinating sidelight of this Florida campaign is that it became the basis for creative adapting in other locations, which helped identify this campaign as a winner.

A statewide campaign in Pennsylvania also used a number of the approaches we have identified. Again, a bright, attractive logo was developed and an effective slogan was used: "Your Public Library: WE HAVE THE ANSWERS."

Pennsylvania worked hard on involving businesses and other state agencies. This approach to partnership not only brought some financial backing, but it also extended the ownership of the project to others. It also greatly increased the exposure of the promotion to the public. For example, Sears, Roebuck and Company printed one of the "how to" flyers which was part of the campaign and distributed it to all customers who purchased items in the home improvement sections of their stores.

An approach to creative financing in Pennsylvania involved the purchase of air time for radio and television spots to guarantee good exposure. Then the planners negotiated for matching public service time (doubling the total airtime available to promote the statewide campaign).

School Ways

Principles do not differ when planners are in different types of libraries. Although PR objectives will be specific for the goals and objectives of the institution, a variety of approaches will be needed to reach the objectives, no matter what kind of a library is involved.

Such was the case in Union Public School District in Tulsa, Oklahoma. When a local grant was secured to upgrade the book collections in the school libraries, the media services department used it as a springboard to publicize the libraries.

The theme Connections was an appropriate one as they proceeded to link each of the target groups they had identified. Administrators, parents, students, staff, and board of education members were all involved in some way. Teachers dressed as characters from their favorite books as part of Project D.E.A.R. (Drop Everything And Read), while library staff members wore T-shirts with reading slogans and book logos. School board members received scrapbooks filled with letters from students thanking them for the new books and explaining how they were using and enjoying the new materials (see figure 1.3). As a result, two more target groups were connected. (Notice once again "Different strokes for different folks.")

Fig. 1.3. Examining scrapbooks of letters to board members. Reprinted with permission of Union Public Schools, Tulsa, Oklahoma.

University Ways

At the University of Texas Health Science Center in San Antonio, circumstances also opened up the way for a carefully planned effort to acquaint specific members of their constituency with new library services. A new building and new online services were the impetus for a complete revamping of services, image, publications, and operations.

The first step was the identification of specific target groups, which included students and faculty, as well as area librarians and health professionals, the local press, former users, and community groups.

A library-wide PR committee was created to determine objectives and activities for the year. The first step taken by this group was to spend three months on internal public relations to inform the staff about all the new changes and to develop an ongoing system of communications. This continuing effort included regular presentations, a calendar of events, weekly staff newsletters, tours of the new building, hands-on demonstrations of the online catalog, regular staff time to discuss upcoming changes, and a special information flyer.

Then the library moved on to its external publics. A monthly newsletter began a regular chronicle of the upcoming move and online potential. Primary users came to a preview presentation where an update report was supported by handouts and a general brochure.

Once the actual move into the new building took place, activities increased. Daily tours were conducted, floor plans and brochures prepared, etc. Shortly after settling in, the staff sponsored Media Day and gave the local press carefully prepared press packets which included black and white photos. This day-long information session was followed by Community Week, which provided tours for community groups twice a day. Library publications were also redesigned with the help of other university departments.

The pattern should be evident. Public relations objectives are based on library goals and objectives, the identification of target publics or audiences, followed by a selection of a variety of approaches to meet those objectives and to reach the target groups.

Texas Style: Big and Bold

A final example of how a winner did it is the Houston Public Library, which received a $135,000 grant from the National Endowment for the Humanities (NEH) to provide a learning and reading program for adults called CITY! (see figure 1.4). They used it as an opportunity to create a blanket PR campaign that employed the full range of PR tools and a variety of approaches to spotlight the library.

Fig. 1.4. CITY! traffic light logo. Reprinted with permission of Houston Public Library, Houston, Texas.

The central thrust of the CITY! project was the cooperative development of programming by the library staff and affiliated humanists, which focused on the history, literature, architecture, films, religion, sociology, and psychology of cities in general. It was so successful, a second grant was approved for a program which highlighted living in Houston.

How was this success achieved? A full range of tools was used to promote the first project. A distinctive and dramatic logo, a traffic light with all three lights in green, gave the project identity. A local graphics artist and library supporter donated his talents, valued at $3,000, to design the logo, as well as the production expenses involved in coordinating the image with the program. This logo was used on all letterheads, press releases, press kit, television public service announcements, publications, posters, flyers, and whatever else was used to represent CITY! to the public.

A major effort was made to inform the staff as well as the public about the entire effort. Staff members were kept informed through workshops, meetings, newsletters, and copies of all press releases (prior to their public release). Switchboard operators, in particular, were targeted to receive all relevant information.

How did they endeavor to reach the population of Houston? They used dramatic posters in all libraries and throughout the community, including one which read, "Loving, Warring, Lying, Scheming, Building, Coping, Dreaming – the City in Fiction and Film."

Events calendars were not only hand delivered throughout Houston, but were also inserted in all Neiman-Marcus mailers, a contribution from the company.

Bus advertising posters were also used to publicize events. Extensive publicity packets went to all members of the local print media, gleaning plenty of coverage for the library. Several different approaches were used to involve the broadcast media. Taped public service announcements were created for radio and television. The advertising agency responsible for these announcements charged only for production expenses, donating its creative resources. Broadcast coverage of significant special events was also sought and obtained.

One of the most impressive special events in the program was a Kickoff reception with 5,000 invitations sent to representative leaders in all fields in the city of Houston. Later a special fund raiser netted $20,000 for the library's humanities collection. The gala featured a nostalgic and current fashion show by Neiman-Marcus, which was narrated by Houston's mayor, and starred library Friends. Included was a dinner dance on the library's plaza. The department store covered the various costs of the special affair, which allowed the library to realize the large financial bonus.

Strong programming, partnerships, creative and eye-catching graphics, and special events were among the different approaches used to reach a wide variety of audiences. Houston did them all, as do other libraries which understand the significance of grand schemes in PR.

2
Winners Form Partnerships

Partnerships, alliances, or joint projects—no matter what they are called, they are important for the continued well being of a library or media center. Many of the winners in the annual John Cotton Dana contest have recognized the strengths that can come from such alliances. It was no accident that a recent president of the American Library Association (ALA) centered his entire year in office around the concept of building coalitions for the public good.

Let's look at the wide variety of ways in which library award winners have built "bridges" in their communities, and the diverse groups with which partnerships have been formed.

BUSINESS LINKS

When the Milwaukee Public Library celebrated its Centennial—and won a Dana award in recognition of its efforts—they forged numerous links with various segments of the local business community. For example, a local lithographic company was also celebrating its 100th birthday, so the library arranged space for a special exhibit which featured the history of the company as well as samples from 200 years of printing. In appreciation of this recognition, the company printed the library's handsome centennial posters for free (see figure 2.1).

Another business link was made with the Milwaukee Downtown Merchant's Association, which sponsored a series of activities in the main shopping district during the library's centennial celebration. For example, there were:

- a used book sale at a bank
- story hours for children at a department store
- Ronald McDonald giving away library balloons at the local McDonald's
- movies from the library's collection shown at the downtown mall
- library information and displays in many banks and stores
- the electric company's prominent sign carrying the library's message

Fig. 2.1. Centennial Committee at work. Reprinted with permission of Milwaukee Public Library, Milwaukee, Wisconsin.

In addition, a local newspaper gave the library a gazebo for permanent displays of pictures in the local history room, and branch celebrations of the anniversary were made possible by donations from neighborhood florists and bakeries.

Another winner that made an alliance with local business was the Illinois Valley Library System, Pekin, Illinois. System staff coordinated a special display about member libraries and system services, which was placed prominently in an area shopping mall. They also recruited state legislators for a breakfast and tour of system headquarters—a smart move, since their funding comes from state appropriations.

Library Card Brings Bargains

The Ralph Ellison Library, Oklahoma City, Oklahoma, used an unusual approach to the business community to raise awareness levels about the library and to increase circulation figures. Also a Dana winner, this library won merchant cooperation in providing discounts or gifts to patrons with library cards. Discounts ranged from 5-30 percent. Other merchants offered one free item with the purchase of others, or reduced admission prices. Cooperating businesses included beauty shops, restaurants, banks, record stores, cleaners, and even the local high school, which offered discounts on lunches and football game tickets. This campaign was quite successful in making the library visible to patrons and the local business community. (See figure 2.2.)

Fig. 2.2. Bumper sticker. Reprinted with permission of Ralph Ellison Library, Oklahoma City, Oklahoma.

Friends Find Friends

Sometimes local library Friends groups can build partnerships with business, as was the case at the Louisville (Kentucky) Public Library. The Friends wanted to establish a gift shop that would serve as an ongoing source of revenue. The establishment of the shop was made easier by the carefully selected gift items which were donated by local businesses to help stock the store. This project garnered a Dana award for Louisville in 1982.

Sometimes when a business district is facing a rough situation, the library can help. The Duluth (Minnesota) Public Library conceived the Digging up Duluth campaign, joining with local merchants in an effort to keep patrons coming downtown despite the heavy construction going on in the central city (see figure 2.3). Capitalizing on a construction theme, library staff members wore hard hats and vests contributed by the city's public works department, while creative programming and special events kept patrons coming to the library. Grateful local merchants supported the effort with door prizes. For this imaginative approach to a difficult situation, the library earned a Dana PR award.

Fig. 2.3. Constructing good will. Reprinted with permission of Duluth Public Library, Duluth, Minnesota.

Corporations can sometimes become underwriters for library projects, which is what American Express did for the Broward County Library, Fort Launderdale, Florida. Not only did they underwrite the Book Bash, a book sale at the library, they also sponsored the Book Bash Dash, a kickoff event in which American Express challenged other corporations. In the dash, each member of a corporate team was assigned to dash to the library, get a specific book, and then sprint back to the finish line. The result? A successful fund raiser as well as a Dana award.

Incidentally, the participation in the library program by American Express was the result of the interest shown by one executive in the corporation. Moral: Corporations are made up of people who benefit from good library service just like everyone else.

Sometimes a partnership can be sought with specific specialized businesses. For example, when the Lincoln Library, Springfield, Illinois, wanted to sponsor a Bicycle Fair (see figure 2.4), they asked local merchants to help set up a display of related merchandise.

They also arranged with the Springfield Police Department to provide registration of bicycles owned by patrons to help prevent bicycle thefts. A nice library tie-in was the compilation of a Bicycle Resource Directory which included the names of local bike shops, bike related organizations, races, tours, registration facts, and library books and magazines about the sport. For this and other creative efforts Lincoln Library earned a Dana award in 1981.

COMMUNITY CONNECTIONS

When the Reading Public Library, Reading, Massachusetts, needed money for the conversion of a facility into a library, they turned to the various community organizations in Reading for help. Twenty-six different groups helped raise over $200,000. The theme that was used to get this kind of support and cooperation was Become Part of the Tradition (see figure 2.5).

Fig. 2.4. Breaking away. Reprinted with permission of Lincoln Library, Springfield, Illinois.

Fig. 2.5. Become part of the tradition (brochure). Reprinted with permission of Reading Public Library, Reading, Massachusetts.

Donations, raffles, carnivals, bowl-a-thons, and Las Vegas nights were some of the ways that money was raised by the groups for the campaign. Especially noteworthy was a flower show held by the local garden club to raise money for landscaping the new library. A strong plus for this kind of fund raising is that all groups share in the effort and the library becomes a true source of community pride and interest.

Other libraries have found unusual ways to raise funds. In Harrodsburg, Kentucky, the Mercer County Public Library took advantage of the keen interest in basketball in their area. A Hoops for Books basketball game between two local teams brought the library $2,000. A special appearance by Coach Joe B. Hill and the University of Kentucky basketball team added to the festivities of the evening. This was a high-scoring Dana success story.

In Ohio sports figures also attracted interest to the Columbus and Franklin County Library in Columbus. Members of the local baseball team were solicited to appear in television public service announcements supporting the library's summer reading program, The Best Game in Town. When baseball players talk about their favorite children's books, the children listen and the library wins.

Literary Link

A statewide program in Florida, coordinated by the Council for Florida Libraries, offered author and book events/programs for local libraries sponsored by local Friends' groups. Authors gave of their time, while publishers helped with their appearances. The council prepared promotional materials, helped set up radio and television interviews, made the contacts, and gave awards to all who were involved. They earned a Dana award in 1984.

Events varied from community to community, ranging from coffees to luncheons and dinners. Key West sponsored a four-day Literary Tour and Seminar, which rapidly outgrew its original 75 capacity facility (see figure 2.6). Friends' groups were especially enthusiastic about this campaign.

for The Third
Annual Literary Seminar

© Karsh, Ottawa

HEMINGWAY: A Moveable Feast

PANEL DISCUSSIONS at Tennessee Williams Fine Arts Center.

RECEPTION at Sloppy Joe's.

BOOK & AUTHOR LUNCHEON with Patrick Hemingway at the East Martello Museum.

TOUR & COCKTAIL PARTY at the Hemingway House.

FILMS & SLIDE SHOW

REMINISCENCES, PHOTO EXHIBIT & MEMORABILIA

FIREWORKS DISPLAY

In addition to George Plimpton, Patrick Hemingway and Charles Scribner, Jr., over a dozen internationally-known Hemingway experts will participate in this four-day homage to Hemingway.

Cosponsored by the Council for Florida Libraries, the Hemingway Society, *The Miami Herald*, the Monroe County Library, the Friends of the Monroe County Library, the Broward County Library. Funded in part by the Florida Endowment for the Humanities with support from the National Endowment for the Humanities, the Florida Endowment for the Arts with support from the National Endowment for the Arts

Council for Florida Libraries, 1700 East Las Olas Boulevard, Fort Lauderdale, FL 33301, 305/525-6899

Fig. 2.6. Author's festival. Reprinted with permission of Council for Florida Libraries, Fort Lauderdale, Florida.

With Friends Like This

Many libraries have Friends' groups that repeatedly prove their worth as partners. The Tucson Public Library has such a group. In support of a special literary campaign, Plant the Seed: Read, Tucson Friends sold bumper stickers, book bags, and T-shirts.

A particularly notable effort was made by the group at the Green Valley branch of the library. In this retirement community they supported the creation and promotion of two nearby trails enabling visitors and residents to enjoy the flora and fauna of the desert. One of these walks was hard surfaced to accommodate wheelchairs and the handicapped. The Dana award was presented to them in 1981 for this and other outstanding PR campaigns.

A combination of Friends and volunteers have given a total of over 9,000 hours of volunteer service to the Handley Library in Winchester, Virginia. These volunteers are responsible for the design and creation of all of the flyers and posters used to promote the library, as well as arranging for the printing. Members of the volunteer corps also write the library column for the local paper, and develop the library's programming efforts as well as publicizing them.

Such efforts have included the development of a series of children's programs which merited a Virginia Humanities Council matching grant. For fund raising the group sold $1 ticket/chances on a large dollhouse which had been built and donated by the local Home Builders' Association and decorated by the Friends. This is an example of a real partnership—a donation of time, talent, and money—which can serve as a model for other small town libraries. Handley Library was honored at the annual H. W. Wilson ceremony as a 1981 winner.

VIP Volunteers

A partnership between the library and its volunteers was the focus of a special campaign waged by the Los Angeles County Public Library of Downey, California, winner of a Dana award in 1985. The library used the theme, Volunteers Are VIPs, and created a videotape which featured actual volunteers on the job. Its purpose was to attract additional volunteers by showing the many and varied tasks volunteers perform—everything from working on displays to helping with storytelling.

The program was so successful the library eventually had to end it because there were more volunteers than they could adequately train. Throughout the effort, the emphasis was on building a sense of belonging and of showing volunteers how much they were needed.

Volunteers were also the keystone to the success of a financial campaign to raise money for a new library for the Westbank Community Library in Austin, Texas. One of the clever approaches used was the creation of a Square Foot campaign, with a logo designed as a squared-off human foot (see figure 2.7). To receive a square foot, donors gave $100 or more.

Fig. 2.7. Buy a foot. Reprinted with permission of Westbank Community Library, Austin, Texas.

Volunteers for Westbank also paid for a special folder for donors, and worked with the local newspaper to get a 16-page supplement included about the campaign. The campaign resulted in a Dana award and $147,000 for the building campaign.

Public relations experts understand the importance of influencing those people in the community who are influential, whose opinions are respected by others. The York County Library System, York, Pennsylvania, made a conscious effort to inform the "key communicators" in their service area. Over 800 individuals were chosen to receive educational materials about library services through monthly mailings. The library system directly credits increased county allocations to these efforts. The lesson for others in this 1985 winning campaign is that libraries can't wait for the movers and shakers to come to them; they have to go out and win them.

Cooperation – Every Which Way

Another library that successfully sought out community groups to help with a funding problem was the Brown County Public Library, Green Bay, Wisconsin. When money for children's programming was threatened with cuts, the library staff sought out other community organizations who were interested in children's programs. Through the support of a variety of these groups, programming was continued.

One particularly successful joint project was with a local hospital junior auxiliary. Called The Body Shop (see figure 2.8), this annual program focuses on wellness, offering a variety of experiences and information for children. They can try out a hospital bed, use crutches or a wheelchair, have their weight and height taken, vision and hearing checked, learn about nutrition, walk through a heart model, and practice calling 911 for emergency help. Promotion is done through schools, churches, day-care centers, and local doctors.

The Brown County Library used other cooperative partnerships in their 1982 winning campaign. Local folklorists and a department store's teen board helped the library with the Blue Jeans and Blue Grass Day, a blue grass concert with an appealing informal tone for teenagers.

At the DePere branch, Future Farmers of America and Four-H clubs assisted with a Family Agri-culture Day, which offered exhibits and family programming. Visitors could make cheese and butter, watch chicks hatch, and see farm animals. The large red tractor on the library's front lawn was a vivid promotion device.

One other program Brown County sponsored which received cooperation from many community leaders and agencies was their Any Time, Any Place, Any Book story hour program. Many people, including members of the Green Bay Packer football team, read and told stories in various places including in ice cream shops, at the Packer Hall of Fame, fire stations, the wildlife sanctuary, a television station conference room, and pediatric wards in the hospitals.

Because Brown County had no line item for children's programming, it was essential that they reach out to other agencies for support, expertise, and help in funding such programs. Although it would be foolish to say that libraries have an advantage in not having a programming budget, the Brown County did not use it as an excuse for doing nothing. And they used the cosponsorships as positive factors in raising public awareness.

Special Help from Special Interests

Sometimes the special interests of service clubs accommodate the needs of the library. In St. Paul, the Junior League had a special interest in the St. Paul Library's Raising Readers (see figure 2.9) program, which encouraged children to read. During Children's Book Week the efforts were extended to reading aloud by celebrities such as the mayor and the police chief. Pleased with this program, the Junior League went on to provide funding for an audiovisual presentation, brochures, booklists, and library workshops. With their efforts the library garnered a 1986 PR award.

Fig. 2.8. Check-up at the library. Reprinted with permission of Brown County Library, Green Bay, Wisconsin.

Fig. 2.9. Encouraging readers. Reprinted with permission of St. Paul Public Library, St. Paul, Minnesota.

When the Louisiana State Library started to plan for the first statewide summer reading program, staff members approached the New Orleans World's Fair organization for permission to use Seymore D. Fair, the fair's official mascot (see figure 2.10). Permission was granted and the fair organization also provided the services of their graphic artist at no cost to the library. Reading and All That Jazz was a success and the library's total statewide effort received a Dana Special Award.

In Kentucky, the Department for Libraries and Archives also understood the value of partnerships and their recent statewide reading program was also a Dana award winner. Using the theme Adventures in Kentucky with Library Jones, they formed an alliance with the Kentucky Department of Tourism. The partnership made possible the production of quality materials, prizes, and activities for the summer program. Even the governor participated by drawing the winning entrant for the grand prize – a weekend adventure in the Kentucky state park of the winner's choice.

The tourism office also negotiated arrangements with the State Fair Midways attraction group, enabling children to get free ride tickets in exchange for books read in the summer program. Also provided were free T-shirts and logo pins for participants.

All Kinds of Partners

One final example of a unique partnership is the Prince George Public Library, Prince George, British Columbia, which arranged a special celebration in honor of the 70th anniversary of the arrival of the railroad in their community (see figure 2.11). Many special events were held including programs, speakers, and exhibits. The focal point, however, was the grand celebration at the library in honor of the opening of the festivities. At this event the local brewery donated all of the Iron Horse beer required for the party. A good time was had by all, and a second celebration held when the entire campaign earned a Dana award for Prince George Public Library.

Fig. 2.10. Seymore D. Fair, Mascot. Reprinted with permission of Louisiana State Library, Baton Rouge, Louisiana.

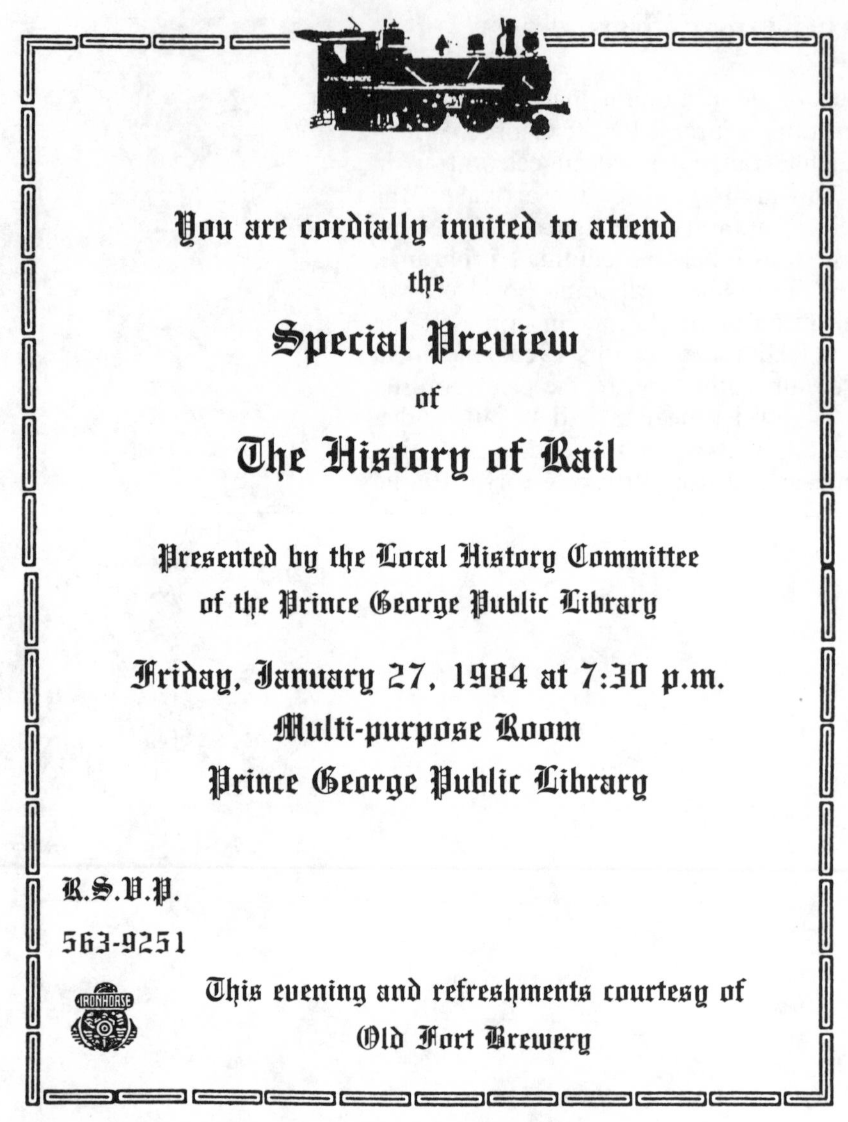

You are cordially invited to attend
the
Special Preview
of
The History of Rail

Presented by the Local History Committee
of the Prince George Public Library

Friday, January 27, 1984 at 7:30 p.m.
Multi-purpose Room
Prince George Public Library

R.S.V.P.
563-9251

This evening and refreshments courtesy of
Old Fort Brewery

Fig. 2.11. Celebrating the railroad. Reprinted with permission of Prince George Public Library, Prince George, British Columbia, Canada.

PARTNERSHIPS:
A Systematic Approach

To paraphrase the late John F. Kennedy, "Ask not what the other group can do for you. Rather, ask what you can do for them." Then you will find that you will end up doing things for and with each other. So that your library can use partnerships well, let's take a look at some of the central concepts for cooperation and communication with partners.

Analyze the Group

There are five principles and procedures that should be adhered to and followed before a renewed effort is launched to increase partnerships, alliances, coalitions, and joint projects. First, spend a considerable amount of time analyzing the group. This first principle is the most important one because it is the basis for the other four which follow.

Be sure you understand the group's purposes. If they publish a newsletter or other kind of publication, either locally or nationally, be sure to scan a number of issues. This will tell you a lot about the thrust of the organization. Look carefully at the membership, considering not just numbers, but age, sex, economic and educational levels, residence, etc.

Please do not misunderstand. We are not suggesting that some groups be ignored because they don't measure up. Rather it is important that the nature of the group's membership is understood so that you do not try to begin cooperative efforts of a kind that are inappropriate. For example, if a group is largely composed of working mothers, don't try for daytime programs requiring their presence. This is a simplistic example, but many efforts fail when the group is not carefully studied to be sure that the suggested cooperative plan is feasible.

When studying the group, also be sure that the way in which the group finances its own activities is examined. If possible, find out what kind of a budget structure they have. Again, this will provide valuable insight when resources and budgets for joint projects are developed.

Do they have frequent fund-raising activities? Do they achieve their own financial goals? If they are having a hard time staying alive, they may not be able to work with you on projects that require financial commitments. But remember, these groups may have other kinds of resources such as expertise or access to a different segment of the community, so don't dismiss them out of hand.

Take a good look at their structure. Do they have any local paid staff? Do they have a physical facility? Are there elected officers? If so, how many, how long do they serve, and at what time of year do they take office?

Beyond the local level, is the group affiliated with a larger district, state, regional and/or national organization? If they are, how autonomous are they in deciding on joint projects? How much support can be expected from a larger affiliate in terms of money, staff talents, equipment, facilities, or even just good publicity for any joint projects?

Again, there are possible pluses and minuses in each type of situation, but you have to know where the power is: who can make the decisions, who can allocate the staff or volunteer efforts, who is needed to make sure the group really does support any venture that is planned.

Urging you to recognize the power base is not meant to sound cynical. Many projects get bogged down in the red tape of group process because the library staff has not done its homework and does not understand why there are problems. It is difficult enough to get a cooperative project off with another group without adding additional difficult hurdles in the path.

Another area to analyze is the geographic area that the group services, or the communities or neighborhoods from which the membership is drawn. If the library is trying to reach a particular group, defined by geographic boundaries, then it is important to choose a partner which serves the same area.

Look at Activities

Principle number two is to take a long look at the other group's major activities. How are they related to their purposes? How active is the group? What percentage of members seem to participate in ongoing meetings and events? Do they offer programs or services to nonmembers? In other words, is this a viable, healthy organization? Or does it have the potential to be so?

Find out about their yearly calendar of events. Is there a high season as well as periods of lower activity? This is important to recognize because some groups may be perfect for joint projects if they are correctly timed. However, the group may be highly pressed for time if asked to take on something else during their most critical project of the year.

Other Liaisons

The third principle is to explore whether or not the potential partner has any other kinds of liaisons or partnerships in place. If so, it is an indication that they are willing to participate in such arrangements. Looking at the type of group with which they have established a cooperative effort may also provide an idea for projects *you* can productively suggest. In addition, you should try to rate the degree of success that these other cooperative activities have attained. In other words, is this group a winner or a potential winner? Or can you find ways to help them become winners through working with your library?

Find Their Needs

The fourth step is a critical one as it focuses on an analysis we suspect is frequently omitted. Once the basic information on the group—their activities and their other liaisons—is in place, then you must relate your strengths to their needs. Too often we only ask, "What can they do for us?" In addition we should ask "What do we have that they might use to enhance their activities or serve their clientele or membership?" Possible answers include:

- specialized information
- staff skills
- facilities
- communication tools or avenues
- equipment on site
- programming in place
- reputation in community

Use Their Strengths

Finally, as a fifth step, relate their strengths to your needs. Identify their areas of expertise, their specialized information and/or staff and membership skills. Consider their methods of communicating with the public or with their members. The fifth step probably won't be difficult since you chose the group because you felt they had something to offer.

By using the five steps, start to consider new and different groups for partnerships and cooperation, and raise your thinking to a higher level of creativity. Do not close off avenues which might be pursued successfully.

The best result is one that finds overlapping needs and areas of interest between two groups or institutions. Then both will have a commitment to any joint effort and both will work diligently to see that it succeeds. And, one successful cooperative project generally leads to another—either with the same group or with an expanded list of partners.

PRESIDENTS' BREAKFAST

An idea for reaching out to community groups on an annual basis is to invite the current presidents of all groups to a Presidents' Breakfast at the library or the school district. This leadership breakfast is an excellent way to honor participants for their contributions to the community and to show off some feature of your library or school. It is also an effective way for you and other staff members to get to know the leaders of your community.

The invitation list for each community will be slightly different, but the list should include all of the various service groups, the parent-teacher organizations, village or city council or board presidents, the library board, and the school board. Also include groups such as American Association of University Women, the garden clubs, the newcomers and women's clubs, and certainly the senior citizens. Additional varieties of groups that might be considered as potential partners are listed at the end of this chapter. Finally, be sure to include editors, appropriate reporters, and photographers from the local newespaper.

The main purpose for such a gathering is to get your message out. Certainly there is some feature of your program that would be of interest to these community leaders, for example a new service, special series, or upcoming event. In selecting your program, remember that it must be one of interest to this diverse audience, one the guests might want to share with their own club members. Also there is the opportunity for future speaking engagements by library staff members resulting from this kind of program.

It is important that just one topic be selected for the program. Don't rehash ongoing activities as it can appear "old" and unappealing. Your topic should also be one that is broad in interest so your target group will feel you are offering something that will affect the community and interest a broad spectrum of citizens. It is not necessary to have a topic that is directly related to the audience. For example, currently there is broad interest in computers, literacy, and reform in American education. You will need to assess your own library setting and community to determine what would be of interest and what messages you wish to communicate.

A program that includes either a demonstration, tour, or audiovisual presentation is particularly effective in that your message is reinforced and the program has added appeal.

How to Organize

The microcomputer is an excellent tool for building a data base of organizations and their addresses, meeting dates, and names, addresses, and phone numbers of current officers. The file needs to be updated annually with the names of new officers, with a series of phone calls which can be accomplished in a few days. Such a mailing list has value for other purposes, but labels can easily be generated for the breakfast invitations.

Before actually scheduling your first breakfast, be sure you have built your data base. If the library does not have an up-to-date list, check with city hall for a list, and screen local newspapers for announcements of club meetings. If the community or school caucuses in your area are made up of representatives from organizations, check these resources. Ask other people who are active in the community for the names of groups.

If you have a microcomputer available, use any of a number of simple computer programs available for mailing lists and labels. You can also use a more complex and versatile program that can be used for other purposes. It is important to ascertain all of the types of information that would be useful to you. For example, do you want the names of the program chairperson or the president-elect as well as the president? Do you want to know the date of elections for new officers? Do you want the groups' meeting date, time, and place?

Time and Place

The next step in planning for a Presidents' Breakfast is to establish the date and time for the affair. Local conditions do vary as does the availability of space. In some suburban communities an 8:30 a.m. start is appropriate. It is also important to set an ending time as well and to include it in the wording of the invitation. Keep the total time under two hours; ninety minutes is even better. In this way guests can determine if their personal schedules will allow them to attend.

When conducting the actual program, it is important to adhere to the time frame established. A natural break in the program for questions or departure for a tour should be provided for guests who wish to depart gracefully. Guests will be more inclined to encourage others to attend the next year if you stick to your schedule. Naturally the schedule will depend upon available facilities and the food service you plan.

With all details in place, it is now time to design and mail the actual invitations. It is important to stress that this is a Presidents' Breakfast and that they are special people.

And Now for the Food

It is possible to get away with juice, sweet rolls, and coffee, and if your budget and facilities are limited, it may be necessary. But if possible try for something more. For many institutions, especially schools, it is often possible to tap the services of the cafeteria staff and offer more in the way of a breakfast menu. Scrambled eggs, sausage, fruit cup, and homemade muffins, served on tables seasonally decorated with napkins and small vases of flowers or greenery will make for a breakfast that is truly designed for special guests.

Because such a breakfast is an important PR effort, library and school boards will often approve extra expenditures. However, a high-priced caterer and an elaborate buffet will bring an adverse reaction from the people you are trying to reach. Isn't this a case where a Friends of the Library group might help?

It Gives Us Great Pleasure

Although the selection of a program topic should be done first and included in the invitation, the details can be refined in the several weeks between the invitations going out and the actual event. Plan to distribute name tags at the door, and be sure that you and other staff members are on hand to mix and mingle. The availability of a pot of coffee for early arrivals will be much appreciated. Encourage staff members to sit at different tables. You may even want to designate a host or hostess for each table to ensure that everyone feels welcome.

Provide a *brief* greeting before serving breakfast. If you have planned carefully, you will know when to start your formal program because it has been timed and rehearsed in advance.

The best evaluation for this type of program is the invitations you receive to carry the message further or the opportunities which are created to explore joint projects.

LIBRARY PARTNERS: A List to Consider

In developing a list of possible partners for your library or media center, you may want to consider this compilation. Not intended to provide dramatic new insights, rather this list provides many groups with which libraries of all types have cooperated over the years. This catalog of categories is intended to stimulate you to start planning explorations in new fields. Only one or two ideas are offered in each category because we have already provided a wide compendium of award-winning partnerships. If you analyze potential groups, you will undoubtedly come up with your own prize-winning ideas.

Government Agencies

Consider boards and commissions of all types, particularly at the most local level. Check out the recreation department as an opportunity for joint programming. Also, concentrate on government's need for valid, up-to-date information.

Police and Fire Departments

School media centers as well as public libraries may find their expertise in video and cable would be appreciated by local police and fire departments. An informative cable or library series with tips from the local police or fire department on avoiding danger, scams, etc., is always a solid offering.

Medical Institutions/Associations

With the current emphasis on health and wellness, medical institutions and/or associations offer many possibilities for joint efforts. For example, one media center produces a cable series in cooperation with the education department of a local hospital. One typical program was on How to Quit Smoking, which was taped before a live audience.

Earlier in this chapter, we described how one library cooperated with a hospital auxiliary to sponsor The Body Shop for children. Consider also medical associations, home nursing services, charity groups related to specific diseases, dental associations, etc.

Service Clubs

The various service clubs are often involved in cooperative efforts with schools and libraries because by their very nature they are seeking to provide service. For these it is especially important to analyze in advance to make sure that your needs match their purposes.

Many service clubs can be helpful in library fund raising if they see a correlation to their own reasons for existing. For example, Sertoma Clubs often support projects and assist with fund raising for activities that serve the handicapped. Research and analysis of such groups is critical if you are going to be successful.

Cultural Agencies

In most communities there are a variety of cultural agencies such as zoos, museums, orchestras, and art leagues. They are natural candidates for cooperation because they often face the same kinds of difficulties as libraries—lack of funding, difficulty in publicizing programs, understaffing, etc. Consider shared expertise or joint program sponsorship.

One obvious way to show your interest and support is to become a member of these other organizations and institutions. If you are interested in them, shouldn't they be interested in you?

Realtors

Realtors have a front-line position when it comes to meeting new or potential residents of a community. In most cases homes are sold through realtors, and often larger firms serve as management agents for apartment complexes as well.

Increasingly these firms are turning to videotape as a tool in selling specific listings. A real estate board might be interested in sponsoring the development of a brief program for clients about the community, particularly its schools and cultural institutions, including libraries. This could even be a four-way cooperative venture among government officials, school staff, library, and the realtors.

Educational Institutions

School and public libraries have long sought and found ways to work together. Increasingly there are partnerships between these libraries and community colleges. Instances of providing loan privileges to college staff and students regardless of local residence or allowing community residents to check out materials at the college is increasing. Public libraries can be the site for off-campus video courses, or, if space permits, even a site for regular late day or evening classes. School and public libraries are natural allies which are important to cultivate.

Business and Industry

Expertise and special facilities and equipment are some of the main benefits of forming partnerships with business and industry. In the case of retail business, these companies often have public spaces that are ideal for promotion of libraries and their services. A mall exhibit, for example, is a good idea. Libraries that have placed branches in shopping malls recognize the value of high traffic. A multiple partner effort, with many different agencies setting up displays in the local mall to highlight their different groups and services, could have a greater impact than one agency by itself. Maybe all it would take is the library staff's ability to organize.

Service Personnel

One group of key communicators that is extremely influential in any community is service personnel, particularly barbers and beauticians. Lots of conversation goes on in barber shops and beauty salons, which is why it is important that these people have accurate information—they are in a position to pass it on. They also have expertise which can provide programs for the library in turn for free publicity.

An analysis of their needs that you can satisfy will be important in building a partnership. One suggestion might be a special seminar on use of microcomputers in small business establishments.

Churches and Synagogues

Libraries have often received special support from churches and church related organizations. In celebrating the many religious holidays throughout the year, they are a ready source of information and materials for programs and displays. Often churches starting church libraries need advice. The expertise of the library staff might save them a lot of headaches in the future. Libraries without meeting rooms have often been welcomed into the social halls or educational wings of local churches. Certainly there are ways they can work together.

Children's and Young Adult Agencies

Local preschools, scouting or campfire programs, the YMCA and the YWCA, and governmental agencies dedicated to serve the welfare of those under 18 are all rich sources for forming alliances. Young adult and children's departments as well as school library media centers share the same clientele as these groups. Therefore this is a critical coalition to build; you need each other for lobbying efforts and will probably find ways to cooperate in programming and publicity as well.

Senior Citizens' Groups

As the demographics of this country continue to show a shift to an older population, we have an obligation as well as an opportunity to look for ways to serve and cooperate with senior citizens' groups. Many institutions are also finding this a rich source of volunteers who are reliable and interested in helping community residents. Skills and experience ought not to be wasted. Here's a good way to find the manpower to establish a talent bank as well as a good source for many of its listings.

Media

Because of the power of the press and of television as well, it is only logical that a continuing liaison should be sought with these groups. One noteworthy idea was a seminar sponsored by a library for the officers of all clubs and organizations in town. The local newspaper staff and representatives of electronic media were invited to present information on how such groups could write effective press releases or public service announcements for their clubs. The program, which was held at the library, benefitted everyone.

And Many More

The preceding list is not exhaustive. Other considerations could include the legal profession, or restaurants, hotels, and motels. For school libraries, there are parent and alumni groups. Public libraries often work closely with special interest clubs such as garden clubs, literary societies, embroidery guilds, collectors, etc. There are many potential partners out there for your library to form a partnership with.

3
Winners Offer Strong Programs

For many libraries the central focus of their public relations effort is the planned schedule of programs offered for the various segments of the community they have identified as targets. There are a number of reasons why these libraries feel that programming is a worthwhile activity. First, such programming can be used to improve the circulation of materials. Certainly, a variety of programs will attract more people to the building. As a result it is also possible to acquaint more people with materials and services. This also helps patrons of all ages to form the library habit. Thus, those who do not usually visit the library can be encouraged to become regular users.

Programming that is targeted toward significant issues will also help enhance the library's image within the community. These kinds of programs demonstrate that the library is a place for lively debate and serious consideration of issues.

Finally, for many libraries, programming is a suitable way to offer various types of cultural enrichment to the community.

WHY DO IT?

There is a long tradition of programming for children by many libraries. However, efforts aimed at the general adult population are generally less frequent. Objections cited by some librarians to providing programming for adults include:

- not enough money, staff, space, or time
- not viewed as part of the library's function
- can't compete with other community groups

Often these are excuses for inactivity, and we feel that the previously mentioned positive results of adult programming outweigh these perceived drawbacks.

Because libraries are in the information business and programming is simply an alternate information source which offers an *active* experience with information, we must automatically be advocates for such efforts for all audiences.

WHAT AND WHO

Let's look at some practical aspects of such programming: How do we decide what to do and who is to do it? Active programmers use a variety of sources to determine potential topics, all selected to keep up with the current interests of patrons. They constantly scan television, radio, and newspapers to see what's going on in the immediate area and what special topics are repeatedly showing up.

For example, one librarian recalled seeing a small article about a Buddy Holly memorabilia collection in the local paper. She called the man and ended up with a program which was not only immensely popular but attracted everyone from teenagers to septugenarians. In addition, the program was free.

Effective programmers also listen to their library patrons and keep track of their reading interests. Often they will suggest potential series that will be popular and provide additional information to those needing it.

Survey techniques are also helpful in identifying program topics. Surveys can be distributed at current program offerings, through library newsletters, organization and club meetings, or given wide distribution by cooperative local newspapers.

Potential library programmers are also encouraged to talk with key community members and to take advantage of studies made by other groups, such as local radio stations which must annually list public service needs that are not met in the community. These lists are generally available upon request.

ANALYZE THE ACTION

After gathering information in these ways, it is necessary to analyze what learning opportunities are already available, not only by topic but type. Although a course on a specific topic may be available locally, don't discard the idea for a one- or two-part program, which may serve the needs of another segment of the population.

Once a topic is determined, the next step is to find a presenter. Once an ongoing level of programming is established, the list of potential presenters usually builds rapidly, with talented people offering themselves, usually at no cost, as future presenters. This is the result of successful programming.

Naturally it is important to do some screening of such offers. Try to talk to someone who has heard the individual. Each potential presenter must be reminded of time limits, should be urged to include a question-and-answer segment, and warned against pushing their own service or product too insistently.

Hunting Grounds

It is also essential to seek out special presenters, generally from local sources. Common "hunting grounds" include schools, colleges, universities, civic groups, local artisans, agencies such as police and fire departments, museums, and businesses. It is also useful to ask staff members, friends, family, and patrons for suggestions. The result can be a rich file of people willing and able to offer quality programs.

One cannot generally expect spontaneous success, however, once a program is scheduled. You should not ignore practical planning components. A detailed discussion of PR planning is provided in chapter 9. However, a simple four-part plan that can be useful in preparing for each library program includes a consideration of:

- community need
- evidence of this need
- efforts currently being made to help meet this need
- what the library should do (if anything)

Once you have determined the program's objectives and considered if the results are worth the effort, you are ready to proceed with related exhibits and booklists.

PROGRAMMER'S LIST

One of the most important items on the programmer's list is room logistics. Nothing can kill an effective program faster than a poorly arranged room, or one that is uncomfortable for an audience. Temperature, ventilation, lighting, acoustics, and properly working audiovisual equipment and microphones must be verified and checked out ahead of time.

A number of other items to consider:

1. Publicity possibilities, both before the program to attract an audience, and after to build awareness of the library's ongoing offerings. The preprogram publicity should be related to the target audience that has been identified.

2. Contents of program and quality of presenter. Careful records should be kept of each offering so that successes can be repeated and less than satisfactory efforts can be improved or avoided.

3. No show speaker. As advocates of the "What if?" school of planning, we must always imagine the unimaginable and determine how to meet such a challenge. In programming, it should be "What if the speaker doesn't arrive?" For a major presentation, you might consider having a local back-up program. Or if the topic lends itself to small group discussion, you should be prepared to dust off your best small group leader skills and let the audience members become their own program. This kind of sharing can be successful and popular.

No Show Audiences

It's equally difficult to handle the no show audience. Sometimes bad weather or unforeseen bad timing cut into the size of an audience. In some ways this is a more difficult situation. Honesty at the moment of scheduling is undoubtedly the best policy. You need to explain to speakers that the size of the audience can vary widely. Sometimes a pre-registration approach can be taken, even if no fee is charged, and a commitment made by audience members to attend. An effective technique is to promise to provide specialized materials and handouts to all those who do make a registration commitment in advance.

Program with Partners

Another good way to guarantee a base of support for an audience is to form partnerships for your programs, as described in the previous chapter. In this way the burden of building an audience is shared with the partners, who also have a membership or clientele that are logical candidates for the audience.

Gauging Opinions

Be sure, also, to build in an evaluation for each program you offer. Have each participant fill out a brief questionnaire at the conclusion of the program. A body count isn't always an effective measure of opinion. A small crowd may indicate weak publicity, bad weather, or poor choice of date, but if the small group is enthusiastic about the program, that is the most meaningful evaluation.

PRIZE WINNERS

Since one of the grand schemes is the importance of programs, let's take a look at a number of prize-winning efforts starting in Oklahoma where the focus was on helping libraries strengthen their programming efforts.

For Adults Only

Because it had been determined that libraries statewide needed experience in programming for adults, the Department of Libraries began a PR program to tap the skills of those experienced in this area and to provide nonthreatening support services for those who were inexperienced. In addition to introducing adult programming, the Department developed program kits which could be used by both small and large libraries in the state. They also launched a program to create a public awareness of library programs available to adults. A monthly guide was begun to stimulate ideas and give suggestions to local programmers.

Once a program package was developed, the state staff wrote a step-by-step handbook for that package, including publicity materials such as news releases, feature stories, clip art, bibliography of books and films, publicity ideas, and special event planning. A speakers' bureau was developed and published for librarians, and information on grants for public library programming was distributed.

The adult program kits were announced to the library community in a unique graphic presentation titled Contains Adult Material (see figure 3.1). Circulating exhibits were available to local libraries and there were also small grants available to help libraries to fund special programs for adults. Once the adult programming was underway statewide with the prepackaged kits, local libraries were invited to develop program kits of their own.

A key element in the success of the PR activity was the networking between libraries that was encouraged through meetings of librarians from across the state at least three times during the year. From the beginning the program planners enlisted input from the librarians in order to answer questions, share concerns, and develop relevant programs. This two-way communication was essential for the supportive effort which culminated in wide acceptance of a type of library service which was new to many of the librarians as well as Oklahoma residents.

Fig. 3.1. Meet the author kit, developed for the "Adults Only" campaign. Reprinted with permission of Oklahoma Department of Libraries, Oklahoma City, Oklahoma.

Prepared with Care

Some of the most striking prize winners are those whose programs were based on grants from the National Endowment for the Humanities (NEH), or from state humanities councils. Because such grants require careful and detailed advance planning as part of the application process, they have a built-in potential to be successful in stimulating wide community interest and participation.

For example, in 1986 the New Hampshire State Library coordinated their first statewide campaign. Called the Mill on Main Street, it focused on cultural, social, architectural, and economic impacts of industry throughout the state and in local communities. The state library led off with several programs and exhibits which presented a statewide view. (See figure 3.2.)

To encourage cooperative planning and resource sharing, participating libraries were required to develop additional programs and/or exhibits focusing on local industry. These local programs also incorporated the partnership concept as they were required to involve at least one local community agency or organization.

Fig. 3.2. Mill on Main Street. Reprinted with permission of New Hampshire State Library, Concord, New Hampshire. Art work by Todd Smith.

To emphasize the statewide aspect, a unifying and identifiable project logo and distinctive image and style were developed for visual pieces. Publicity was primarily on a local level, although the unifying graphics and the availability of the state project director as a consultant helped to ensure the extent and quality of the publicity. Posters, calendars, exhibit guides, and essays were uniformly designed and produced. Flyers and bibliographies were done in-house, keeping costs down. A three-month calendar was mailed to those on the mailing lists of the state library, the state historical society, and the state humanities council. In addition, each public and academic library received one calendar for display, while participating libraries received 250 for distribution. Thus, even patrons of nonparticipating libraries became aware of the campaign going on within their state. In all, the project produced 35 programs, two traveling exhibits, and six local exhibits as well as pamphlets written by local historians in support of the project.

The Dana award judges cited the New Hampshire efforts for its excellent organization, visual appeal, use of volunteers, and wide dissemination of information. Undoubtedly, the nature of the theme the Mill on Main Street, which touched on the central role of industry in the life of New Hampshire communities, contributed greatly to the success of this programming effort.

Heritage and History

Several NEH grants were responsible for programming that met specific community needs. In the early 1980s the Tucson Public Library won a Dana award for their three-year Sonoran Heritage Project. Because of the impact of the Sonora Desert on the lives of the people in the Tucson area, the library offered programs and related materials about the people, ecology, history, plants, and animals of the desert. Study guides helped participants to take advantage of all kinds of resources in addition to the formal public programs.

In Rhode Island, a series of programs about the state's past, present, and future called A Lively Experiment was also an NEH funded project (see figure 3.3). This first cooperative, statewide effort at library programming in Rhode Island won a PR award "... because the project offered a lively example of how a humanities grant and concept can be used to enhance library programming."[1] Research and publication of original support materials for use at the local level was an important component of this project.

Fig. 3.3. A Lively Experiment. Reprinted with permission of Providence Public Library, Providence, Rhode Island.

Similarly, the DeKalb Library System, Decatur, Georgia, won a Dana award for "a year long campaign bringing local scholars, writers, publishers and readers together for humanities programs in the public libraries of the system."[2] The three goals established by DeKalb for the campaign were: to explore the current writing of the Atlanta area; to provide a forum in which local writers could be encouraged; and to gain public attention for southern literature.

The program titles in this series suggested the nature of the project—Roots in Old South—Reflections of the New, and A Southern Fried Festival of Local Authors (see figure 3.4). To guarantee that there would be a continuing impact from their grant, the library system arranged to tape book reviews of 39 related titles that the public could borrow.

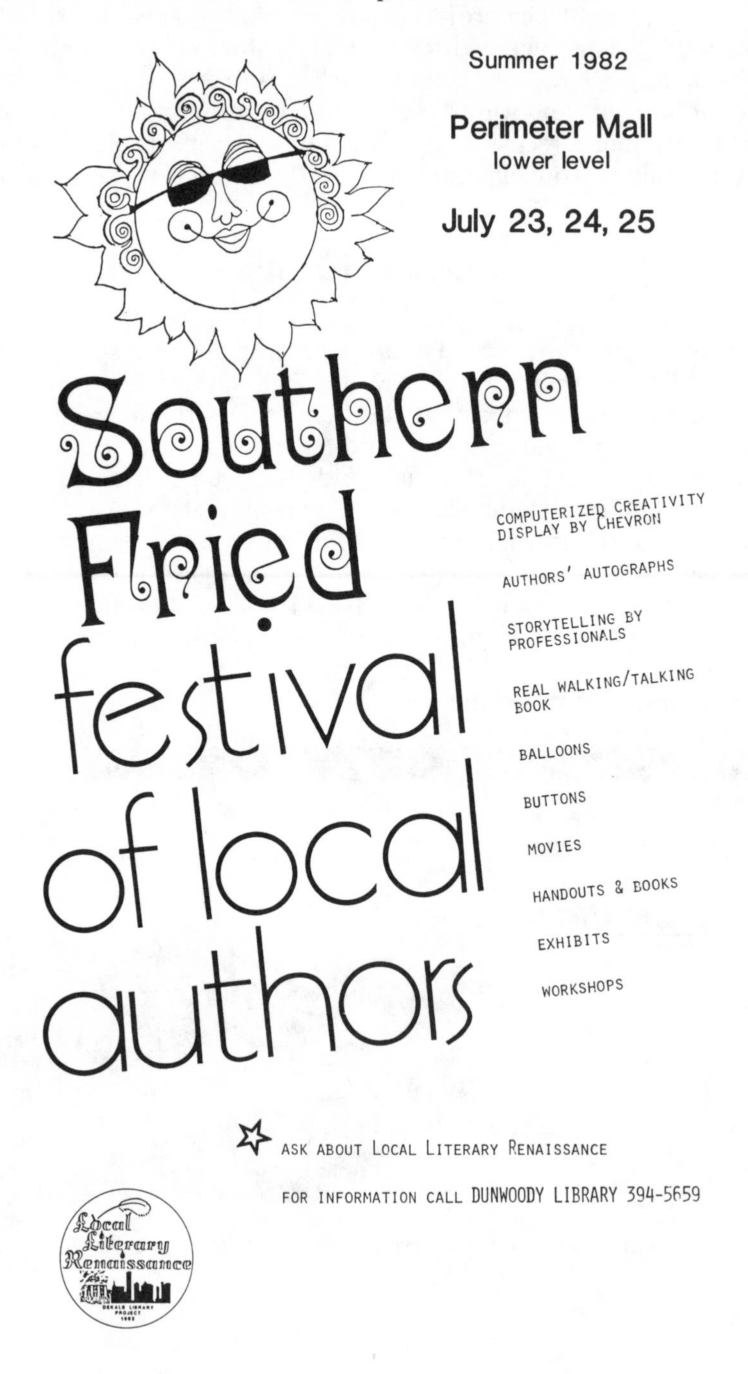

Fig. 3.4. Roots in the Old South. Reprinted with permission of DeKalb Library System, Decatur, Georgia.

Schools can also benefit from humanities grants. The Riverside-Brookfield High School Media Center, Riverside, Illinois, coordinated programming for the entire community with a grant received from the Illinois Humanities Council. Built upon the theme Alone Together: Conversations about Relating (see figure 3.5), several elements were incorporated:

1. Four humanists from the Chicago area gave lectures on the subject of alienation, with a focus on families.

2. Community actors and actresses auditioned for roles in four dramatic productions based on relevant dramatic literature. The productions were taped in the school's television studio.

3. A professional television producer and theater director were employed to work with student crews.

4. Volunteers were trained to lead small group discussion following the presentation by the humanists and the playback of the related videotape production. Over 400 residents signed up for the series, which was offered at no charge.

Fig. 3.5. Community outreach. Reprinted with permission of Riverside-Brookfield High School, Riverside, Illinois.

For this and other programs, the school was awarded the National School Library Media Program of the Year. As we have seen, the key to success in these programming efforts is the selection of a central core or theme that is significant for the community, the region or the state.

On the Track

Another winner that selected a unifying theme for year-long library programming was the Spokane Public Library, Spokane, Washington. The Year of the Train provided residents a look at the impact of railroads on the city's growth.

Starting with a proclamation by the mayor which marked the official opening of the celebration, the library offered a wide diversity of programs and activities in support of the "train year." For example, nine Sunday afternoon events were presented at the library by scholars and other experts and then repeated at community centers. A film series which focused on trains was offered in combination with background commentaries by railroad experts.

The Spokane Public Library also tied in traditional annual library events such as National Library Week and the summer reading program, which ended with a hobo party for all children who participated. Other related efforts helped to provide a continuing spotlight on the year-long program, in which nearly 10,000 people were involved. It's obvious that this library's programming was on the right track.

Tied to Special Events

Although many libraries use their anniversaries or "birthdays" as occasions for special events, some will build a major programming effort around the date. For the Milwaukee Public Library, Milwaukee, Wisconsin, their centennial prompted a series of related programs. For example, branches offered sessions on tracing one's roots, with the assistance of a local genealogical society. Other program topics included the history and uses of herbs and spices, tatting and rug braiding demonstrations, and the art of spinning and weaving. Barbership quartet concerts were enhanced by stereopticon slide viewing and homemade ice cream and birthday cake.

Houston Public Library was honored for an "exemplary, totally coordinated public relations program that focused on community interests and needs and one that was researched, planned, and executed in an extraordinary manner."[3] The Dana judges noted that Houston offered programs that were notable in both quantity and quality. (See figure 3.6.) Their topics included filmmaking and screenwriting, architecture, parenting, magnet schools, alcohol abuse, and marriage issues. Some unusual topics were also a part of their calendar: coffee tastings, a car show featuring "low riders," and appropriate for Houston, a cowboy demonstration of roping skills.

Not Just One Approach

It is important to note that successful programming does not fit a single mold. Local conditions and timing are factors to be considered. For Milwaukee, the library's centennial was a suitable occasion around which a whole year of programs and events could be built. On the other hand, Houston Public Library targeted programs to specific segments of their population and offered a wide variety of topics which would appeal to a broad spectrum of residents.

Another library that has consistently offered a wide range of programs with great success is the Lincoln Library, Springfield, Illinois. In addition to a variety of film series, they have held workshops on writing resumés; offered a sign language course; sponsored a chess tournament; provided workshops on stained glass, calligraphy, and furniture refinishing; and offered programs by a science fiction author. This whole range of programs was promoted through exemplary graphics, another consistent hallmark of the Lincoln Library's PR efforts.

AGE GROUP PROGRAMMING: Seniors

Good library programming is often targeted to special audiences delineated by age. In addition to the offerings for the adult patrons, libraries have traditionally striven to provide stimulating programming for preschoolers and elementary age children. Many libraries also schedule programs for young adults. Recently there has been a growing interest in making specialized efforts toward the programming needs of senior citizens.

In order to be successful with these kinds of age related programs, it is important to consider the unique qualities of each targeted group. When considering programming for senior citizens, it is important to avoid lumping all of them into one group. There are many diversities within the over-55 age group. Effective planning for programs requires that we remember that this is not a homogeneous but a diverse population which may stretch from 55 to 95. A second caveat is that when serving senior citizens, one must refrain from even a hint of a patronizing attitude, which is both insulting and demeaning.

Fig. 3.6. Diverse programming. Reprinted with permission of Houston Public Library, Houston, Texas.

Perhaps the most useful approach is one that could be characterized as holistic. Libraries exist to improve the quality of life for patrons, either through access to information or educational and cultural programs. Programming, then, should be focused on topics which offer enhancement to the lives of participants. Remembering our diverse population, we need to look for variety in our programs, and in each case we must ask, "For whom is this targeted?" The interests of senior citizens are often not different from the interests of the rest of the adult population. In fact, some members of this age group are turned off if a program is labeled, "For the aged."

Bring on the New, Too

Senior citizens are also interested in new things, not always just those that are reminiscences. There is often a misconception that programming is meant to fill their empty hours. Rather, senior citizens are looking for things to do that are meaningful, that will enrich their lives. When planning programs for senior citizens, there are other related items which planners must take into account.

There are physical changes that accompany aging, which need to be taken into account. For example, there must be accessible bathrooms. Higher levels of illumination are generally needed, and careful consideration given to sound systems as hearing problems are common. Program areas need to be easily accessible, chairs need to be comfortable, and parking areas well illuminated and safe. Some libraries, when offering programs, attempt to provide free rides for senior citizens, within the constraints of always scarce funds.

When programming for seniors, as with other services, library staffers should seek partnerships with outside agencies that also serve this population group. In this way, the efforts of all such organizations, including the library, are strengthened.

PROGRAMMING FOR CHILDREN

Few would argue against libraries serving children because there is the recognition that how libraries treat children will be carried over in their minds when they are adults. They will view the library as they have always seen it, either as a comfortable, welcoming place for learning and fun, or as an unwelcome, cold, austere place.

One of the most compelling reasons that children's librarians are ardent advocates of programming is that it contributes so significantly to high visibility for the library and helps build strong community support. Programs bring large numbers of children through the library doors. Unfortunately few, if any, statistics are available to prove that children's programs produce lifelong library users. Conversely, there are no statistics available to prove that they do not. But one thing can be said for sure; if programs do little more, they at least expose children and their parents to the library.

Libraries are always seeking good publicity, and children's activities bring in plenty. Within this book there are a number of detailed descriptions of Dana award winners which won those awards on the basis of special kinds of programs for children.

Children's librarians also recognize that libraries are in the information business and that a good program has information. Programming is a continuation of this central library function and a key method to make children aware of all the materials the library has, a reinforcement of the variety the library has to offer.

An important element in children's programming is knowing the audience in order to prepare the best program. We can't use our childhood or even our children as a basis for knowing the audience. Time and communities change and so do forces working on children. A knowledge of the clientele is important for material's selection, for other services, as well as for programming.

YOUNG ADULT PROGRAMMING

Advocates for specific library services for young adults speak out loud and clear on the importance of recognizing that this is a specific age group that ought to be served. An obvious benefit is that every teenager who becomes a regular library user is a strong candidate to become a library advocate as an adult. Schools and public libraries are natural allies in providing services to youth of all ages, and both types of libraries share the opportunity to do so, including library programming.

Young adult (YA) programming is not necessarily easy; it takes time, commitment, and a clear understanding of purpose. Unfortunately, with budget cuts in both school districts and public libraries, the first areas usually hit are the media center or the YA department. Part-time staff with divided duties are often harried and need guidance in serving this age group. Consequently, the following discussion on YA programming will prove helpful.

How do winners do it? One model is what was done by the Albany Public Library, Albany, New York. The staff developed a teenage promotion which "combined school visits and programming, to bring 'em into the library."[4] They began with a needs assessment whereby YA librarians visited schools and conducted a poll of teenage interests. In one year this resulted in 25 programs and seven series of workshops, films, videos, and games that attracted 1,500 young adults. Popular topics included computers, music, fashion make overs, arts and crafts, and trivia.

Goals for Guidance

At the Prince Georges County Memorial Library System, Hyattsville, Maryland, six goals were identified for their YA programming:

1. To give teenagers opportunities to discuss ideas they have acquired from reading, viewing, and listening.

2. To introduce new interests and broaden existing ones.

3. To stimulate reading and the use of library materials.

4. To stimulate creativity.

5. To attract young people to the libraries.

6. To establish the library as a dynamic and integral part of the community.

From years of experience these Maryland YA programmers feel there are certain prerequisites to successful programming. First, know your teenagers. What are they interested in? What talents do they possess? What problems worry them? What kinds of questions are they asking each other, their parents, their communities? And equally important, what kinds of questions don't they even know how to ask?

Second, know your community. What other agencies serve teens, either directly or indirectly? Are there recreation centers, crisis centers, and/or youth groups in the area? How do young people get around? Do they own cars or bikes, or are they dependent on buses, parents, or walking? Where do teens congregate? Is there a column for youth in the local paper? Is the community hostile, supportive, belligerent, or tremendously positive toward teens?

Third, take a good look at your own library. How much time is available? What are your resources? How much support can you expect (or work to get) from the rest of the library staff and administration?

Finally, what's missing for young people in your community? What can I as a librarian and we as a library do to supplement (not duplicate) and originate YA activities?

Common Mistakes

According to Maria Pedak-Kari, YA specialist, two of the biggest mistakes in YA programming occur in planning. One is not allowing enough time to take care of all the varied responsibilities involved while still allowing for human limitations and unexpected emergencies. Whenever possible allow three months to develop a YA program. Work out a tentative schedule that allows for:

- locating people and equipment
- drafting, typing, and mailing correspondence
- allowing time for responses
- designing posters and flyers
- distributing posters, mailing, and distributing flyers
- assigning specific responsibilities

The other common mistake in planning is assuming that you can do it all yourself. It's not possible to be in three places at once, and it never hurts to invite an extra set of hands and feet to be there just in case. Decide who is going to create the displays, move the furniture, do the introductions, handle the photography, control the crowd, run the projector, etc. Help can come from an infinite variety of sources: fellow staff, teenage patrons, best friends, family, and any other willing workers.

Ask for Advice

Planning actually starts with seeking input from young people. Without their advice you stand a 50-50 chance of producing a tremendous program for an absent audience. There are a number of ways to find out what your teens think:

- Talk to them informally wherever you encounter them.
- Hold a tape-in or write-in session where they can express their opinions without adult interference.
- Form a teen advisory board which can also help later when programs are offered.
- Develop programs based on teen participation. Young adults have tons of talent, more energy than most of us, and a willingness to share both if properly asked.

Input, however, is only half of the communication process. In this initial phase, be ready to present your own interests, thoughts, and talents to them as well as asking questions. It is often easier for teens to react to a concrete idea than to come up with an original one. Work at developing a mutual interest in YA programming, with you and the teens as partners in this process. Set goals and objectives for yourself and your young adults. Are you aiming for one specific audience agewise and geographically? Are you presenting an issue, filling a void? Spell out your theme and purpose in the beginning for and with your teen clients.

Plan the Time

If you're in touch with both the community and the young adults, you will be able to avoid scheduling your program during conflict times such as midterms, vacations, date nights, the night a popular rock group is performing three blocks away, or when Susie, Tommy, or Joey is throwing the party of the season.

As a matter of fact, it's a good idea to ask teens what day and time is best, and if you want to start an addictive YA program habit, find one time that fits both teens and the library, every week or every month.

It also is a good idea to make some phone calls to church groups and youth agency contacts. Explain what you're planning and ask if they have any conflicts with the date or know of other conflicting events.

The time of day is another factor to consider. Evenings may be easiest for you, but if the young adults in your community depend on public transportation or the area has a crime problem, they may not come. Look at this issue from your patrons' vantage point and your community's habits and needs.

Choose a Spot

Where a program is to be held must also be considered. If a library meeting room is not available consider holding a program:

- on the floor of the YA section (if you have one), at a time when the library is closed or not busy

- at a recreation center

- in a church, warehouse, or school

- in a home

Be sure to consult with supervisors for approval before plunging ahead with definite bookings.

Using a locale outside the library often leads to cosponsors for the program, who can share the work load and expand your supply of resources. Other agencies, community groups, or libraries may all be considered possible cosponsors. Remember, it is important to include a cosponsor in the programming effort from its inception to conclusion. It is also important to determine in writing exactly who is responsible for what by when. This is to avoid last minute discoveries that usually start with, "But I thought you were going to do that."

Put Out the Word

It is imperative to the success of YA programs that the word be put out in the right places in order to reach the target audience. There are a variety of ways to let teens know about your program, including:

- posters and flyers
- articles and listings in local papers
- displays in the library, schools, stores
- announcements on local cable and radio
- church and other local newsletters
- public address announcements in schools
- letters to teachers and school library media specialists
- word of mouth (a good function of a teen advisory board)

Direct this publicity to key spots in the community such as grocery stores, bookstores, pizza parlors, community bulletin boards, and schools. Don't forget to alert the entire library staff to the program. One of the best PR tools is if you and the rest of the staff can share the excitement about a program with the public.

Remember the potential of displays on books and objects relating to the program which can arouse interest ahead of time, and don't forget to post the program information at these displays.

A Few More Hints

Other steps that should be taken before planning a YA program include:

1. Put things in writing. Invite outside resource people in writing, after you have spoken to them. Ask for written confirmation of time, place, date, and who is going to bring and do what.

2. Test any equipment before the day of the program to be sure you are a smooth operator and that no repairs are needed.

3. Set up as early as possible on the day of the event. If there's anything you can do the day before, do it. There will be plenty of other details to take care of just before the program.

4. Be there. But in the event you become ill the night before, appoint someone else as a stand-in. Keep that person aware of what's going on throughout the planning and implementing process. If no staff member is available, find a patron or trustee who'll troubleshoot for you.

And When It's Over

The program ends and you're entitled to a momentary collapse, but within 24 hours sit down and evaluate the program. Evaluation is probably the weakest element in all kinds of programming, but it is especially true for YA programs. If your program was a failure, don't spend weeks brooding about it. Everybody has failures; the idea is to avoid having them regularly.

In evaluation, ask yourself the following questions and write down the answers for your own reference.

- Did the program meet its objective?
- What problem(s) did I have?
- What would I do differently if I had it to do over again?
- What went right?
- Could a different or additional medium or format have been used?
- What feedback did I get from the audience?
- How many teens came?
- Would I do it again?
- Would I recommend it to other programmers?

If your audience didn't turn out, ask yourself:

- What other activities were going on?
- Was the program really in response to teenager's interests and needs?
- Was the program duplicating something else that had been recently presented elsewhere?
- Where did the publicity efforts go? Did teens see or hear about it?
- Were teens involved from the inception of the idea?

Develop a standard evaluation form to use for all of your programs. Keep these on file and reread them before planning your next program, and share them with the rest of the staff.

Programming for teenagers offers the library profession the opportunity to become a positive catalyst at the time in their lives when the doors of childhood are closing and doors to adulthood have not yet opened. When those doors *do* open, the young adult audiences will be ready for the excellent adult programs that libraries offer.

NOTES

[1]John Cotton Dana Award citation, Providence Public Library, Providence, Rhode Island, presented by H. W. Wilson Company, 1983.

[2]John Cotton Dana Award citation, DeKalb Library System, Decatur, Georgia, presented by H. W. Wilson Company, 1983.

[3]John Cotton Dana Award citation, Houston Public Library, Houston, Texas, presented by H. W. Wilson Company, 1984.

[4]John Cotton Dana Award citation, Albany Public Library, Albany, New York, presented by H. W. Wilson Company, 1985.

4
Winners Capture Attention with Creative Ideas

As children one of our favorite folktales was the story of King Midas. Having his golden touch, enabling the accumulation of untold wealth, has been a fantasy we have often appreciated, anticipated, and coveted. But, as adults, we realize the way to success is not through gold production by whim.

However, another type of magic touch is shown in the success of many John Cotton Dana award winners. These top-level libraries demonstrate a special ability to use their talents in a unique way. Creativity is their special gift; they know how to appeal through captivating phrases; they exercise their imaginations, and, in the process, seize the imaginations of others. They plan unusual events, seize unusual opportunities, develop programs untried by others, or change tried and true events into something out of the ordinary.

This special touch we feel involves a special way of thinking and of solving problems. It means looking at ideas with an eye and ear open for a step that's different from the moves tried before. It entails taking risks, a willingness to do something different, to take a chance, to go where no one has gone before.

Creativity in library public relations also necessitates knowing the audience. By understanding how a community thinks, what appeals to them, what experiences they've had, what they've responded to in the past, one gains a basis for knowing how much risk can be taken before venturing too far. What works in one community may not work in another. Then again, it may work with some modifications or adaptations.

It's impossible for us to delineate how one can be creative. We cannot say do this, think that, follow these steps and voila—the results will be unlike the ideas others have had. However, creativity in library public relations may be developed by reading, by watching what others do, by communicating with fellow professionals, and by being attuned to whatever may be a different twist to an old idea. Such activities help make one sensitive to what is unusual or unique. Certainly, perusing some of the entries of Dana award winners can inspire those who are lacking in the creative touch to notice how creative talent can be used for the good of libraries and programs.

THE "TOUCH" IN PRACTICE

Creativity and imagination abound in the activities of two-time Dana award winner Bad Axe (Michigan) Public Library. Bad Axe demonstrates that creativity and enthusiasm are excellent substitutes for a lack of funds to hire professional PR assistance. Armed with a small budget and a big imagination, the Bad Axe Public Library decided to make itself a focal point for the community, a place filled with interesting materials and services, overflowing with fun and fresh ideas.

A whodunit contest geared for young adults quickly captured the attention and cooperation of many local residents. The mystery revolved around who stole the original "bad axe" from the library. Recognizable personalities were spotlighted over several weeks through features in the local paper, which simply inquired if these individuals could be guilty but always left the question open. For example, the newspaper editor was pictured in a Superman T-shirt coming out of a phone booth with the caption: "Was it the young newspaper editor who needed an axe to grind?" In another feature, the school principal was shown above the caption: "Was it the school principal, noted for his strict discipline?"

While the paper identified suspects, only the library gave clues, which were printed on bibliographies of mysteries that were available near displays of mystery books. The contest brought the library attention, a change of image, and a chance to make friends within the community.

Another special promotion was developed for the video cassette collection. Posters styled after movie advertisements promoted the service with a flair typical of Bad Axe's efforts. The classic shot of Gable and Leigh featured in *Gone with the Wind* promos was recaptioned: "Frankly my dear, I'd rather check out a video cassette from the Bad Axe Public Library." In another, Katherine Hepburn, as a prim little missionary, tells the disheveled Humphrey Bogart as he tends the *African Queen*, "Pour on the steam, Mr. Allnut. I want to go to the Bad Axe Public Library and check out a video cassette."

The library promoted its movie collection with a somewhat different touch. While old film photos once again appeared with modified captions, a unique approach was worked out with the newspaper and the local grocer. The paper carried ads about the film service with the caption, "Now all you need is the popcorn." The grocer agreed to include in customers' grocery bags small packets of popcorn which carried the note "Now all you need is a movie. Bax Axe Public Library loans films."

Easter Carols?

Programming has been somewhat nontraditional for Bad Axe, too. For the children, the library offered a very confused Easter Bunny who came at Christmas. He led Easter carols, skits, and passed out Easter baskets. Another offering was Dr. Knock Knocks' Official Joke and Riddle Convention. A big event was the Medieval Pleasure Fair, an afternoon event which offered food, crafts, a Christmas shop, jesters, troubadours, costumes, and all the fanfare and festivity of a medieval pageant.

Bad Axe began a Skill File. Local residents were asked to fill out a form which indicated a skill they had and would share. These forms were filed, allowing interested groups to contact the person, identify the skill, and determine a fee and any other information needed to obtain the person's cooperation in a program.

In a subsequent winning entry, Bad Axe used humor – sometimes subtle, sometimes dark, sometimes childlike – to exemplify its PR efforts in a year when budget cuts reflected a bleak economic environment. The library had the right touch; they received a 40 percent increase in funding.

De-wey Have It?

A paid ad campaign in the local papers, which eventually paid off for the library, featured the theme We Deliver emblazoned on a bold bookmobile. Included on the bookmobile's side was a strange tale of the library's failure to obtain a reference. For example, one ad focused on the library's chagrin at not being able to obtain through interlibrary loan an obscure book of cannibal recipes created by a bizarre doctor located in outer Samoa. But, the ad concluded, we can get *most* books for you in three days.

Personal letters were sent to local businesses. The letter's tone was "we know you're here and important and busy and we think we can help you. Here are some things we could do; can you think of anything else?" Even businessmen who didn't begin to directly use the library were more aware of its services.

Public officials were invited to a special brunch at the library where the theme De-wey Have It – You Bet We Do was exemplified in a show and tell of the library's services and collections. Officials who attended were sent thank-yous for their time, along with library pens.

Humor was once again the focus of a Bad Axe bulletin board which featured Video To Go. Videotapes were displayed inside "to go" cartons from McDonald's, A & W, Burger King, etc., along with a fork, spoon, and knife. Then there was the display Did You Lose a Bookmark? – a bulletin board full of the various items left in books. Bad Axe's creativity displays two important, consistent features, humor and an understanding of what appeals to their target public.

UP FROM THE ASHES

Another library that used its creative touch to reverse a negative image in the community was Dauphin Public Library in Harrisburg, Pennsylvania. Utilizing as its logo a Phoenix – the legendary bird that rises from its own ashes – Dauphin summarized its own PR efforts (see figure 4.1). Financial difficulties resulting in furloughed staff, shorter library hours, and a lack of purchases, had brought about drastically reduced library use and a lack of attention from both staff and public.

Fig. 4.1. Up from the ashes. Reprinted with permission of Dauphin County Library System, Harrisburg, Pennsylvania.

The library began with itself, improving its physical appearance, adding services in new technology, and maintaining a steady flow of fresh programs. It then increased interest from younger readers and built support among new clientele by targeting programs for special groups.

An inexpensive but effective slide show was created to demonstrate to community groups, including the city council, the mission of the library for the total populace. One especially effective portion of the presentation consisted of scenes of various users shown in slides masked in the shape of an open book. Slides of services offered, clear graphics, and attractive shots added to the overall appeal.

One targeted program area illustrates an imaginative approach in children's services. A character named Mrs. Pockets acquainted children with library services. She visited schools where she handed out her Mrs. Pockets' Packet, a collection of program brochures, a coloring book, and a flyer for parents explaining her purpose. (See figure 4.2.)

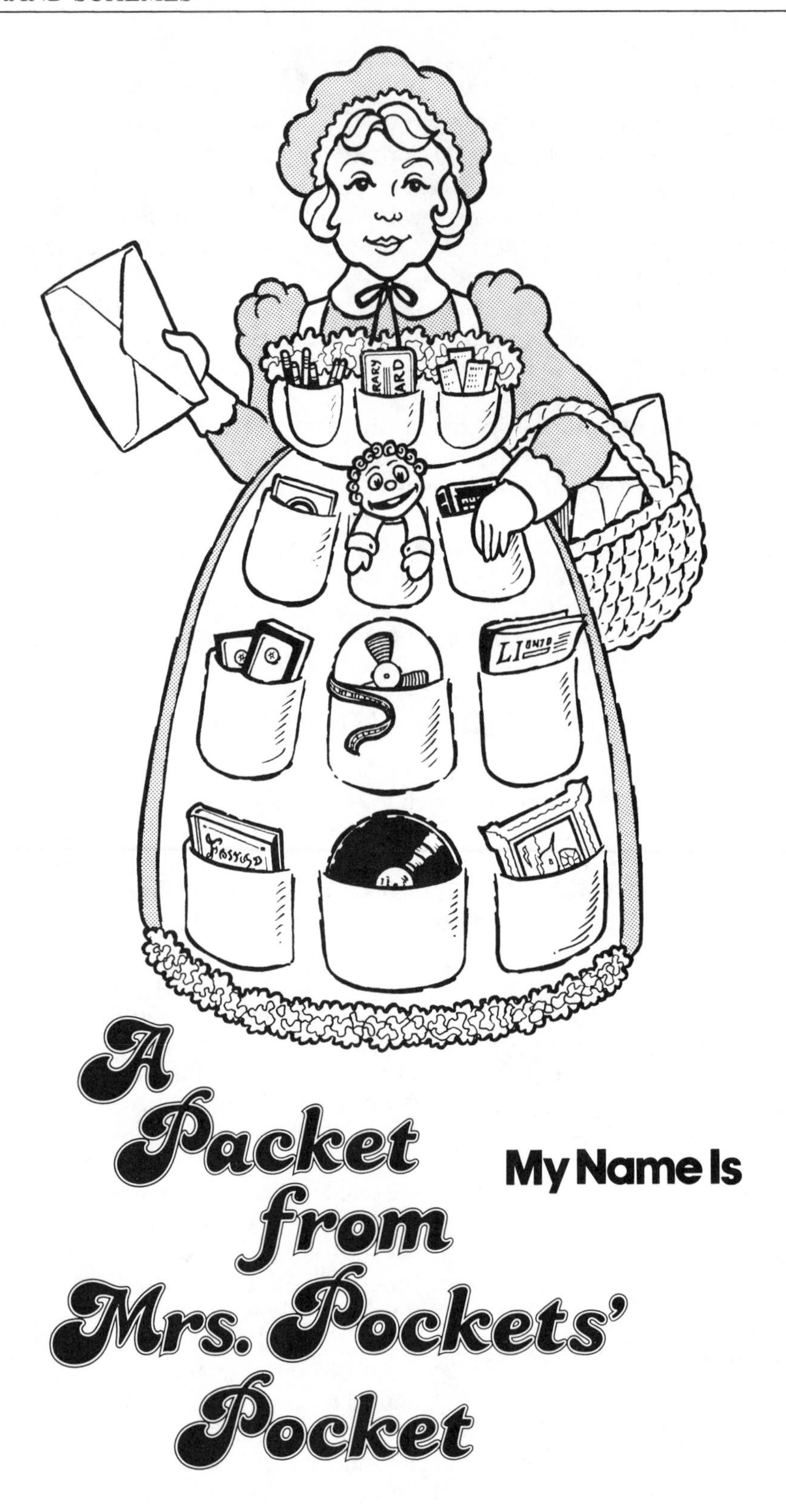

Fig. 4.2. A pocketful. Reprinted with permission of Dauphin County Library System, Harrisburg, Pennsylvania.

Teenagers became involved with the library through Teen Issues Phone-In, live radio programs focused on specific topics of interest to teens with suggested reading lists and discussions of pertinent fiction.

Adult programming included a Layman's Law series and a Grant Information Center. Pennsylvania Portfolio, a library magazine focusing on Pennsylvania authors, books, and libraries was begun. In summary, Dauphin did what it set out to do: focus attention on the library and encourage maximum utilization through atypical activities.

MILITARY ENERGY

Another two-time winner which bursts with creativity is Clark Air Force Base (Philippines). In its first entry, Clark prided itself on "A to Z" public relations. Programs included "A," the Animal Photo Contest whereby participants brought photos with captions of their pets for display and subsequent voting by patrons. The winner received a sketch of his or her animal created by a library technician at no cost to the library. "C" was the Chili Cook-Off, the Christmas Cookie Cook-Off, and the Christmas Centerpiece Contest, which were held at little or minimal cost due to contributions from local merchants. "H" was the Home Computer Show where patrons shared their own computers with others. Two shows were held with over 500 people in attendance.

"O" was the Overdue Campaign. Bookmarks were given to each patron and the staff wore buttons which had logos featuring police saying "STOP Overdues." This program resulted in overdue books dropping by 50 percent. (See figure 4.3.)

Using a menu format in posters, Fare for the Family (see figure 4.4) offered specials in the appetizer section such as investment information (an Inflation Fighter) and car repair books (the Take Home Special). Other special events included a Mystery Month with a contest to match authors with the detectives they created. As part of a Recreation Month, a Fiction Fair was held with displays for special reading tastes. There was a Name the Face contest, with photographs of 30 movie stars of now and then to be identified. The library also made an appearance at the annual coffee held by officers' wives.

Taking Aim

The exuberance of military libraries is also shown in the entry of Nellis Air Force Base (Nevada). Nellis tackled head-on the problems of being a combination special, academic, and public library. Nellis sponsored a Unit of the Month, spotlighting a different base unit complete with a bulletin board explaining the unit's mission, photos introducing key unit personnel, and a display of related materials and books. During a particular unit's display, the members of that unit could register for door prizes each day they visited the library. Prizes were practical but unique: a day of free golf on the base course, three free lanes at the bowling alley, a free dinner, and so forth.

Other activities included Munch a Book, a summer reading program of special projects. Children who completed the projects received a Sweet Smell of Success Certificate, complete with a scratch and sniff seal. Their projects were displayed in the library. Life, Be in It month featured a What's Your Bag? contest wherein participants decorated a library book bag. The 172 entries were suspended from the library's ceiling.

Fig. 4.3. "O" is for overdue. Reprinted with permission of Clark Air Force Base, The Philippines.

Fig. 4.4. A full menu. Reprinted with permission of Clark Air Force Base, The Philippines.

THE AUDIOVISUAL WAY

The Chicago Metropolitan Library System also demonstrated creativity in their excellent television public service announcements (PSAs) for the Dial Law series. Chicago used John Housman, noted for his role as Professor Kingsford in the television series *Paper Chase*, to help launch an awareness campaign.

In the ad, Housman stood authoritatively in front of a statue of Abraham Lincoln, discussing Lincoln's role in giving assistance on legal matters. As the camera moves in, Housman indicates that Dial Law is a continuation of the type of help Lincoln provided. Proudly looking back at Lincoln, Housman confides, "He'd be *proud* of it."

Another audiovisual entry that was also imaginative but even harder hitting was submitted by the Alabama Public Library and the Alabama State Department of Education in Montgomery, Alabama. The two formed a partnership to fight against public ignorance of illiteracy. In addition to posters and flyers, a film for schools and public groups was developed to make people aware of the problem of illiteracy and its effects on all involved. The group used excerpts from the movie as PSAs to encourage target audiences to borrow the film.

In one PSA, a little girl is "read to" by her father, who can't read and talks his way through the story using the pictures to help him. As the child becomes dismayed and upset, the narrator explains that she is well aware her father cannot read and chances are she will not learn to read either.

Another PSA shows a tired, young woman standing in line for her welfare check holding her little girl. The narrator tells us, "Julie left school, her husband left her and now she depends on us for her income." He emphasizes that if Julie knew how to read she and the thousands of others like her on welfare could get jobs and take care of themselves. He also reminds us that Julie's daughter probably won't learn to read either. The PSA ends with a close-up of the child's face.

Yet another PSA features Danny, a young man who dropped out of school, entering a cell. We are reminded we paid for Danny's judge and trial, and are now responsible for his room and board as well. If Danny doesn't get an education, we are warned, he'll be in and out of jail all his life. The cell door then clangs shut. The impact of this imaginative effort is extraordinary.

IN THE SPECIAL WORLD

Public libraries aren't the only ones to exhibit imagination in PR. The High Street Christian Church Library in Akron, Ohio, demonstrated the same enthusiasm, dedication, and inspiration noted in many Dana award winners. This library chalked up over 47,000 volunteer hours, had its librarian selected outstanding librarian by the Church and Synagogue Library Association, and made every individual within the church aware of its services and materials.

The library offers tapes of all Sunday sermons for those individuals unable to attend services. They have also developed a program not typical of a church library – an art festival featuring an artist of the week from among the church's members. Each artist's works are displayed and an informal reception held in the library to give people a chance to meet the individual artist.

The library also regularly sponsors story hours, a reading club, and displays. A newsletter, the *Book Nook*, is issued 10 times per year, and a calendar of events is provided. Library activities are announced in the church bulletin. Departments of the church can obtain bibliographies in their interest areas, as well as other services. Each new member of the church receives a personal welcoming letter and a folder introducing the library. During Christian Literature Sunday, all church members receive a folder reminding them about their library.

The library has held a number of workshops, including one for church school teachers which features book reviews on good literature to recommend to students. Other workshops were for storytellers, and a library quiz was held to arouse reader interest. During the winter months (so not to conflict with public libraries) the church sponsors a reading club. The library recognizes not only children who read and adults who read to children, but also the church department that read the most.

Hold High the Flame

Yet another church oriented library with an imaginative approach is the Lutheran Church Library Association in Minneapolis, Minnesota. The group developed a total publications program around the theme Hold High the Flame (see figure 4.5). Stationery, membership brochures, and flyers incorporated the theme. Three regional association conferences encouraged member chapters to create banners interpreting the theme to bring for display. Commemorative bookmarks were developed as a lasting reminder of the conference. Another memento was a stained glass suncatcher in the shape of the flame for workshop instructors and leaders.

The Illinois Valley Library System in Pekin, Illinois, launched an awareness campaign intended for the general population, whom it felt needed to know the importance of a library system to an individual library patron. They used the simple theme Not Alone But Together, and a logo composed of a single bird and a flock of birds, which appeared on all their efforts to contact the public (see figure 4.6).

A slide show of system services was shown at clubs, open houses, and an outdoor festival. A display with photos demonstrating cooperation graced shopping malls. The focus of all activities was on materials to be found, questions to be answered, and special services to be offered by all libraries working together through the system. Illinois Valley exemplified their theme by passing out samples of all materials to member libraries.

Fig. 4.5. Conference theme. Reprinted with permission of Lutheran Church Library Association, Minneapolis, Minnesota.

Fig. 4.6. System style. Reprinted with permission of Illinois Valley Library System, Pekin, Illinois.

READING TIME

Many Dana award winners most effectively demonstrate their creativity and imagination in their reading programs. Tacoma (Washington) Public Library is one such example. Its material, activities, and programs were keyed to the theme 20,000 Books under the Sea (see figure 4.7). Programs on sea creatures, a display window filled with underwater items, stickers, bookmarks, and T-shirts all carried out the theme. An activity book was offered to each child to keep him or her occupied and interested. Included were word puzzles, mazes, coloring sheets, fill-in-the-blanks, and other activities children love.

As a companion to the regular reading club, Tacoma created the Tadpole Club especially for preschoolers (see figure 4.8). As each child read a book or had a book read to him or her, he or she received coloring pages which showed in sequence the development of the tadpole into a frog.

20,000 BOOKS UNDER THE SEA

Join the summer sea-readers at the Tacoma Public Library

Fig. 4.7. Sea-readers Club. Reprinted with permission of Tacoma Public Library, Tacoma, Washington.

CERTIFICATE of AWARD

This is to certify that

____

has participated in the

Tacoma Public Library

TADPOLE CLUB

____________________ _______________

Children's Specialist Date

Fig. 4.8. For the little ones. Reprinted with permission of Tacoma Public Library, Tacoma, Washington.

Ventura County (California) Library also used an effective summer reading program: The Mysterious Beasts of Dr. Geest. As children read their books, they were awarded stickers which featured drawings of assorted beasts. Each child was given a clue with every sticker so he or she could try to guess the beast's identity. Each book read earned a guess, but there were a limited number of types of stickers. The beast was kept in a sealed crate in the library. Each week a new clue was added to the side of the crate. Children's guesses were placed in a receptacle for a final drawing for prizes.

The summer reading program kickoff included a shadow puppet play, a hand puppet play, and a melodrama. The building equipment mechanic played Dr. Geest and children looked forward to his unveiling the Mystery Beast at the final summer program. As an added touch, the library concentrated on involving visually impaired youngsters through support of the local Lions Club. The program kept the children busy and mystified all summer. The element of suspense was just the motivation they needed.

Read On

North Carolina embarked on a statewide campaign for reading. Just Open a Book featured a froggy character, JOAB, who hopped his way through all the fun and activities (see figure 4.9). The state library asked the governor to launch the program with a televised public service announcement. Sitting at his desk surrounded by children, the governor was an effective and concerned spokesman for the benefits of summer reading. Materials for the program included reading records, game sheets for different ages, bicycle decals, buttons, and a certificate signed by the governor.

Fig. 4.9. JOAB invites readers. Reprinted with permission of North Carolina State Library, Raleigh, North Carolina. Artist: Ron Jones.

Plaza Junior High School in Virginia Beach, Virginia, focused its creative efforts on increasing circulation by fostering positive attitudes about reading. A videotape documenting various activities planned and executed by the library testified to the year-long events which constantly reminded students and teachers to read. Japanese Culture Week, special story hours, and a biweekly news show helped to promote books and authors and relate them to topics of interest. A clever series of photographs showed kids reading in every conceivable place and position – from the huddle in a football game to standing on one's head.

MONEY, MONEY, MONEY

Not all creative efforts are related to children. The St. Louis County (Missouri) Library wanted to appeal to adults who would be voting for an upcoming library tax issue. However, the library wanted to avoid the vote yes motto while at the same time instilling a yes message in the voters. They simply took a current issue, back to the basics, and shaped it into a usable concept. The library staff felt Yes, Books Are Basic stated the one thing taxpayers would understand and support – buying books (see figure 4.10). With brochures, bumper stickers, direct mail, and volunteers, the library got the message out that a defeated referendum would also defeat buying more books. Shortly before the election, the library sponsored a library election: children and adults voted for their favorite books. The step had a great psychological effect – voting for a book right before the election. The referendum passed and a grateful staff posted thank-you signs in the library and assured the voters through the newspaper that book purchases would remain a priority.

The Brooklyn (New York) Public Library also needed to increase the public's awareness of the library's need to purchase books, but they used a unique plan to solicit donations. They focused on present donors, as well as new ones. Individual direct appeals were mailed to those who had donated in the past. Parent-teacher associations were sent requests, and five well-known authors wrote statements about the importance of public libraries. A semi-annual book sale, Books By the Pound, was enthusiastically received. Even canisters with wrap-around messages were used to solicit small donations at the library check-out counter.

Another fund-raising effort noted for its ambitious creativity is that of Eufaula (Oklahoma) Memorial Library. The library accepted an overwhelming challenge – to raise $250,000 within 120 days in order to keep a federal grant. The library staff of two so infected the town with their enthusiasm, energy, and spirit that the community actually raised $322,000 in the designated time. The entire concept was a potpourri of unique, unusual, and sometimes bizarre schemes to raise funds. (See figure 4.11.)

Fig. 4.10. Back to basics. Reprinted with permission of St. Louis County Library, St. Louis, Missouri.

Fig. 4.11. Fundraising community style. Reprinted with permission of Eufaula Memorial Library, Eufaula, Oklahoma.

Among the activities:

1. Meals. The library sponsored a kickoff dinner at $100 a plate with the director acting as speaker. Local restaurants sponsored meals and contributed the profits to the fund-raising. One pizza parlor regularly contributed 50 cents for each pizza purchased on certain nights. One lady opened her home for an elegant luncheon she prepared herself, giving all the money she raised to the library. A group of high school students sponsored a pie supper.

2. Entertainment. The Veterans of Foreign Wars sponsored a dance at which the band donated its services. A group of university professors donated their time for a German music concert. Cheerleaders sold chances for a stadium blanket. School children obtained sponsors for a bike-a-thon and rode miles for dollars. Children weighed in at one school and donated a penny a pound to the library. (See figure 4.12.)

3. Special activities. A beauty parlor raffled a permanent. A local cattle farm raffled a steer. A local library lover issued a challenge–for every individual who would donate $1,000, she would match it, up to $100,000. (She spent all $100,000.)

Eufaula showed creativity is often the child of enthusiasm.

Fig. 4.12. Penny a pound. Reprinted with permission of Eufaula Memorial Library, Eufaula, Oklahoma.

IT'S ACADEMIC

At the academic level, the Albert R. Mann Library, Cornell University (Ithaca, New York), took an inventive approach to stop food, drink, and litter problems in the library. They first established a policy restricting food and drink in the library and then began a campaign to make students aware of the policy, and to educate students about the problems which forced strict adherence to the rule.

To kick off their campaign, the library resorted to a shock technique. The staff filled the library's glass display cases with all the debris collected within the library in one day. Each day the new accumulation was added to the cases. A bold STOP sign was posted above the display.

Additional exhibits indicated the type of pests attracted by the debris and the type of damage they perpetuated in the materials (see figure 4.13). A trash analysis begun before the campaign continued throughout, with specific documentation offered on a constant basis. Actual counts of item types and numbers found were posted next to photographs of debris left behind.

Fig. 4.13. Don't bug us. Reprinted with permission of Albert R. Mann Library, Cornell University, Ithaca, New York.

A saturation campaign featuring a clever logo of a happy bug destroying materials while eating and drinking was spread throughout the campus. The unique campaign caught the attention of the local press. Students were bombarded with the facts of the damage their neglect was causing. By the end of the project, 71 percent of the students surveyed indicated they knew about the new rule and 83 percent indicated they were now following it. The food related waste in the library dropped by over 52 percent.

A final example of a unique approach is John McIntire Public Library in Zanesville, Ohio, which used radio announcements to increase usage of its audiovisual collection. AM and FM channels, rotated throughout the week, aired a total of 10 different spots produced each month. Impersonations of Cheech and Chong, Marlon Brando as the Godfather, Sherlock Holmes and Watson, and even President Reagan, were heard extolling the benefits of using the audiovisual collection. In one spot, Bogey played records borrowed from the library, repeating "One more time, Sam."

There are some who may question if all these examples demonstrate creativity. But creativity is like beauty, it's all in the eye of the beholder. To us, creativity is, as we stated earlier, that sense which elevates the ordinary to the unusual. It involves understanding and energy, and looking and acting and being different from everyone else. Above all, it involves having the confidence to try whatever seems appropriate to the target audience whose support is needed.

5
Winners Spotlight Special Events

It is only natural that any public relations campaign includes at least one activity which draws total attention to the library. Usually, this is a carefully planned, skillfully executed, and dynamically publicized special event which attracts both people and media coverage. A special event is exactly what its name implies, an activity that is, at least momentarily, set apart from other ongoing library efforts in such a way that its purpose is uniquely and individually noted.

Special events are like people, they come in all sizes and shapes. They may be special events with small letters or SPECIAL EVENTS in all caps. Their purpose within the overall scheme determines how they look. But, in each case they are concentrated, unusual, or unique activities that merit the attention they receive.

A special event can be a mini-event, a pleasant, seemingly informal happening that demonstrates a significant moment in a library's life. Or a special event can be an extravaganza, a highly orchestrated, perhaps heftily funded, event which is impossible to overlook. A special event can be a stand alone, an activity that is in and of itself. Finally, a special event can be part of other activities.

MINI-VERSIONS

One example of a small-scale, mini-type event can be the library's involvement in a parade. The building of the entry itself can be a focal point for staff and patrons. When the Tucson Public Library celebrated its 100th birthday, their chuckwagon float in the Rodeo Day parade was a mini-event, one small happening in the midst of a lot of others. But, their reminder that they had been "cooking up" good library service for a hundred years was greeted by shouts and applause all along the parade route.

One library, while not a John Cotton Dana award winner, sponsors a mini-event to kick off their summer reading program. Each year on the first day of registration for summer reading, the library invites the winners of the local school district's Young Authors contest to a reception. The Young Authors donate autographed copies of their books (compliments of the school system) to the children's collection, and the librarians collectively thank the youthful writers. After this formal and traditional ceremony, writers, their families, library staff and media representatives casually gather together, enjoying small talk, cookies, and punch.

EXTRAVAGANZAS

An extravaganza special event takes a great deal of planning and time. It is highly involved, in terms of staff commitment and attention to detail. It usually is created with a high attendance in mind and is geared to keep people talking about it for some time afterward. The most frequent extravaganza events are library anniversary celebrations or fund raisers.

Clearly representative of the extravaganza events is the Dana award-winning Chili Cook-Off sponsored by Clark County Library District in Las Vegas, Nevada (see figure 5.1). While the primary purpose was fundraising, the underlying accomplishment was an increase of the library's visibility with a population segment which rarely considered the library's importance to the community. The success of the event was that it was unusual as well as fun. But, the library's careful planning, studious monitoring, and all-out involvement ensured everyone had a good time and got a good impression.

Fig. 5.1. The good, the bad, the ugly. Reprinted with permission of Las Vegas-Clark County Library District, Las Vegas, Nevada.

To guarantee receptive participants, the library applied for and received an endorsement from the International Chili Society. Thus, a built-in recognition factor was set up, as well as a logical reason to request entry fees. The library also solicited and received cooperation from local businesses. Business "friends" gave merchandise for prizes, helped underwrite many of the gimmicks, entertainment, and publicity, and assisted in the planning.

An appropriate theme and logo were soon developed. Now You're Cookin' Hot Stuff featured the good (a tomato), the bad (a chili pepper), and the ugly (an onion). Souvenir T-shirts, buttons, mugs, hats, and aprons were for sale, each decorated with the clever graphic, as were all publicity pieces for the event.

When the day arrived, each team of chili cookers, many sponsored by local groups or restaurants, staked out their spot in the library parking lot, then built and decorated their booths, trying to "hype" the spectators into support for their culinary efforts. Spectators paid $5.00 admission to watch the dicing, slicing, and cooking while listening to country western and bluegrass bands. A Miss Chili Pepper beauty contest and drawings for prizes filled out the day's activities until the moment of judging. Concession stands offered souvenirs, food, and drink.

Library staff members, attired in western clothes, helped keep the day moving smoothly, assuring that participants, spectators, and media representatives got their fill. The library raised a significant amount of money, the image of the library definitely improved, and many businesses and individuals who hadn't thought a great deal about library services suddenly gained a whole new perspective.

Extravagant, but Classy

Another example of an extravaganza is the fund-raising effort of the Salt Lake City Public Library. Focusing on books, the library found an innovative twist which aroused community interest and involvement.

Responding to the community's emphasis on culture, the library decided to sponsor a gala, Favorite Books of the Famous, which combined an elegant reception and an exciting auction (see figure 5.2). A list of 575 notable individuals, ranging from movie stars to writers to political figures to sports heroes and heroines were contacted by the library. Each was asked to explain in writing what book made a difference in his or her life. The library staff then determined which responses were the best, in terms of content and interest in the person. The favorite books were purchased and then designated to be auctioned, along with the letter from the celebrity, at the gala reception.

Extensive publicity was used to encourage participation at this highly organized and appropriately festive celebration. The library made certain the event was elegant with lovely music, catered refreshments, evening attire, and an atmosphere of style. A stylized logo was developed, programs were distributed as souvenirs, and the media were ecstatic over the unusual activity. Reminiscent of the style of the movies of the 1930s, the auction offered participants the unusual opportunity to bid for letters from such celebrities as Alan Alda and Sir Alec Guinness.

It took a great deal of work on the part of the staff not only to plan the event and to coordinate the necessary components to develop the atmosphere desired, but also to track down individuals who would respond to the request for letters. Then came the task of deciding which ones should be auctioned and purchasing the titles.

Fig. 5.2. A classy event. Reprinted with permission of Salt Lake City Public Library, Salt Lake City, Utah.

STAND ALONE EVENTS

Both the Clark County and the Salt Lake City events are examples of yet another aspect of special events – the stand alone event. Stand alone events are not part of an ongoing program. They are, as the term implies, a single event of and by themselves. They are conceived, planned, and executed as a totally separate entity. Frequently, they are like extravaganzas in that they are fund raisers or anniversary celebrations.

Pig Mania

An exception to the fundraiser or anniversary event is the Dana award-winning effort of Needham (Massachusetts) Free Public Library. Eventually known as Pig Day, this stand alone event began as an opportunity to meet a local author, Susan Fleming, on the occasion of the publication of her book *The Pig at 37 Pinecrest Drive.* Then someone suggested the original Disney version of *The Three Little Pigs* be shown for variety. After that, events and ideas began to snowball; and the staff retreated to develop, with the library board and the Friends groups, a special event for the whole community.

Soon the notion of an Oinktion, an auction of assorted pig paraphernalia, was launched. Books about pigs were placed in the auction catalog as well as a lavendar glove from none other than Miss Piggy. Pigs – papier-mâché, pottery, ceramic, and bank versions – appeared from everywhere. Soon an enthusiastic search began for any pig connection in local history. It was quickly discovered that pigs were indeed deeply rooted in Needham. Rumors even sprouted about a man who was so fond of his pigs that he placed them in beds with satin sheets.

A local sheltered workshop for the mentally disabled made buttons for the event with the motto "Oink If You Love Books." The governor became a hogreave (sort of a sheriff upholding pigs' rights). The *Today* show heard about the day, and Needham received national coverage. The event was planned joyfully, performed exuberantly, and left the happy afterglow of a job well done.

PART OF THE ACTION

Many special events, however, are part of an event, a segment of a total program – an ongoing campaign or project ranging over a time period of a week to a year. Some are kickoffs to draw attention to the total package; others are final occasions designed to bring a recognizable conclusion to a worthwhile undertaking. And a few are incorporated as part of the continuing series of events to sustain interest along the way.

Kickoff Events

To launch their statewide reading program, the Kentucky Department for Libraries used a special event and consequently ended up making a regular event special. The department asked the governor to endorse their program by focusing on one of her campaign goals: to increase funding for education, specifically, the education available through the public libraries and their summer reading programs. The governor agreed and her office helped organize a press conference to kick off the year's summer reading program.

The governor introduced Library Jones, a lop-eared, happy-go-lucky adventurer (in the tradition of Indiana Jones) to the press and outlined the activities plans for the summer (see figure 5.3). Library Jones was a hit with the press and the governor was so delighted with the favorable publicity she invited Library Jones to help her at two events scheduled later in the summer.

Fig. 5.3. Readers of the Lost Ark. Reprinted with permission of Kentucky Department for Libraries and Archives, Frankfort, Kentucky.

After the press conference, Library Jones attended the regularly scheduled state library association conference. There, Library Jones posed with librarians throughout the state for photographs that were sent back to local papers. Thus, from the press conference with the governor to the library association conference, Library Jones became an easily identifiable library advocate, and a delightful character to urge Kentucky children to read. All in all, this entire campaign illustrated positivism, energy, enthusiasm, planning, and attention to detail.

Concluding and in the Middle Events

On the opposite end of kickoff events, Spokane Public Library's main event was at the conclusion of their year-long effort focusing on the impact of railroads within the community. After the lectures, films, displays, book lists, and reading programs, the finale of The Year of the Train was, appropriately, a Day of the Train (see figure 5.4).

The Union Pacific Railroad cooperated with the library and hosted this occasion, providing a diesel locomotive and a caboose for display. Demonstrations included the operation of a crane car as well as the computerized maneuvers of today's railroad. Movies and exhibits rounded out this final tribute to a cooperative involvement wherein the entire community rediscovered its roots.

Another type of special event is the one that occurs midway in a series, usually to add or renew interest to an ongoing effort that may be becoming stale. For example, the Tacoma Public Library participated in a local shopping mall's Youth Information Fair. The library set up a Quick Info Service which included a telephone hook-up to the reference desk. Shoppers asked questions which were immediately fed to the reference department and the reference staff had to respond in five minutes or less to beat the questioner. A large tally board informed everyone of the scores, while videotapes featuring library services and programs were played to occupy waiting time.

Fig. 5.4. On track. Reprinted with permission of Spokane Public Library, Spokane, Washington.

ALL IN A BUNDLE

Many special events become intermingled. Stand alone programs are extravaganzas and mini-events become part of an ongoing theme. Occasionally there are several types of special events within one project, such as a mini kickoff or ending event, an extravaganza midway, and a stand alone event which is related to but not really part of a specific campaign.

A good example of a series of special events is the Dana award-winner submitted by Osceola High School in Seminole, Florida. Deciding that the best way to attract high school students was through all-out saturation, the librarian made National Library Week an occasion which could not be overlooked.

A bombardment of special events occurred. There were contests, tokens, a videotape, and a constant barrage of flyers and posters. Each period of each school day a presentation was offered from some significant person or group: television commentators, authors, folk singers, artists, actors, journalists, photographers, and Japanese dancers. Each day became bigger, more active, and, if possible, more special than the day before.

Students were astounded by the wide range of constantly changing events which surrounded the Library Media Center (LMC). The librarian wisely pointed out that the LMC is actively involved in all aspects and all types of information on all topics. This special-upon-special event was impressive to the faculty and students. The yearbook featured a five-page spread on the library, and the librarian was nominated by faculty and students as outstanding educator of the year.

HOW TO DO IT

There are endless examples among the Dana award winners of special events of all the types mentioned. But, before looking at other specific examples of special events, first consider the all-important question: How do we do it? Taking for granted that we have some special occasion which we wish to recognize, then what must be done to ensure that we have managed to do this occasion justice?

The best way is through proper planning. Advance planning means having a clear idea of what we're doing and why, and how to know if we've accomplished what we wanted to. Planning also involves knowing what resources are needed and what considerations must be made so the event proceeds without unanticipated disasters that doom it to failure.

No special event should ever be considered without a reason. Even when Andy Hardy urged his friends to "Come on, gang. Let's have a show!" he had a reason. Perhaps it was to raise money, perhaps to raise spirits, but there was always something the gang was trying to accomplish. A library considering an event also must have a purpose in mind.

The why will usually determine the what, the where, and the how. Therefore, we must specify why the event is worth the trouble, the staff time, and perhaps the money. In addition to the principal reason for sponsoring the activity, there may be a second reason; or even a third reason, but it shouldn't go any further. If we try to make one event "all things to all people," it can become so all-encompassing it can actually be an event with no obvious purpose. The target audience will recognize such a flaw. It is important, therefore, to recognize the difference between accomplishing what we set out to do and just shooting off into a vacuum hoping to hit something.

What is the *primary* purpose in having this event? If it is to get press recognition, then we do startling things to get their attention, such as the worm race sponsored by Dauphin County Library System midway through their summer reading program.

Perhaps the purpose is to raise money. Salt Lake City and Clark County libraries have already been cited as examples for their ability in that area. Another example is the Alameda County Library System in Hayward, California, which launched a campaign specifically geared to purchase books for the children's department. They did not feature a specific special event. Instead, one library in the system offered a weekend special for Cabbage Patch Kids™. For a nominal fee, the dolls spent the weekend at the library, where library staff read them stories. The dolls were given new ribbons and "had a wonderful time." The event was low key, but unique, and quietly focused attention on the need for books to replace worn out ones that the dolls "heard."

Or maybe the special event is to celebrate a date of significance to the library – a community or library anniversary, the opening of a new building or a new wing, or the highlighting of a specific collection area. The occasion can be anything the library feels is worth noticing, but exactly what the occasion is and why the library wants to celebrate it must be determined.

Details, Details, Details

Once the library staff decides why they want to have an event, the next critical decision is when to hold it. If the decision is made today to have a special event next week, or even next month, the event better be low-key, small scale, and of no major importance to the library since there isn't sufficient time to plan. Planning takes time, and holding an event too soon is a sure way to make it falter.

Planning involves consideration of what resources are needed, who must assist, how much money will be required, how much publicity is needed and where it should be placed, as well as the simple logistics of how everything will fit together on the day of the event. If a decision has not been made about where to put the speaker's podium or the punch bowl, or how to arrange the chairs, the event is going to appear poorly planned and badly organized, no matter how well-intentioned.

One of the best ways to work with a time factor is to first decide when the event will occur and then work backwards, determining what needs to be done at each step before the event. If people need to hear about the event at least two weeks in advance in order to plan their attendance, then that day goes on the planning board as the day to release the publicity. If the publicity is going to consist of posters, then the next item backward is the day the posters must be ready to allow time for their distribution. And the date before that is when the poster content is due to the artist. Before that is the date the idea for the event must be approved. Before that is the time necessary to brainstorm and establish the idea, with a built-in time factor in case the first idea is rejected.

This backward system, called Program Evaluation and Review Technique (PERT), should be used for any other aspects of planning, from the logistics of the room, to the ordering of the refreshments, to the scheduling of the speaker, to the writing of the thank you notes when it's all over. (A more detailed discussion of PERT is in chapter 9.)

If time is taken to organize as much as possible in advance, then few things, if anything, will go wrong. We should role play the entire event in advance in order to anticipate as much as possible what will and might happen. Like graduations or weddings, a special event should be rehearsed.

Who's to Do It?

When possible, planning should also include the division of labor. An event of any consequence will involve a great deal of effort and time, which needs to be distributed among staff as much as possible without affecting program. Assignments should be given with an eye to who has time, who has talent, who has interest rather than simply on the basis of which department seems logical. The more individuals involved with the event, the more in-house advocates, and the more assistants available during the event itself. Also we will have input in the planning, especially in the idea stage. Much of what makes an event successful in terms of what to do, how to do it, and how to publicize is best generated through involvement of people.

Assignments need not be limited to paid staff. Volunteers, board members, students, faculty, friends, and any other interested parties can be used. A note of caution is in order, however. Assignments need to be clearly spelled out, deadlines understood, and a coordinator appointed who knows what each individual is doing. This coordinator must see to it that people keep on schedule, progress reports are rendered, and problems are identified and solved.

MORE EXAMPLES

Some special events which have won Dana awards stand as examples of good planning. The Salt Lake City School District was faced with an ignorance on the part of the administrators about what a library media professional does. The library media staff decided to meet the problem head-on and educate the educators with a breakfast for school administrators and board members. Planning included a carefully crafted invitation, an easy-to-serve breakfast menu, table decorations which focused on storytelling, a clever program with a definite message, and an opportunity for guests to meet with the library media staff. This stand alone event was developed around the single purpose of making administrators aware of the importance of the staff.

After the meal and some conversation, the program featured an original tale which illustrated the roles of the library media specialist—a teacher, curriculum specialist, materials' producer, administrator, and technical processor. Through live action and videotape an original tale was told about a king who discovered that the royal librarian could not possibly perform her job all by herself. She enlisted the help of her sisters so that she could become the "all things to all people" type of person that was expected of her. The administrators got the message and the library media staff got the understanding they sought.

DAY OF INFAMY

an exhibit of
WW II posters

and

War Department films

December 6 and 7, 1981

LOUISIANA STATE LIBRARY

Fig. 5.6. That fateful Sunday. Reprinted with permission of Louisiana State Library, Baton Rouge, Louisiana.

Super Saturday included:

- a rocket-shaped information booth on the front lawn
- an exhibit of winning entries in the children's poster contest about the library
- theater and mime for children
- arts and crafts demonstrations, including sculpting, furniture making, spinning, tole painting, portraiture, and sheepshearing
- a pet parade of stuffed animals (see figure 5.7)
- music ensembles including the high school jazz combo and folk musicians.

Fig. 5.7. Stuffed animal parade. Reprinted with permission of Martinsburg-Berkeley County Public Library, Martinsburg, West Virginia.

Renaissance Today

Another special event which illustrates the necessary time, care, and planning to activate a special event is the Renaissance Pleasure Faire of Sheridan County (Wyoming) Fulmer Public Library (see figure 5.8). While there are many such festivals, this may well be the first one ever sponsored by a library. No players or actors were hired: the community, led by the library, created this "faire" themselves.

Local civic groups participated in the creation. The local paper covered the coming events, including recipes and a guide for making Renaissance clothes. Because everyone was urged to appear in costume, the library offered a workshop to turn modern styles into Elizabethan costumes, and created a costume guide.

Flyers and public service announcements encouraged involvement. The day of the event nearly 2,000 people showed up, most in costume. The participants strolled through the local park amid storytellers, puppeteers, arts and crafts exhibits, games, food, and drink.

Prizes were awarded for the best booths and costumes, but the smiles, the happiness, the excitement reflected on the faces of those attending were the best prize any library could have. The success of the event was best summarized in an editorial in the local paper, which lauded the library in its efforts to develop a community get-together which truly got the community together.

All of these special events are examples of what careful planning, staff commitment, community awareness, and creative thinking can do to feature a library in a positive manner within its community. Any library can create an event as meaningful, as enjoyable, or as dramatic as those mentioned. All that is needed is an idea, planning, and a commitment to doing it and doing it well.

Fig. 5.8. The Pleasure Faire. Reprinted with permission of Sheridan County Fulmer Public Library, Sheridan, Wyoming.

6
Winners Use Eye-catching Graphics

Those of us who work in the library field are busily involved in the day-to-day trials and turmoils of our profession. Offering our patrons our best service demands much from us, leaving little time to learn about and perfect other skills often necessary to assist our efforts but out of the immediate realm of our training. One such area is the field of graphics.

Good slides, brochures, flyers, notices, displays and other eye-catching pieces are dependent on knowledge of graphic design and execution. Yet few libraries can afford the services of a graphic artist, thus forcing the library to settle for less than quality graphics or the librarian to take courses or read books to try to develop the needed technique.

While warm, cheerful facilities may welcome patrons and encourage their return, librarians must first convince potential users to make that initial visit. To reach out and touch them usually means communicating with them through some form of media. On the one hand, we must convey our eagerness to offer materials and services. On the other hand, we must keep an eye on our competitors, television, radio, newspapers, and magazines, so that we know how they are dealing with the public and how we might use them to help us communicate.

VISUAL IMPACT

Communication is a key to effective graphics. We are trying, through visual technique, to capture people's attention, to make them stop and notice us in a positive fashion, and to make them want to use our services. We want patrons to be aware of a project, event, service, or collection that will have value for them. Consequently, we must communicate with them rather than with each other. All too often ideas for visual impact are effective with fellow librarians but have little or no meaning to patrons.

We have to know where to find those patrons. Trying to get nonusers into the library by placing inviting brochures on the check-out desk is like encouraging parents to join the PTA by making a plea at the PTA meeting. We also must look critically at our efforts, remembering the amount of junk mail received in a day, the number of television commercials viewed, and the countless articles and ads in the newspapers. To appeal to our hurry-up, throw-away society, we have to be brief, using graphics which will make the target audience stop, look, and remember. Graphic content must be accurate, neat, and aesthetically appealing. That's a pretty tall order for a group of people who never had graphics training.

Consequently, many John Cotton Dana award winners do turn to the professionals for graphic assistance. Some are lucky enough to have such talent within their libraries; some are fortunate enough to have available funds to hire expertise; and some use their own creativity in figuring out a way to obtain the help without taxing their budgets.

Some winners made graphics a priority, designating a major portion of their budget for artwork while sacrificing other aspects. Other winners appealed directly to graphic artists in their community for help, often at no cost. The "partnering" aspect mentioned in chapter 2 worked with some libraries, which convinced local businesses to donate money for graphic development or to donate their own graphic talent to assist the library. Some libraries bargain with artists, offering free exhibit space in the library, or free publicity by featuring the artist's name prominently on all publication pieces in exchange for the artist's help.

Other libraries tap into the talents of the local college or high school art classes. There are librarians who spend hours scanning through available copyright-free clip art until they find that one piece that conveys the message they feel will appeal to their patrons. Sometimes libraries in a particular area will join together to contract for the services of a professional graphic designer. Although graphic development is not a part of library training, there are ways to find it and use it for the good of the library program.

FOR EXAMPLE

Timberland Regional Library in Olympia, Washington, decided that centralizing design was the best way to develop quality and consistency in the graphic style of their member libraries. They began with an evaluation of their existing logo, working and reworking it until it had a new look more reflective of the image they wished to portray. The new logo was incorporated into all pieces which were created, using the saturation strategy typical of prominent advertising. Stationery, envelopes, press release forms, bulletins, memos, reserve notices, flyers, cover designs for vertical files, and periodical holdings—everything incorporated the new, professional-looking design. (See figure 6.1.)

New directional signs were created for all member libraries. Each sign was done in a color scheme which complemented the individual library's decor. Seasonal flyers and advertising pieces were created by the regional staff, as well as bookmarks and book lists. Spaces were left blank in each piece so the local library could fill in whatever information was appropriate to their services.

Fig. 6.1. Coordinated design. Reprinted with permission of Timberland Regional Library, Olympia, Washington.

The graphics were simple but strong, and the regional production made an impact because of its consistency throughout the five-county area. Timberland demonstrated that cooperation among libraries was one way to find a professional graphic identity.

St. Louis Public Library is yet another example of the centralizing of graphic development. The main library's PR department assists the branches with their publicity and coordinates all publications. One goal has been to develop consistent, high-quality pieces with visual appeal. The monthly events calendar is an example of such coordination. In booklet style, the calendar unfolds to an 11-by-17-inch list of all events, while the first-fold highlights special events or materials. The calendar is sent to the media and local businesses. Patrons obtain it at their library.

A series of "focus" posters has been another popular service. The ideas for these posters, which appear four times a year, come from a committee of four librarians within the system. Each poster's theme is different and is further developed by supportive programming suggested and refined by the same committee. Topics used thus far have included a black writer's program, featuring the works of black writers, and the small business resource centers at the branch libraries. In the latter case, posters captioned Stick Our Knows Into Your (Small) Business advertised sessions in the various branches where speakers gave information on how the library's resources could assist a small business.

On the Automated Front

The University of Texas Health Science Center at San Antonio Library also used a committee to plan its campaign to introduce a new building, a new online catalog, and subsequent changes to its patrons. Systematically and with judicious planning they attacked their project. Once again, all publications were centralized and a coordinated look was developed for all pieces. The art department helped in this effort and even submitted their work to an art contest. A simple grid with bold lettering was chosen as the coordinating component—brief, bold, concise, and professional.

Elmer Holmes Bobst Library at New York University was seeking an effective way to help users make the transition from the traditional card catalog to the user-friendly online catalog. They adopted a lovable, grinning mascot, affectionately called Bob Cat after the Bobst catalog. Bob Cat appeared on press releases, flyers, and posters. He was featured in a paycheck insert encouraging personnel to buy an I'm Behind Bobcat T-shirt to help complete conversion of titles from the old card catalog (see figure 6.2). He became so popular he was adopted by the newly created varsity basketball team as their mascot. And he was such great PR, users became convinced the online system was friendly. He even appeared in the *New York Times*.

The J. Paul Leonard Library at San Francisco State also found that they had to deal with their patrons' ignorance when it came time to complete the conversion to a computerized circulation system. They had to build awareness throughout the university community of 30,000 that their campus ID cards had to be tagged with a bar-coded zebra label so books could be checked out from the library.

Foremost in promoting the Zebra Your ID campaign was the hanging of a huge red, white, and black banner in front of the library (see figure 6.3). This banner, which features an enormous replica of a zebra bar code along with the slogan of the campaign, is reusable each semester for new students. Sign holders in elevators and stairwells also conveyed the message to "zebra." Bookmarks were passed out and soon converted by innovative library staffers into jaunty hats at the circulation desk as another way to communicate to patrons. An unusual graphic technique was employed in the form of an electronic message board outside the student union, which constantly flashed the students with its bar code message.

Fig. 6.2. Meet Bob Cat. Reprinted with permission of Elmer Holmes Bobst Library, New York University, New York City.

Fig. 6.3. The Zebra technique. Reprinted with permission of J. Paul Leonard Library, San Francisco State University, San Francisco, California.

Get It Together

Akron-Summit Library decided that their image needed a little refreshening. They identified three areas of concern, one of which was development of a new logo. Their final design was a contemporary, stylized A with extended serifs which give the appearance of a mountain with a summit (see figure 6.4). Therefore, they updated their image but retained components representative of their name. Their new logo first premiered on the bookmobile. It was so effective the library decided to modify the color scheme and use it on all printed pieces, as well as library vehicles, maintenance staff uniforms, employee badges, and service awards.

Fig. 6.4. Stylized logo. Reprinted with permission of Akron-Summit County Public Library, Akron, Ohio.

Houston Public Library also decided to take a good, hard look at its visual image and impact. They wished to improve the quality and reduce the quantity of the library's primary communication tools—print media. The method they used was, again, coordination. The library decided that uniform design and systemwide impact were important for their publications. The system calendar of events and the central calendar of events became one piece. The branch calendars were standardized and a bimonthly newsletter with good visual appeal was created from the office of the library's director.

The visual components used by the library had a great effect. Occasionally, even the newspapers used the graphics. Unusual objects became part of the package, such as an actual fan which advertised an exhibit of fans and yet served a practical purpose. Press releases were often coordinated in terms of style, color, and illustrations with the flyers and posters announcing events. While the calendars (see figure 6.5) and the newsletter retained a uniform appearance, there was some variety in the design so that each piece did not look like the one preceding it. Still, the standardization of approach left no doubt as to the source.

Graphic Standards

Irvine Library at the University of California also decided that the best way to promote campus and public awareness of the library and its programs was to establish a special committee to develop and maintain graphic and editorial standards for materials. Primarily, the group was to produce a series of publications, using coordinated designs that would be recognized as distinctive to the library. The group developed guidelines, requested a budget, and established a committee to plan publications in cooperation with the campus publications office.

Fig. 6.5. Coordinated design. Reprinted with permission of Houston Public Library, Houston, Texas.

This approach to the development of library publications resulted in a coordinated design scheme, quality and quantity control of publications, as well as systematic review and updating. Several different categories of publications were established: general library information, department and branch library descriptions, service descriptions, reference guides, newsletters and acquisitions lists, and maps. Each had its own distinctive look but all featured a basic coordinated design developed especially for the library. The emphasis was to make the pieces eye-catching and professional. (See figure 6.6.)

Individual Efforts

Other Dana award winners were not involved in a complete revamping of their visual image but were trying to communicate a specific project or service to the community. Several examples of these projects have been mentioned in other chapters. We urge the reader to notice effective graphics that may be illustrated elsewhere in this book. However, we will look at a few more winners to analyze their effective use of graphics.

A consistent winner in the graphics area is the Lincoln Library. It has been cited three times in the last six years for its graphic excellence. Their graphics are bold and sometimes controversial, as is their method of using them. Initially, the library bought ad space in the Saturday magazine section to expose their style.

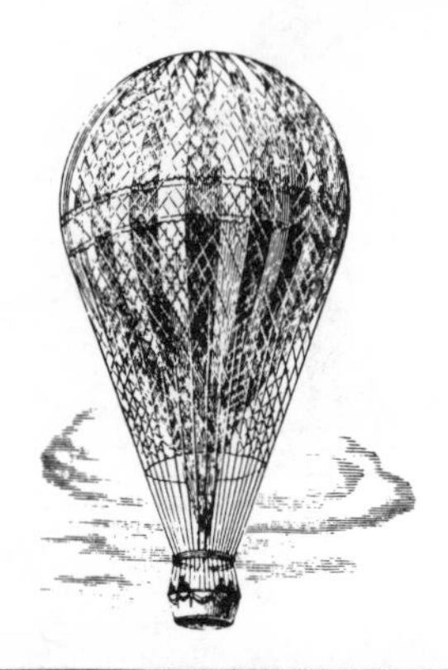

New Orange County Aerial Photography Collection

Research on Orange County, increasing dramatically in the past few years, will be enhanced by two sets of aerial photography now available in the Library's Orange County Collection located in the Government Publications and Microforms Department.

From the first photographs made of Paris in the 1860s using an untethered balloon, aerial photography has developed into a highly technical skill requiring excellent coordination between photographer and pilot. Carefully selecting the best weather conditions for maximum clarity of ground contours, the pilot flies a slow, high-wing aircraft or helicopter with slide windows at an altitude of about 5000 feet and the photographer uses cameras with wide-angle lenses. The prevalent applications of aerial photography today are in geographical and geological surveying, agriculture, the military, and real estate development.

The recently acquired resources include the *Orange County Aerial Atlas* (1985) and the WAC aerial photographs collection. Produced by Rupp Photographics in Orange and shot at a photoscale of 1″ = 1200′, the *Orange County Aerial Atlas* is an oversized spiral atlas with the following overlay guides: Traffic Analysis Flow Map; Census Tract Map; Acreage Overlay; plus an ordering grid with coordinates to be used as an accompanying photo guide to specific locations. City and county zoning is also provided for all coverage of the maps in Orange County.

The second resource is a set of 140, 9″x9″ aerial photographs shot at a photoscale of 1″ = 2640′ and produced by WAC Corporation in Eugene, Oregon. This collection includes a map index with photo number and map coordinates. Earlier collections for 1964 and 1974 are also available in spiral atlas format.

These collections afford the researcher a unique view of the development of Orange County over time including building and construction, highway development, and changes in agricultural patterns. Aerial photographic collections for other California counties and time periods are located at appropriate UC libraries. A stereoviewer, recommended for viewing in order to maximize the three-

UC Irvine Physical Sciences Library

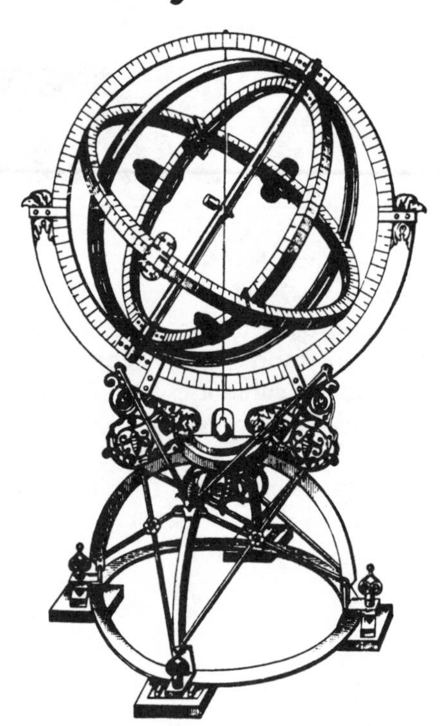

From *Lore and Lure of Outer Space*

University of California, Irvine

Fig. 6.6. Unified visuals. Reprinted with permission of University of California, Irvine Library, Irvine, California.

One of Lincoln's annual reports is a sample of their bright way of handling printed pieces. The cover style was in the form of paper money (value = $7.17 bill), with a "winkin' Lincoln" in the center (see figure 6.7). The $7.17 figure was the calculated retail cost of services provided by the library. Included was the message that the taxpayers were getting a 600 percent return, or $7.17 worth of services, for every tax dollar.

Fig. 6.7. Winkin' Lincoln. Reprinted with permission of Lincoln Library, Springfield, Illinois.

Delightful posters and flyers are another trademark of Lincoln's style. For example, there was the winged tennis shoe urging teenagers to "get a running start on your term paper" (see figure 6.8). Teens are also featured in the publication *Original Neat Stuff*, which compiles their writing efforts.

The State Library of Pennsylvania designed a graphic piece to be used over the entire state. The printed pieces were not for a visual identification of a particular library or group of libraries, but rather were for a specific project to increase public awareness of library services. The colorful and bold graphics consisted of a lightning bolt streaking out of a cloud, imparting a god-like power with the motto "We have the answers!" (see figure 6.9). Bright gold, orange, green, and white on a black background grabs one's eyes and refuses to let go. The state library also prepared a kit for all other libraries giving hints on how to kick off promos, work with people, and use the posters and other materials for maximum effect.

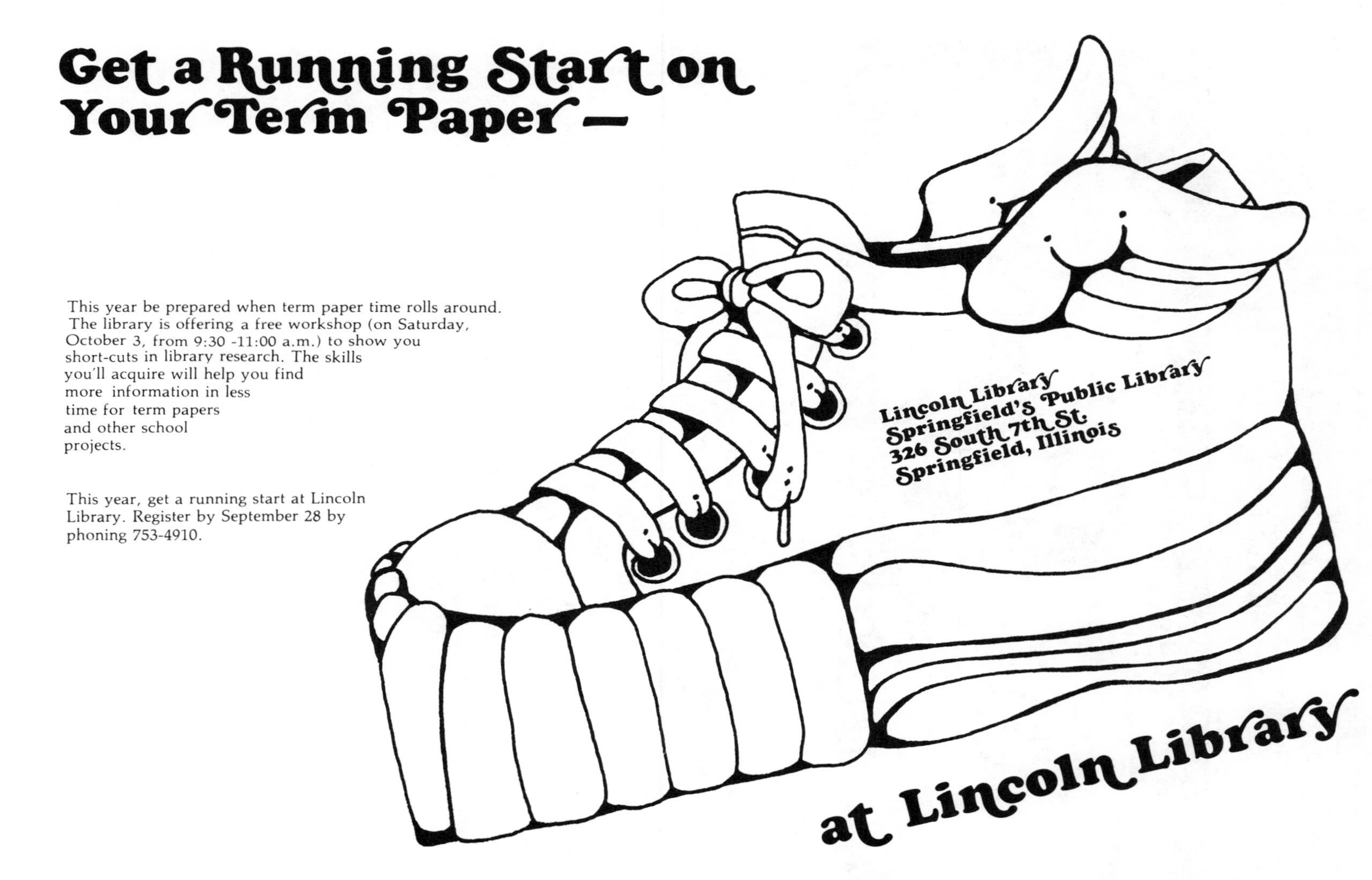

Fig. 6.8. Research workshop. Reprinted with permission of Lincoln Library, Springfield, Illinois. Art work from Dynamic Graphics Clipper service.

Fig. 6.9. Ask the library. Reprinted with permission of State Library of Pennsylvania, Harrisburg, Pennsylvania.

Reading Time

Carlsbad (California) City Library publicized its innovative, in-house summer reading program with a series of "Supervet" comics which incorporated exciting graphics (see figure 6.10). Capitalizing on the local interest in zoos and animal care generated by the nearness of the San Diego Zoo and a wild animal park, the staff developed a series of high quality cartoons which children could obtain after reading specified numbers of books. In these cartoons, children became Supervets and saved little-known animals from assorted problems. The library's graphic artist worked closely with the children's staff to identify and research unusual animals the children would not know. In the final adventure the artist created a new species, the Fuzzheads, which saved the Supervet when he or she got into trouble. The realistic and high quality illustrations were a delight not only to the children, but to all who saw them.

Alameda County also used highly appealing graphics in their campaign to rebuild a deteriorating children's picture book collection. Picturebooks Are a Family Affair was coordinated around a family of mice who enjoyed books together (see figure 6.11). The lovable family appeared on posters, bookmarks, brochures, bookplates, and birthday cards. Their obvious enjoyment of reading was an encouragement to patrons to help them keep the collection viable by donating funds to help purchase books. The target audience was families with small children. The plight of the collection was reinforced by displays of "well-loved but well-worn books" in strategic locations within the libraries.

Reeves Memorial Library at Seton Hill College in Greensburg, Pennsylvania, wanted to find an effective way to appeal to their students. Their technique brought them quality graphics at low prices, plus a visibility on campus. The library appealed to a graphic arts class to take them on as a client. The library was seeking a series of bookmarks which would relate to college students and would emphasize the services and collections of the library (see figure 6.12). Budget, physical dimensions, type of design, and image that was not appealing were discussed with the potential artists.

The students completed their designs and presented them to the library staff for review. Selections and corrections were made, and the final designs were reviewed a last time. During National Library Week, the best designs were displayed, followed by their printing and distribution. The resulting series were fresh, timeless, and uniquely the property of Reeves' student artists.

Fig. 6.10. Supervets to the rescue. Reprinted with permission of Carlsbad City Library, Carlsbad, California. Art work by Janell Cannon.

Fig. 6.11. Picture book promotion. Reprinted with permission of Alameda County Library, Hayward, California.

Fig. 6.12. Student designs. Reprinted with permission of Reeves Memorial Library, Seton Hill College, Greensburg, Pennsylvania.

Another appealing program was sponsored by the Travis Air Force Base during its silver anniversary. The library adopted an appropriate mascot/logo—the well-read Baron. Flamboyantly pictured in his biplane with helmet, goggles, and scarf, the Baron was accompanied with the logo, "25 Years at the Front" (see figure 6.13). The anniversary celebrations incorporated a series of events to commemorate the birth of the library, including a rededication of the library.

Fig. 6.13. High flyer. Reprinted with permission of Library, Travis Air Force Base, California.

IN THE AUDIOVISUAL WORLD

No coverage of graphics can be complete without a look at that companion to print components: audiovisual. Several Dana award winners have effectively used slide shows and video to portray a library message. For example, Mid-Hudson Library System billed itself as the "Libraries' Library" in a slide show designed to explain the organization and purpose of this library system. Excellent visuals and a well-written script, which compared library networking to broadcasting networks to convey the concept, made this presentation a winner. Particularly noteworthy were the series of slides using silhouetted figures of typical patrons asking questions about the system. A brightly illuminated projection screen, with people standing or sitting in front of it in the desired poses, was the technique used to create these effective slides.

King County Library System in Seattle, Washington, also used a slide show to introduce children to the library. In Pingo Visits the Library a tiny space visitor whose spaceship malfunctions discovers the library. He lands near the library, meets children who show him around, and encounters a librarian who helps him find the sources he needs to fix his ship. He goes home but vows to return to this wonderful place—the library.

The distinctive element of this single screen, two projector slide presentation was imagination. Use of common elements such as an outdoor sculpture for a spaceship, of clean, well-planned and creative shots, of a good sound track with a believable voice full of expression, and of timely sound effects, helped create an effective show which the children loved.

King County also created a public service announcement for television. Featuring a basketball star from the Seattle Supersonics, the spot details all the materials available in the library. As the player walks through the stacks, he lists the subjects covered by the collection. As he talks, hands appear out of the books, working on the subjects being mentioned—from operating machine tools to holding paintbrushes to bouncing basketballs. The hands help illustrate the message, the library is where information comes to life.

Santa Ana Public Library also created a lively slide show which gave a comprehensive overview of the library's services and resources. The faces of all kinds of users are shown in the opening segments. Originally produced for a two projector/dissolve setup, the library also prepared a single projector version for easy use by interested community groups. The most intriguing aspect of the slide show was the use of a professional mime to act as the universal patron. Thus, the patron is represented regardless of racial or ethnic background. The scripting technique used questions from the mime with voice-over responses from a person knowledgeable about the library.

Audiovisuals for Training

The University of Texas Health Science Center, cited earlier for its graphics, also created a specialized slide show to help their new users become familiar with their LIS, an online catalog which provides access to the library's book, journal, and audiovisual holdings. The library felt the versatility of a slide show would be effective on an individual, small group, or large group basis.

The center used superb graphics, a step-by-step technique, and visual clues. For example, when the second slide was shown, the first slide was present in a reduced format in the upper left corner. Thus, the viewer could focus on the new information but have a clear sense of previous information. This particular technique saved time on the part of the library staff in training users, allowing a user to return to information which needed repeating. It also standardized the information presented.

Video Version

McBride Library from Kessler Air Force Base executed an imaginative video program with excellent special effects to bring books to life, sparking interest in the library and increasing usage. Cooperating with the training center's television studio, the library staff developed a 7-minute tape about services using the theme Look to Your Library. The tape focused on actual patrons who consistently used the library, particularly high use subject areas. A different patron was shown in each section. Practical uses as well as educational ones relating to base operations were featured. Recreational uses like periodicals, art prints, and records were highlighted.

An interesting video technique was live action superimposed on the open pages of the book. For example, someone looking for military history opened a book and discovered the Civil War going on before his or her eyes. The tape's message was that if one looks to the library, he will quickly discover that a Reader Is a Leader.

Richmond Public Schools developed a multi-image slide show. The original version incorporated two screens, four projectors, and a tape recorder, activated by a dissolver. The basis of the show was a behind-the-scenes look at district media services. Slides utilizing bold colors and Kodalith film pointed out each service area. In each case, a request was made by a patron and the solution was the delivery of the services, which was revealed through clear, sequential shots that delineated all the necessary steps. The show used varied camera angles, gradually building close-in shots, and two projectors to create a panorama-type scene.

The graphics of all these winners are bold, unique, eye-catching, and yet simple. In each case the visual component serves a clear, identifiable purpose. The resulting graphic is neat and has aesthetic appeal. A single point of emphasis is apparent to capture, but not confuse, the viewer. In other words, the graphic has excitement and simplicity. Each effectively places the library before the public. Many award winners have worked hard to coordinate their publications with the visual image, avoiding a shotgun, scatter approach. Their visual emblems incorporate the spirit of the library and the purpose of the project.

7

Winners Demonstrate a "We Care" Attitude and Create an Appealing Environment

A concern for people is another significant hallmark of the winners in the John Cotton Dana library public relations contest. It is, in fact, not a separate ingredient added to the library's efforts at the end of their planning, as a creative cook might stir in a pinch of special seasoning. It is the very basis of their approach to library service on a daily basis.

This sensitivity to people of all types and of all ages, to staff and to the public, is a grand scheme that is important in the other grand schemes: it is a part of many of the partnerships these libraries are committed to; it is reflected in the programming efforts that they offer; and it shines through in special events and in the pervasive atmosphere of the library.

It is difficult to isolate this quality of concern. Just as the seasoning in the creative cook's culinary masterpiece is blended thoroughly with all of the other ingredients, so the library's concern quotient cannot be separated from other aspects of its program of services.

But we can find hints, suggestions, and clues through their work for "By their works ye shall know them." What we cannot know absolutely without being a patron of the library is how the staff feels about serving the public. How is each patron treated? Is it a happy, purposeful place? Is there an atmosphere that suggests that people enjoy working here?

A FIRST CLUE

Looking for clues about the treatment of staff is undoubtedly a good place to begin. While it is possible for staff members who are treated well, with consideration and sensitivity, to growl and snap at patrons and each other, this is the exception rather than the rule. However, the antithesis certainly has a higher degree of probability: staff members who are treated poorly, who are ignored or bullied, are likely to treat patrons and each other in a similar manner. Those who can rise above such insensitivity on the part of bosses or coworkers are likely candidates for sainthood.

Look at some clues as to the treatment of staff members among the PR winners; this will provide some significant signposts that show how these libraries do, in fact, show concern for people.

Staff Involvement

Administrators of the library at the University of Texas Health Science Center, San Antonio, knew where to begin when they were making plans to introduce a new building to the various groups of users on campus. They started with the library staff, establishing a library PR committee composed of people from various departments, and making sure in the first three months that their employees knew about all of the building's features and understood the online catalog as well. Only then did they turn to their external publics, the library's patrons.

Another library where the same kind of approach to staff was used is the Milwaukee Public Library. Their award-winning centennial celebration was characterized by attention to employees. For example, a staff party was held at the Central Library the night before the Kickoff Centennial Open House, as a sort of pep rally for the year's celebration.

Sneak Preview was the title of the special centennial newsletter issued six times a year to keep all employees up to date (see figure 7.1). As an added touch, the mailing list included retired staff members, who were included in the festivities. The newsletter was in addition to the regular staff publication, *Book Truck*.

A campaign to revitalize and coordinate the library's entire public relations efforts at Houston Public Library began with the recognition that external PR efforts were not enough. They concentrated on their own communications as part of the process, visiting the branches to talk about communications concerns. They also established an ongoing PR Advisory Committee. A staff workshop on graphics was sponsored as part of a continuing PR inservice program. In other words, they developed a total PR effort, recognizing that the best plans will go astray if the staff is not committed and involved in them.

One other aspect of the Houston effort was press releases on the various members of the library staff, their unique talents and interests, etc. They even found one staff member who moonlighted as a shoemaker. Personalizing personnel is the way to describe this approach.

As part of the 25th anniversary of the library at Travis Air Force Base, California, the library adapted a European concept of "Ausflug," scheduling a variety of activities outside of the library that allowed library staff members to get to know each other better. Roughly translated as "fly-out," the idea was that those who play together, talk together, and spend time together are much more likely to work together well. At Travis it was reflected in the staff enthusiasm for the 25 different activities scheduled during the silver anniversary to call attention to the base library's services.

Clark Air Force Base Library, The Philippines, compiled a scrapbook with an A-Z format to log activities. At the end of the scrapbook the X-Y-Z section was inscribed: XYZ = E**x**traordinary, **Y**oung-at-heart, and **Z**est-for-working staff. They went on to say, "Good service is the key to good public relations and a well-trained happy staff is vital to good service. We appreciate our staff and so do our patrons. They deserve three letters in the alphabet—and much more."[1]

SENSITIVITY TO THE SCENE

Another way libraries show their concern for people is the sensitivity they display toward their community. An awareness of what is happening in that community to the library patrons is vital. It could be called the "Avoiding the Marie Antoinette syndrome," or "Don't offer them cake if they need bread." At Bad Axe Public Library, Michigan, the library administration recognized that area farmers were suffering through hard times, so they targeted this group for some special efforts. The library placed a cartoon about wheat and bread prices (wheat goes up and down; bread just goes up) in local farm-interest newspapers and magazines. Flyers were distributed through the county cooperative service. A special calendar of events was created and distributed with a focus on areas where a farmer might need some information. The slogan was, "If you need to know something, all you need to know is our telephone number."

No. 5 August 16, 1978

THE DOWNTOWN ASSOCIATION SALUTES A 100-YEAR-OLD NEIGHBOR

THE MILWAUKEE PUBLIC LIBRARY

Locations up and down Wisconsin Avenue and a few side streets as well will be the setting as the Central Library takes the Centennial celebration into its own neighborhood — downtown Milwaukee. The date: Thursday, August 24 — one of the periodic "Downtown Days" sponsored by the Downtown Association. Besides all the special sales in the stores, it will also include a variety of library activities as "The Downtown Association Salutes a 100-Year-Old Neighbor — the Milwaukee Public Library." A flyer advertising the day's events is being distributed all over downtown and throughout the library system as well, but here are a few additional details.

— LIBRARY USED BOOK SALE.
It will be a scaled-down version of our famous book bargain sale, including about 4000 books (10 times that many have been sold at Central Library over a two or three-day period), but the selection is a wide one and all items are priced at 25¢ as usual. The place will be the First Wisconsin Center at 777 E. Wisconsin Ave. (That's the 42-story building.)* It will be on the Galleria Level, just up the escalator from the main bank lobby. The hours are 10 a.m. to 4 p.m.; members of The Bookfellows-Friends of the Milwaukee Public Library System will handle book sales and have plastic book bags available, for 25¢ as well. (See back page for a look at the new bag design.)

— CHILDREN'S STORYHOURS GIVEN BY LIBRARIANS
Nobody can tell a story like a professional children's librarian and several will be doing so at department stores. At T.A. Chapman Co., near the fireplace on the first floor, Florence Kilaru of the Mill Road Library will be telling stories. A few blocks west, at Gimbels, in the children's area on the third floor, Lynn Williams of the Oklahoma Library will be "on stage." And at J.C. Penney Co., on the balcony children's department, Meredith Bishop of Tippecanoe Library will be the storyteller. All these storyhours will be held at 1:30, and afterwards, the librarians will distribute booklists and balloons with the library's new logo on them. A special performance by the Library Players will take place at the Boston Store in the children's area on the third floor, also at 1:30. Boys and girls in the audience will get a chance to perform, too.

— MOVIES: "Tut — Boy King" and "The King and I"
If you've been in the recently renovated Plankinton Building Mall (still called the Arcade by downtowners), you know that it's become a popular meeting and eating place during the

Fig. 7.1. Keep them posted. Reprinted with permission of Milwaukee Public Library, Milwaukee, Wisconsin.

At the Brown County Public Library in Green Bay, Wisconsin, the children's department extended its programming efforts to include signed story hours for deaf children in the community. Again, the library demonstrated a special concern for a segment of the population which can easily be overlooked.

In a similar fashion, the Ventura County Library, California, made special efforts through parents and teachers to reach visually impaired children for its summer reading program. Building on a partnership, they worked with the local Lions Club.

FOR ALL OF US

Sensitive, caring library administrators and staff members realize that libraries are for all of us. To help libraries in Oklahoma realize that lofty dream, the Oklahoma Department of Libraries began a campaign with the motto "Libraries for All of Us" (see figure 7.2). This statewide project targeted Blacks, Hispanics, and Native Americans, building appropriate collections of materials which were available to circulate to 12 pilot libraries in the state. The Oklahoma Department of Libraries also designed and provided the publicity for the program as well as all types of promotional materials.

Most effective was the active seeking out of ethnic groups for their input and support. Leaders of each group offered suggestions and assisted in obtaining coverage within their ethnic community. Their word-of-mouth enthusiasm greatly assisted the project, as did the unveiling of the appropriate collection at ethnic group conferences and the appearance of librarians on conference programs to explain the project's purposes.

This approach illustrates that it is important to work in concert with such groups: don't do it *to* them or *for* them, but do it *with* them.

PROGRAMS POINT THE WAY

The programs offered by prize-winning libraries often show the kind of empathy that is characteristic of those with the human touch. Consider the stated purpose of the National Endowment for the Humanities (NEH) project called CITY!, which was the multiyear project of the Houston Public Library: "... to help city dwellers be aware of the challenges and problems which confront them daily and to help them live a humane and sense-filled life in the city."[2] This project's very core was to increase the humaneness of the lives of patrons.

Incidentally, the planners also showed their concern for people in the ways staff were treated in regard to the CITY! project. There were carefully delineated plans to keep staff informed. One group that was a special target was the switchboard operators, since it was obvious that these people would be in "the trenches" in terms of answering patrons' questions about all phases of the NEH grant activities. Houston planners knew that a lot of hard work can go for naught if patrons do not get answers quickly and accurately when they call in response to publicity or promotion.

When the command at Nellis Air Force Base put together a Win with Wellness program as an entire base project, the base library moved into high gear to support that project with activities, collections, and even an Operation Exer-Cycle which library patrons could use. An award was given to the patron who logged the most miles. In this case, the program was initiated by an outside agency or group. Libraries in tune with the times will certainly support and enhance such activities. No wonder the Nellis Air Force Library's motto is "Flies high and proud."

Fig. 7.2. Statewide project. Reprinted with permission of Oklahoma Department of Libraries, Oklahoma City, Oklahoma.

THEY NEED KNOW-HOW

"Need some know-how? Check out the library!" was the motto adopted by the Alameda County Library System, for their self-help campaign (see figure 7.3). The target was to inform residents of the variety of highly practical resources which the library could provide to assist them. The use of a wrench as a logo was appropriate for it gave an instant "fix-it" quality to the campaign. The central objective of the plan was to impress upon residents the practical, utilitarian value of information.

Fig. 7.3. Promoting the practical. Reprinted with permission of Alameda County Library, Hayward, California.

Programs at local branch libraries featured self-help topics such as legal self-help and tax preparation information. The involvement of staff was critical since outreach speeches were given by staff members to clubs in the communities served. Also booths were set up in shopping malls and even community parades were used to gain public attention.

In terms of publicity, Friends groups were utilized and a concerted effort was made to get speakers on local radio and television shows, as well as coverage in all print media. Billboards, bus cars, posters, bumper stickers all carried the know-how library logo. Even the paychecks of all 93,000 county employees carried the special campaign theme. The lesson to be learned from the Alameda campaign is that programs that show concern need to be promoted as well as planned.

KIDS AND DADS

An entirely different kind of project was conceived and executed by the Laurel Bay School Library, Laurel Bay, South Carolina. This unique reading involvement project revolved around the theme, Daddy, Will You Read to Me? (see figure 7.4). Objectives of the program, initiated to celebrate the Year of the Child, were: to offer the opportunity for fathers to enjoy a book with their children, to promote the reading habit for life, and to encourage fathers to spend an uninterrupted 15 minutes with their children.

Participants enrolled at the library and agreed to read for 15 minutes per week to their children. Fathers were chosen specifically because this is a U.S. Marine Corp library and children are often separated from their fathers due to military assignments.

Attractive flyers showing two happy children being read to by their father were distributed throughout the base area. Children whose fathers were overseas obtained surrogate fathers through a sign-up campaign whereby those on base agreed to read to their temporary adoptees. This adoption program was coordinated by the guidance department. To build schoolwide support, various other departments and classes were involved. In art class, children designed buttons and shopping bags about their father reading to them. In English classes they reported on the books they shared with their fathers.

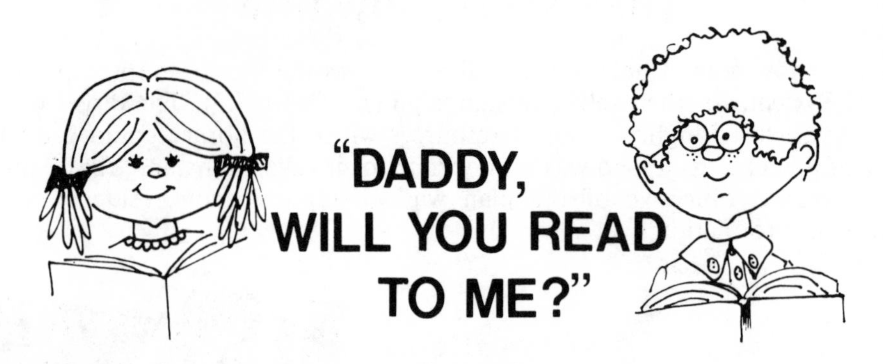

A PARENT INVOLVEMENT PROGRAM

LAUREL BAY SCHOOL
LIBRARIES

Our Program
for
The International Year of the Child

WHY?	To enjoy a book together with your child To help promote the reading habit for life To spend 15 enjoyable minutes with your child
WHEN?	You can join anytime from September, 1979 – May, 1980
WHERE?	Join at either Laurel Bay School Library. Complete the attached Membership form and send it to school with your child
WHAT DO I DO?	* * * * * * READ A BOOK OR STORY TO YOUR CHILD FOR AT LEAST 15 MINUTES A WEEK
HOW?	CHOOSE A BOOK OR A STORY FROM ANY LIBRARY, READ IT TO YOUR CHILD ANYTIME, ANYPLACE. THAT'S UP TO YOU. ONLY 15 MINUTES A WEEK.

- -

MEMBERSHIP FORM

☐ YES, I want to BELONG TO THE "DADDY, WILL YOU READ TO ME?" Program

NAME OF CHILD ______________________________

GRADE ______________________________

TEACHER ______________________________

PARENT SIGNATURE ______________________________

BONUS FOR MEMBERS

MEMORIES YOU CAN KEEP FOR A LIFETIME

Fig. 7.4. Reading together. Reprinted with permission of Laurel Bay School Libraries, Laurel Bay, South Carolina. Art work by Rodger Steele.

Teachers sent home notes reporting the progress of the project. They also provided hints on how to read to children. The librarian prepared a special bibliography of suggested titles for those parents who needed hints on what to read.

The Laurel Bay School librarian reported that the best thing about the project was that in its year-long efforts, it truly created an opportunity for special moments between fathers and children, in addition to encouraging an interest and pleasure in reading. The entire project cost just over $200, a figure which the librarian indicated could have been even lower. As Laurel Bay Schools show, concern doesn't cost money as much as it takes an appropriate mindset about service to people.

TURNING IT AROUND

A special kind of serendipity was at work at the Genesee District Library, Flint, Michigan, when the staff was faced with a censorship issue regarding materials for children. As we are all aware from our reading of professional literature, these issues may become "the times that try our souls," and nothing is needed more than a cool head and a professional demeanor. At Genesee, they were able to create a caring, concerned atmosphere out of what often turns out to be a devisive, corrosive situation.

After directly responding to the specific challenge by declaring they wouldn't ban the books, they conceived and launched a positive response to the censorship issue (see figure 7.5). Targeted to the community at large, the message was that parents have a responsibility to supervise their children's reading. They also incorporated the concept that the library could help parents who wish to get involved in such choices for their children, and that the library had materials which could provide guidance.

They created several types of audiovisual materials for the campaign. Radio and television public service announcements were designed to inform the public at large about the campaign. This was important since censorship issues always receive extensive media coverage. A brief slide-cassette program was produced so that staff members would have an interesting starting point as they presented speeches to community groups and organizations.

Effective, low-keyed, and positive were the words the Dana jury used in describing this effort. Those in charge understood how to turn a potentially negative situation into a program with promise for parents.

PEOPLE PROGRAMS

Let's look at several other examples of "people programs" among the Dana award winners. The Louisville Free Public Library received a grant from the Kentucky Humanities Council to sponsor the program Why Did Grandpa Have to Die? (see figure 7.6) to help parents explain death to their children. At Louisville there was also the establishment of library services specifically for the deaf. What made this program outstanding was that 26 staffers spent over a year learning sign language prior to the program's start.

The Alabama Public Library Service, Montgomery, at the forefront of a multimedia campaign to combat illiteracy, successfully enlisted wide community support for their efforts. When Westfield High School, Westfield, New Jersey, won a Dana award, the judges cited their "People are important" attitude which characterized all of their efforts, from travelogues to faculty-student parties to brunches for volunteers.

Fig. 7.5. A positive response. Reprinted with permission of Genesee District Library, Flint, Michigan.

Fig. 7.6. Dealing with death. Reprinted with permission of Louisville Free Public Library, Louisville, Kentucky.

Women in Poverty

A multiyear winner, the Brown County Library, Green Bay, Wisconsin, recently focused special efforts on a concern about the feminization of poverty as a local trend. They created a videotape in response to this concern and the Video Implementation Committee looked upon the project as a dual opportunity: to bring an awareness to Green Bay citizens of a growing social problem, and to demonstrate the quality and availability of the library's video services.

Their highly acclaimed and moving tape focuses on the lives of four women who live in the fairly well-to-do Green Bay area but are far from affluent themselves. The videotapes stimulated extensive television coverage and overwhelming requests from community and civic groups to use the tape at their meetings. The production itself was well prepared and has stimulated an interest in creating other productions on the part of community residents with unique interests or talents. The impressive statistics on the numbers of people who have seen the tape as well as its frequent playback on cable television illustrate the power of the production.

Dauphin Cares

The Dauphin County Library System, Harrisburg, Pennsylvania, has often demonstrated a concerned and caring attitude. When a U.S. commemorative stamp was issued honoring volunteers, the library was quick to send out "You Have Our Stamp of Approval" invitations to their library volunteers and to entertain them at an appreciation party (see figure 7.7). In another program school children were visited by Mrs. Pockets, a friendly symbol of the library and what it has to offer. Young adults and adults in the community were also targets for programming. A live radio program series, which focused on topics of interest to teenagers, included a phone-in segment. Adult programs included a layman's law series and the establishment of a grant information center. Using the slogan "Library Cards Are Priceless," the library proved their worth when they added a job and career information center for residents.

HOW DOES IT HAPPEN?

A concern for people and sensitivity to their individual needs, how does it happen? What makes it a hallmark for service in some libraries and strangely absent in others? Can it be fostered, encouraged, instilled? The answer is, "Yes!" and the place to start is with you and the rest of the staff. All too often when dealing with PR, librarians encounter that old "Can't see the forest for the trees" syndrome. They get so involved with the public they forget the individual, especially in terms of their own personal roles in the process. If we deluge our public with appealing brochures, promising posters, and enticing flyers, only to have them eagerly visit the library and encounter a library staff person who is neither promising nor enticing, we have a serious credibility problem.

Before getting too enthralled with our outreach efforts, we should conduct a quick survey of our personal PR, the way each of us personally and individually affects the public's attitude towards the library. Most patrons will judge the library, its program, and the library profession by their reaction to the library staff.

DEAR VOLUNTEER,
Please Accept Our Stamp Of Approval...

Fig. 7.7. Volunteer appreciation. Reprinted with permission of Dauphin County Library System, Harrisburg, Pennsylvania.

In Case of Doubt

If you hesitate to accept this and think the only thing that matters is a caring heart, consider a hypothetical situation: Your loved one is scheduled for serious brain surgery. You have an appointment with the doctor to discuss the technique, the risks, and the alternatives. You wait in the office. A door opens and the doctor enters, a man with shaggy hair, a scraggly beard, and dirty fingernails. He is wearing tattered blue jeans, sandals, and a T-shirt emblazoned "Doctors do it with their hands." Knowing nothing about his competence, what's your first impression? How do you feel about his operating on your loved one? What do you think about the hospital who hired him?

So, too, do you reflect on your profession.

Here's Looking at You

This personal inventory will help you analyze the way you may look to others and thus help you pinpoint the impression you are making:

- Do I look so young patrons can't separate me from the YA users?
- Do I dress like I am unaware of style changes over the years? If I haven't changed with the times in my dress, a patron may feel my thinking is outdated too.

- Am I sloppy and careless? If I don't care about my appearance, a patron may think I don't care about my work either.

- Do I look fussy and overdone? Do I call attention to myself by the way I look rather than the service I render. Am I going to work or to a party?

- Do I dress too sensual? Do I boggle my patrons' minds and quicken their heartbeats with tight shirts and slacks or low-cut blouses.

- In summary, do I look like a competent professional, aware of my position and concerned about it?

Appearance is also more than clothes. Hair styles and use of accessories all help to form an impression. Even a briefcase or purse says something, as does office decor. We don't believe in a single style or corporate uniform, but it is important that you become aware of these facets of personal PR.

Just as our appearance will cause others to react in certain ways to us, so will we react to them in the same manner. Be aware of forming opinions which could color the type of service rendered and the type of attitude conveyed. As professionals, we must strive to provide appropriate service to every patron, regardless of appearance.

The Next Voice You Hear

Once patrons see you, the next step is that they'll hear you. Ask yourself:

- Do I use slang, flippant remarks, or jargon? The latter is a special problem in our acronym oriented profession.

- Do I swear, even if patrons are around?

- Do I speak so softly that a patron must strain to hear me?

- Am I so loud I disturb those who are reading?

- Is my tone preachy, as if I am delivering sermons rather than giving assistance?

- Is my tone so cold that patrons feel I don't wish to help them?

- Am I so gushy with my friendly, chatty voice that I seem phony?

- Does my phone voice make me seem approachable or unbearable?

Our voice should reflect confidence and concern in a fashion understood positively by whatever age patron encountered.

A Rose Is a Rose

The next area involves a sense which logically follows sight and sound but is often overlooked because it seems uncouth to mention. How do you smell? Natural odors come to mind, but more often we assault our patron's noses with overdone perfume or after-shave lotion. Musk is especially hard on people with allergies. Another problem is the heavy smoker whose clothes and breath may be obnoxious to those sensitive to tobacco.

Nothing More Than Feelings

Another area to explore is how you feel, or what is your attitude? Ask yourself the questions:

- Am I obviously sick and tired of my job? Do I complain constantly, and loudly?
- Am I uneasy about helping people? Do I prefer to stay in the back room, busy with superficial details?
- Am I always so busy that patrons are reluctant to interrupt me for the help they need and deserve?
- Am I bored? Do I spend time on personal matters, including phone calls?
- Do I seem to have to be forced to work? Am I always somewhere other than where I'm supposed to be?
- Do I gossip or do things behind the backs of my employer or fellow employees?
- Am I inconsistent – helpful to a patron one day, distant, occupied, and rude the next?
- Am I so enthusiastic that patrons avoid me rather than have me occupy their time with my views?
- Do I try to show I am interested in my work and reveal by my attitude that I want to be helpful and useful to those seeking my assistance?

The Old Switcheroo

It's now time for you to look at yourself from another perspective. You've considered how you might appear to others. Now ask yourself:

- Am I an empire builder, viewing each patron as another stepping stone to my success?
- Do I live in a fairyland, unable to see the realities, the problems, and difficulties of my position and of my patrons?
- Do I seem to know it all? Is there never a time when I admit ignorance or acknowledge another's efforts and interests?
- Do I demand that everyone agree with me and become a tyrant if they don't?

Hearing or Listening?

There is a difference between hearing and listening. When you hear, you're aware there is sound, but when you listen, you seek meaning in what's being said. How do I hear?

- Do I tune out noise so completely that I am indifferent to anything going on, no matter how much of a ruckus?
- Do I actually contribute to a noisy environment, giggling and carrying on in a fashion disturbing to library users?
- Do I refuse to hear anyone's views or issues? If there's disagreement, do I make up my mind before I hear both sides?
- Do I hear only when forced to? Am I so busy concentrating on what I want to say that I never listen to what others contribute?

Yes, Caring

The ability to do a job well requires more than skill and talent; it also demands commitment. How much do I care?

- Do I willingly give my time to my job, and occasionally a little extra?
- Do I never have enough time in the day? Do I get so involved that my hours fly by?
- Am I willing to get involved in the nitty-gritty, if need be? Will I move the chairs, clean the coffee pot, and dirty my hands if that's what's necessary to get the job done?
- Do I join professional groups to learn from and support fellow professionals?
- Am I willing to cooperate with the various individuals and groups whose joint efforts are often needed?
- Am I willing to tolerate what I can't change, aggressively work for those things I can, and fight impossible odds, if need be, to render the library service I know is essential?

Daring

How do I *dare*? How far will I go to do the best for my job and profession?

- Will I dare to apologize if I'm wrong?
- Will I dare to mediate if a dispute springs up?
- Will I dare to be one of the group for the common good?
- Will I dare to go to extremes to gain the recognition the library needs?
- Will I dare to work harder, care more, complain less, and love my profession long after other folks have given up?

The questions asked in this inventory provide a picture of the type of people, who, just by being available, create good PR for the library. In other words, competent staff members who enjoy a job, work hard, are warm and helpful to patrons, and sincerely care about what they are doing are worth more than a month of public service announcements or a dozen attractive flyers. PR is a people business, and libraries that consistently demonstrate a concern for people know it.

Actions: Louder Than Words

All of us react to the body signals of those around us. People communicate by the way they walk, stand, and sit. Caring library staffers are aware of the impact of their body language on bosses, coworkers, and patrons. They also know that their body posture can scream "Don't bother me!" in a definitive way to patrons. The answer is to use positive kinds of nonverbal communication to reinforce the positive words we speak.

The most expressive form of nonverbal communication is made with the eyes. Confident people, for example, make more eye contact. We also look at people more when we're truly listening to them. Caring people signal their interest with appropriate "eyetalk."

Stay off My Turf

We also have a sense of territoriality which affects how we act towards others. This is demonstrated when people choose the same seats for monthly meetings or the same daily parking place and get disturbed if someone else occupies "their" spot. There are five "distance zones" wherein we allow people to operate according to their relation to us. These range from a public zone of about 12 feet normally used when we encounter a stranger, to an intimate zone of less than two feet, reserved only for special people. The middle or social zone, four to seven feet, is where most library patrons will feel comfortable. It is permissible territory in which to conduct the necessary interchanges of the library without invading closer or privileged space. However, caring librarians must learn to read the signals being given nonverbally by a patron and to react appropriately. If for example we approach at a limit closer than that person chooses, chances are the patron will back up, literally.

On the other hand, if we force a more formal distance, the patron will sense our discomfort and have a feeling of rejection. Nonverbal clues—eyes, gestures, movements, or hands—will tell people how we feel and how we think. It's up to us to decide what we want to telegraph to them.

Encounters of the Ordinary Kind?

There is another factor that can either hinder or enhance a library's chances for winning a "we care" award—the sticky issues that all libraries wrestle with. For example, what is the general response in your library to the patron who asks for materials on highly controversial topics? It seems easy until the patron is a young adult or a child and then the response may be different. The attitude that is conveyed by staff members is important in responding to this type of request.

What happens when a patron asks the library to purchase a book for the collection that does not meet the library's selection criteria? Does the patron get the feeling that his or her taste is inferior and that the library is only for those with refined tastes? How does the staff handle the patron who comes in with a gift book that he or she wants to add to the library's collection when it is obvious that it would not meet selection criteria? How does the reference staff handle a patron who comes in with an extensive research project and wants step-by-step assistance? And ask yourself, would the treatment be different if the patron were the city mayor, school principal, or college president?

Sticky Wickets

There are other difficult situations which deal with different types of clients. For example, how does the staff react to a patron who has difficulty in expressing a question? How do they treat a patron who appears to be retarded, has a speech impediment, or is hearing impaired? How do they react to a person who does not speak English? Remember, even the most kind-hearted staffer can react adversely when under stress.

How does the staff handle angry or rude patrons? No one should be expected to tolerate abusive language or threats from another, but there are techniques which can be used to defuse anger in others. On the other hand, there are behaviors that only escalate such situations into the opening rumbles of World War III. How do staff members handle complaints from patrons? What is the treatment given to a patron at the circulation desk who insists he returned the three books your records show he still has checked out? How does the staff handle a patron who complains about the quality of service received?

We do not presume to dictate the correct responses to these questions since many of them will depend upon the policies that have been established in a particular library. But it is critical that such policies have been established. That's the first step. The second step is discussion of these kinds of situations by staff. Role playing might even be considered so when the real thing comes along, they can react reasonably and not emotionally.

Every day in libraries of all types across the country, library staff members are interacting with patrons. These encounters have both positive and negative possibilities in terms of building good will. Libraries with a reputation for a caring attitude don't leave that possibility to the whim of fate or chance; they establish a staff development program that will meet both the needs of the library and of the individual employees. They also recognize that education is not the total answer in staff development because there are many people who know how but won't. The motivation problem and the rewards structure must also be considered. Administrators in these libraries understand that people want to feel that they are doing something worthwhile.

An outstanding model in personnel management is the philosophy and approach used by J. W. Marriott of the famous Marriott hotel/restaurant corporation. He believes that service is what the company is all about and recognizes that its success depends upon the service it offers. In turn, this service must depend upon their employees and how they interact with the customers.

PUTTING EMPLOYEES FIRST

On the average, the Marriott Corporation employs an average of more than eight million people. For that reason, the company puts employees first–ahead of management, ahead of shareholders, and even ahead of customers. Without the favorable impression that employees make on people, there would be no customers, no management, and no stockholders. The methods used by Marriott to develop a positive working climate for employees, with the goal of ensuring positive and profitable relationships between employees and customers are applicable to library personnel management.

Systems and Standards

First, they have developed systems and standards for delivering their products, and for teaching people how to meet those standards and deliver quality services. They have developed detailed employee training manuals for every position. The manuals are tied into individual development programs of tasks to be mastered, and a trainer signs off on each task when a new employee completes it satisfactorily. A new employee cannot take over full responsibility for the job until the trainer approves his or her work. In libraries it may not be possible to set up a completely regimented system for training, but we surely could profit from spelling out in writing just how certain tasks ought to be performed. We can also insist that time for training be allowed instead of it being a "catch as catch can" affair. This is doubly important for those positions that have immediate and frequent public contact – answering the telephone, in the reference area, and at the circulation desk.

A second Marriott principle of personnel management is that they include employees in opportunities for expansion and growth. There may not be many advancement opportunities in smaller libraries, but we can encourage all employees to learn new skills, continue their formal education, and participate in planning for the library's future as well as their own.

Lead by Doing

A third principle that Marriott subscribes to involves the role of the manager in the day-to-day operation. Because they believe managers set the work climate, they are constantly in the field observing, inspecting, teaching, and motivating. These managers also know how to do the tasks they are managing; they have to learn what it is like "in the trenches" before they can give the orders. Therefore, they can value the contribution of each and every employee. Library managers, too, could profit from a turn on the shelving truck, at the reference desk on a busy night, on a weekend shift, etc.

The fourth Marriott principle is that it is important to encourage effective employee communications and participation. A good working climate dictates that people must know how they are doing and what they can do to improve and be promoted.

Key Is Communication

Not only are there monthly evaluations of performance, but managers have regular rap sessions with employees to find out how to improve the organization and climate in which they work. This kind of communication gives recognition to people. It allows them to participate in the decisions that affect them. Library managers, too, will find that they can't do much to improve employee satisfaction unless they know what is troubling them.

In order to be sure that employee feedback is reaching management, the Marriott Corporation conducts annual employee attitude surveys through anonymous questionnaires. They also have extensive systems to guarantee each employee fair treatment, allowing an employee to go all the way up the ladder to the president's office if necessary to settle a concern.

These principles of training, planning, sharing, and communicating are ones that we can all profit from, and library patrons will receive better service if we apply them.

AND A "WE CARE" ENVIRONMENT

Another grand scheme that is common to libraries with winning ways is the importance of an appealing library environment. Just as personal appearance has an immediate affect on those with whom you come in contact, so does the library's appearance. Just as we suggested a personal inventory to determine your personal PR, so we would like to suggest you conduct an institutional inventory as though you had never been there before to help you see your library with a fresh viewpoint. You could even ask someone who really is not familiar with the library to do the inventory also, so you can get a truly unbiased opinion.

Who's Got a Library?

Did you have trouble locating the library? Were there signs posted on main arteries to direct you to either a branch or central library? Did a friendly service station operator have to point you in the right direction? Is the library marked on city maps?

We have circled, struggled, circumnavigated, and generally been exceedingly frustrated in trying to find libraries in some communities. Churches, local service clubs, and other groups find it useful to post information signs. You should join the growing numbers of libraries who are posting library logo directional signs. This is especially true if the location is out-of-the-way or reached only by one-way streets. College and university libraries should be clearly marked on campus maps as well as having directional signs at campus entrances. The locations of library media centers within school buildings should also be designated by signs and on maps, even when school policies require visitors to obtain passes at central offices.

Are We Here–or Where?

Could you identify the library? Could you find parking? Once you arrived at the building, was there a large, clearly visible sign or name that could be read from the street by a driver who is watching traffic at the same time. Are there clearly marked signs for parking lot, or even parking suggestions posted, especially in congested business locations? Is there adequate accommodation for handicapped patrons, with signs indicating parking and entrance areas that are accessible?

We know that parking space is a real problem for many libraries and schools, but if there are parking lots within several blocks and patrons are so informed by signs and arrows, the frustration level will be reduced. The worst thing to do is pretend no problem exists. A librarian said to us recently, "I'll be looking forward to your visit, but I have no idea where you'll park!"

Where Do I Go from Here?

Could you find the main entrance? Could you find other areas of the library easily? Was the entrance well marked from both the street and the parking lot? What was your initial impression of the atmosphere? Did you feel welcome? Was there a map or pamphlet handy near the entrance that explained the layout?

What is said about "first impressions" is very true–they count.

Can You Find Your Way Around?

Could you locate major areas within the library easily? Were signs prominently placed directing you to the card catalog, current periodicals, government documents, pamphlets, recordings, information services, etc. Were the signs large enough to be seen easily, even by the visually impaired? Were they attractive and in keeping with the library's decor?

If librarians have one particular failing, it is that they take too much for granted. We use our own jargon and often are unaware that patrons really don't know what we mean. Ask an infrequent user in your library to find his or her way around. All people find it unpleasant to feel unsure of themselves, and if potential patrons feel this discomfort they'll come back only reluctantly if at all.

The Sharper Image

As you proceeded on your inventory, did you notice the physical condition of such areas as the parking lot, the grounds, and the exterior of the building? In the parking lot, did weeds, cracked pavement, and debris mar the scene? In winter are the walks cleared? Did the grounds appear well cared for? Is the building in need of paint or repair? Is there graffiti? Inside the entrance, is the floor clean? Is there evidence of good housekeeping on a regular basis or are materials scattered all over on tables, shelves, or any other convenient spot? Are the rest rooms clean and well maintained?

Yes, what we are speaks louder than any words. We do need caring hearts to reach out and serve, but we also need to show that we care by the effort we put into our appearance, our attitude, and the library surroundings. Winners know it and in both these grand schemes, all libraries can be winners.

NOTES

[1]Scrapbook entry, John Cotton Dana Award contest, Clark Air Force Base, The Philippines, 1981.

[2]Scrapbook entry, John Cotton Dana Award contest, Houston Public Library, 1977.

8
Winners Practice Creative Adapting

There are many clever people in the world – people who dream up themes and schemes, plans and promotions. Often these creative people are involved in library work, as evidenced by those libraries described so far.

Many librarians read library publications, attend conferences, and visit with colleagues in neighboring institutions in order to keep up to date and to pick up a hint or a tip on a way to do it better. Fortunately, the work of these creators is not diminished by the use of their ideas. Rather the creators are often the best of creative adapters as well. Sharing ideas makes it possible for all of us to do a better job.

That is why we believe so strongly in the concept of creative adapting. It is a premise upon which our bimonthly newsletter *Library Insights, Promotion, and Programs* (*LIPP*) is based. We frequently include a feature, "Here and There," which highlights specific ideas that individual libraries across the country are using and that other libraries can use effectively. Suggestions on how such adapting might be accomplished, particularly by libraries of other types, are frequently included.

PIRATE'S ALLEY

It is also obvious to us that there are a great many creative people working in a wide range of vocations and in all types of businesses, industries, sales, and services. However, it takes a bit more insight to recognize the creative adapting potential of the ideas created by people in fields other than librarianship. That's why in *LIPP* we periodically feature some interesting, stimulating, and attractive approaches from the wide world outside the library's doors. These ideas have potential for creative adapting for libraries if they are staffed by people with an adventurous spirit and an open mind.

The Smart One

Let's look at one idea which originated in the library world and was later picked up by other library agencies. The Council for Florida Libraries developed a statewide promotion which used as its theme It's OK to Get Smart with Us! (see figure 8.1). John Cotton Dana judges characterized their entry as "... an imaginative, well-organized, and well conducted campaign focusing on a clever theme and utilizing all media to increase library use across the state."[1]

An overview of their campaign illustrates that effective awareness packages sometimes take time to get started. The Florida campaign started at a Florida Governor's Conference when a resolution was passed citing the need for a statewide library promotion. It wasn't until three years later that funding was secured to develop the promotion; the campaign began the next year.

A central feature of the promotion was the emphasis on those library services not commonly associated with the traditional book oriented role the public might expect. All stops were pulled out to incorporate a wide variety of approaches in the campaign, everything from buttons to billboards, items in print to segments on radio and television.

Adding It Up

An important component was the monitoring which they did during the campaign, watching which releases and special feature articles were picked up by metropolitan papers, and logging the amount of coverage the campaign was receiving. This was an important aspect of their evaluation efforts.

Outside consultants conducted random surveys of libraries across Florida to determine the results of the project. An average increase of over 25 percent in calls to libraries was determined. One library indicated a 96 percent increase in one month. Another indication of Florida's success is shown by the fact that a library in California and the state library in Arizona have requested permission and assistance in utilizing the same campaign within their areas.

The library public information officer for this project commented that her biggest reward was having assisted small independent libraries with no PR staff to have high quality promotion of their services. However, she was confident they had a winner for the Dana competition when she received the requests from California and Arizona.

School/College Smarts

This theme is a natural for school library media centers and college and university libraries. The theme provides a clever turn-of-phrase to a familiar scene – an adult waving a forefinger under a teenager's nose exclaiming, "Don't get smart with me!" It also lends itself to promoting a wide variety of ways patrons *can* get smart at the library: Special review classes for SAT tests? Certainly. Teenage babysitting clinics? Why not? Orientation sessions on online search service? Of course.

In other words, identify what you want to promote, and then tie it to this kind of thematic campaign.

Fig. 8.1. Billboard blitz. Reprinted with permission of Council for Florida Libraries, Fort Lauderdale, Florida.

DISHING OUT SERVICES

Now let's look at a library that borrowed a bright idea from business.

Drive down any main street in any town in the United States today and what is the prevailing architecture? Answer: fast-food franchise. Turn on any network television channel and who are the big-budget advertisers? Answer: the makers of Big Macs and Whoppers. Billboards, magazine ads, direct mail advertising in this country, and now even in London, Paris, and Tokyo, all promote the Colonel from Kentucky and his competitors.

One smart library "entrepreneur" built on this pervasive element in contemporary life. Mobile Public Library, Alabama, produced an award-winning slide cassette show that capitalized on the fast-food industry, using the slogan "Read In or Take Out!" to promote lively library service. The entire script for the slide show was done in verse and highlights the wide range of services and materials available to patrons at the Mobile Public Library, a "fast-info" outlet. (See figure 8.2.)

The show's audio tract featured an appropriately fast-paced narration which was backed up by the steady, jazzy beat of snare drums. Visuals were related to the materials described and were shown quickly to suggest the quick nature of a "fast-info" library.

Fig. 8.2. Lively library service. Reprinted with permission of Mobile Public Library, Mobile, Alabama.

Read In or Take Out!

by Teko Wiseman

We have art, history, and mystery to go.
Big print books for people who must read slow.
Gothics and westerns and science fiction books.
Thrillers and chillers and young reader's books.
There's Van Gogh and Picasso framed for your walls
El Greco, da Vinci and Andy Warhol
Christian Science Monitor, Birmingham News
Wall Street Journal and Times Picayunes.
New Yorker, Fortune, and Harper's Bazaar
Hot Rod, McCall's, Mechanics Popular.

Shirley Temple, Humphrey Bogart, Chaplin and Garbo
Little Rascals, Charles Boyer, and Marilyn Monroe
Dolly Parton, Paganini, Z.Z. Top and Pendergrass
Elvis Presley, Beatles, and Beethoven all have class.

Our private eyes in Business and Science
Have all the answers. They're fact-finding giants.
They'll track down the answer to questions you pose
And come up with answers from someone who knows.
Like Dun & Bradstreet or Standard and Poor
Catalogues, almanacs and directories galore.
A computer that finds you a college or career
And phone books from 400 towns far and near.

No take-outs allowed in this reference center
But a dime buys a copy so you needn't remember.
We've encyclopedias and guides to the media
Who's Who and Film Revue
Bartlett's Quotations and Lincoln's orations
And travel guides by Fodor and Fielding too.

We have government documents coming out our ears
from patents to copyrights to spotting racketeers
regulations, compilations, charts and statistics
bulletins on marketing, graphs on ballistics.

For persons desirous of climbing family trees
We've censuses and registers on genealogy.
Ireland, Scotland, where'd you come from?
France perchance or Germany's lowland?
We've coats of arms and county records,
Army rosters, lineage charts.
Histories of wars and famines,
Ships in port from foreign parts.
Old newspapers, Dixiana, recipes grandmother used.
Marriage, birth and burial records
Anything you might choose.

Our talking books are read by ear
And delivered by mail to folks who can hear
But not see to read the standard print word
Plus sign language books that are seen but not heard.

Our children's menu is too long to repeat
So we'll just mention a few special treats.
We've books on
snakes as pets and spinning tops
secret codes and collection rocks
fixing bikes and making kites and
stirring up potions for dinosaur bites.
Not to mention
Black Beauty, Annie Oakley, Huckleberry Finn
Paul Bunyan, Olga Korbet and Rumpelstiltskin
those Hardy Boys and Nancy Drew
and Kipling's Jungle Book
plus Winnie the Pooh, Doctor Seuss
Peter Pan and Captain Hook

If you can't come to us, we'll come to you
We have a roving library too.
It covers the county all over on wheels
Everybody watches for our bookmobile

All rhyming aside, let us now put before you
Our major intent. We don't want to bore you.
Just read in or take out, it won't cost a dime.
We've got the books if you've got the time.[2]

Other libraries can adapt the fast-food idea for a promotion. Notice that the Mobile Public Library's script incorporated references that seem out of date today. This is because the slide show was meant to show the currency and relevance of their collection and their services. A slide show should be designed to serve its purpose at that time and in that place. In adapting, just update with the appropriate references for your library, for today.

WINDMILLS OF THEIR MINDS

Dana award winners often illustrate the creative adapting concept. The following examples were selected to show the different approaches creative people take as they design new activities for their libraries.

Titles are always important, whether a library is creating a new audiovisual presentation, a summer reading theme, a special series of concerts, or a library rededication extravaganza. When adapted from titles of other sources, they have the advantage of ready identification by patrons, and are memorable if designers incorporate a clever twist or play on words.

For example, the Chicago Public Library wanted an idea for their reading club and selected Invasion of the Book Snatchers (see figure 8.3), a good attention grabber for children. Similarly, Tacoma, Washington, used 20,000 Books under the Sea and prepared all materials, activities, and programs to reinforce this theme. When the Handley Library, Winchester, Virginia, needed a title for their new concert series, which was scheduled for the lunch hour, they chose A Little Noon Music (see figure 8.4).

Fig. 8.3. Invasion of the book snatchers. Reprinted with permission of Chicago Public Library, Chicago, Illinois.

Friends of the Handley Library present

A LITTLE NOON MUSIC

Tuesdays at the Library/12:15 to 1:00 p.m.

October 2 – "The Irish Contra Band"

Contra Dance music, forerunner of the Square Dance, brought to this country by the Irish, is revived by a multi-talented group playing the fiddle, guitar, hammered dulcimer, mandolin, auto-harp, flute and tin whistle. (On the Terrace, weather permitting; otherwise, in the Auditorium.)

October 9 – Madeline MacNeil, Folk Musician

Miss MacNeil sings ballads from the British Isles and Southern Appalachia, and some of her own compositions, accompanying herself on the guitar and mountain dulcimer. In the Auditorium.

October 16 – Shenandoah Faculty Jazz Ensemble

Trombone, Trumpet, Clarinet, Electric Guitar, Piano and Drums. On the Terrace, weather permitting.

October 23 – Shenandoah Woodwind Ensemble

Flute, Oboe, French Horn, and a Piano in a showcase of styles: Duos and Trios will highlight Classical, Baroque, Romantic and Twentieth Century music. In the Auditorium.

October 30 – Music Theatre from Shenandoah

Songs from popular musicals. On the Terrace.

November 6 – Glen Caluda, Classical Guitar

In the Auditorium.

Bring a bag lunch and enjoy this series of free recitals tailored to fit neatly into your lunch break . . . Beverage can be purchased in downstairs lobby. Discover what's going on with the performing arts in Winchester . . . It's happening at the Library!

Fig. 8.4. Midday music. Reprinted with permission of Handley Public Library, Winchester, Virginia.

Far Out

In Garland, Texas, the staff of the Nicholson Memorial Library wanted a vehicle to introduce first through sixth graders to all library resources available to them. They designed a slide show with the theme Close Encounters of the Library Kind, based on the Upstart promotion, which had been adapted from that award-winning film. The result was an award-winning slide show as well. Yes, they had a flying saucer in their story which took 80 hours to construct. It now has a permanent home in the children's department. They also had little space creatures with bug-eyed faces, ray-like shoulders, and silver-booted feet. Their tiny voices were computer-like, thanks to a flanger for voice distortion loaned by the local music store during production. The librarians were good managers as well as creative adapters as they spent less than $90 to put together this effective slide show.

Popular figures in the news—rock stars, nighttime soap opera stars, sports celebrities—receive much media attention and hype. One library decided to capitalize on the royalty fervor and had lots of fun with the phenomenon. Columbus and Franklin County Library, Columbus, Ohio, created a television public service announcement that spoofed the Lady Di craze by employing a local look-alike to promote services for women. The theme was Your Library Treats Every New Mother Just Like a Princess. The text encouraged the borrowing of library materials about children, marital problems, and dealing with in-laws. The public service announcement was picked up by CBS and beamed to BBC for showing in London.

Another library borrowed from the hype surrounding the Super Bowl and Super Sunday for their theme. The Martinsburg-Berkeley County Library, Martinsburg, West Virginia, was planning the dedication of a new wing and the rededication of the rest of the facility. They assembled their own cast of super stars—mimes, music ensembles, Morris (an English dance) dancers, and gifted artisans (see figure 8.5)—to perform and share their talents. Their Super Saturday, when the community was invited to tour, to share, and to celebrate, was a sell-out.

Pride of Place

The Elk Grove Village Public Library, Illinois, wanted a summer reading program idea that would encourage diversified and selective reading as well as provide information about nearby Chicago. They designed an adaptation of the Monopoly playing board and called their program the CTA Reading Program (CTA in this case stood for Chicago Travel Adventure instead of Chicago Transit Authority). Children "traveled around" by reading. Spaces on the game board were Chicago landmarks, identified also by appropriate Dewey subject numbers: Adlar Planetarium, 500's, Wrigley Field, 700's, etc. (see figure 8.6). This Dana award winner provides a great idea for other libraries to adapt. Just change the landmarks to those in your locale.

Keep It Clean

Sometimes libraries show creative adapting in the creation of a logo with elements combined from a number of different sources. Such was the case at the National Geographic Society Library in Washington, D.C. With a major library renovation and move planned, the librarians wanted a logo which would identify both the organization and their part in it. The result was an adaptation of the national library logo: the familiar National Geographic Society stylized globe with the logo superimposed. The integrity of the library logo was preserved and the result was graphically pleasing. A word of caution, wildly creative variations on this symbol are not encouraged.

Fig. 8.5. Artisan at work. Reprinted with permission of Martinsburg – Berkeley County Public Library, Martinsburg, West Virginia.

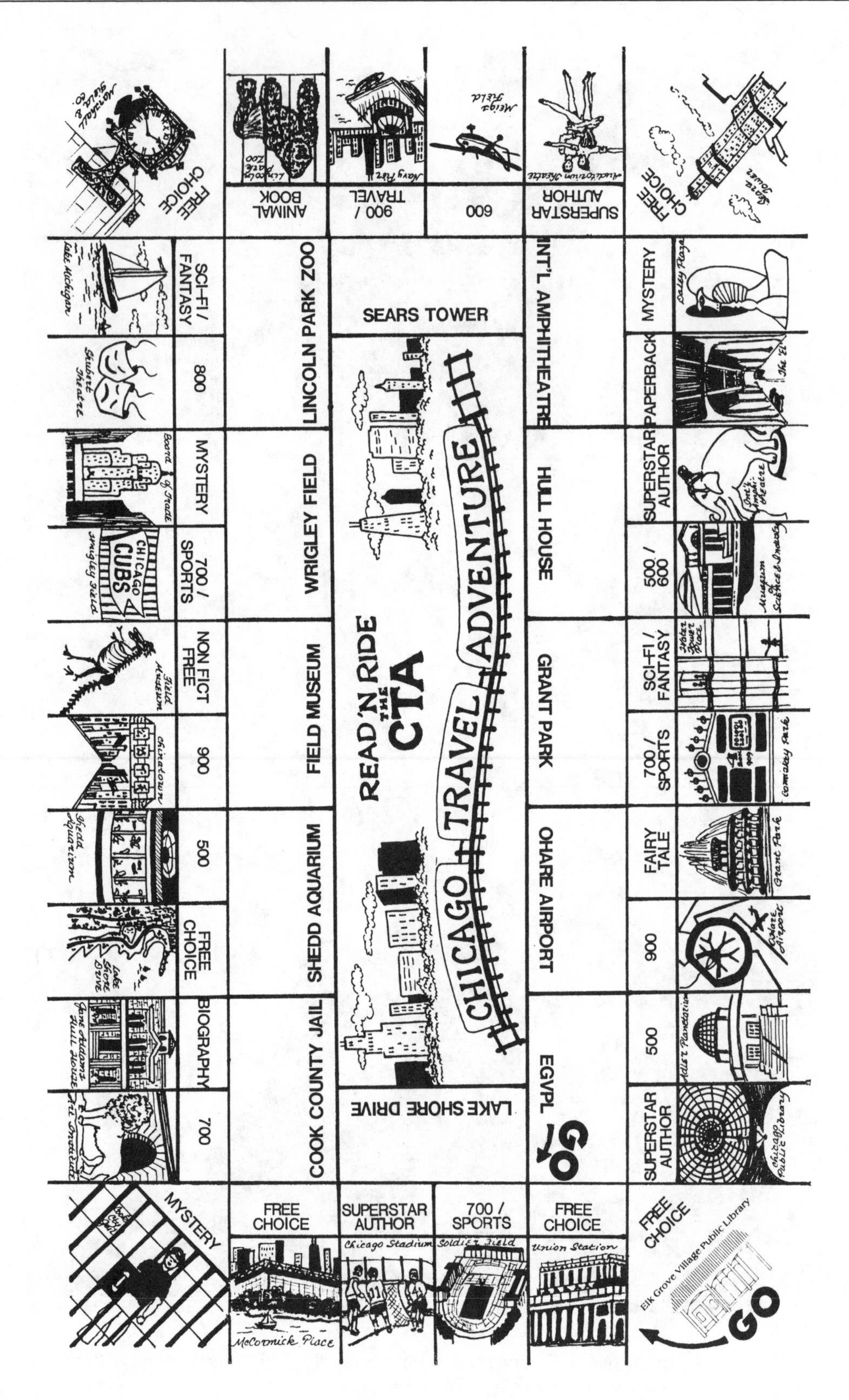

Fig. 8.6. Chicago travel adventure. Reprinted with permission of Elk Grove Village Public Library, Elk Grove Village, Illinois.

One final example of creative adapting is the theme around which the Travis Air Force Base library staff built an entire campaign for their silver anniversary. Who is it Snoopy is always chasing when he climbs into his Sopwith Camel? Who is always recognized by his red biplane? That Red Baron, of course. But at Travis he became The Well-Read Baron – Twenty-five Years at the Front. A clever caricature of the Baron became the symbol and theme for their year-long celebration. History and folklore were drawn upon and the result was an outstanding flight of imagination. The Well-Read Baron has become so popular that each year the library alters the logo to reflect the year's promotional emphasis (see figure 8.7).

ARE YOU AWARE?

Libraries can borrow winning entries in the Dana contest that seem to offer possible ideas for their own adaptation. Use a standard ALA interlibrary loan form and send your request to Headquarters Library, ALA, 50 East Huron Street, Chicago, Illinois, 60611. This is especially recommended if you are planning to enter the Dana contest because it is helpful to see how other scrapbooks have been put together.

Fig. 8.7. Flight of imagination. Reprinted with permission of Library, Travis Air Force Base, California.

PIRATE SHIPS, AHOY

Conferences are wonderful opportunities to learn new techniques and theories; to meet old and new friends; to find a simple solution to an unsolvable problem, and to relax with a group that talks our language. When we attend conferences, we've always got our skull and crossbones flag flying, looking for ideas that other libraries can pirate and adapt.

We are often successful in our raiding parties. At a recent conference of the Illinois Association for Media in Education, a section of the Illinois Library Association, we found an idea that was a bit different. The conference exhibits committee was encouraging attendees into the exhibits hall with an especially appealing approach. They placed poems throughout the hotel, by doors, stairs, in elevators, meeting rooms, etc. The humorous verses caught everyone's attention and provided a reminder to visit the exhibits. An approach such as this might be adapted by a library to get attention for a special program, a display, or a specific book collection. The possibilities are endless. You might even start the library Burma Shave jingle collection. To get you started, here's one from Illinois Association for Media in Education:

No matter what your budget prohibits,
There's something for you ... in the exhibits.

This would be especially popular in schools. It even has potential for a contest to see which student could write the best couplet for National Library Week or School Library Media Month. Another tact would be to use the Kilroy approach, having the poems mysteriously appear. Get a small group of students to be the secret band that posts the poems about the school. Be sure to honor school rules about posting, however, and clear the activity with the principal first.

Business Buried Treasure

True devotees of creative adapting have a field day when they contemplate the treasure chests of ideas that they can discover and loot from the brightest and best minds in the business community. Sometimes it's just a name or title that sets off the imagination. For example, we visited South Bend, Indiana, for a Notre Dame football game and spotted a firm named Imagineering. From that title, two years later, was born an entire workshop for librarians on creativity and management. When one sees something that strikes a spark or an instant recognition, it's important to file the idea away for future use. Don't rely on memory because as a creative adapter you are going to accumulate many treasures, and not all of them will be instantly useful to you. Two tips: First, always carry a small spiral notebook with you. Jot down ideas about anything you see that might be suitable for pirating. Forget loose slips of paper as they just get lost in the paper shuffle. Second, start a file folder or desk drawer which you can toss materials into that seem to have potential for the future. Then when you are generating ideas for a new program, campaign, flyer, or you-name-it, start going through the stack. Also check those spiral notebooks. Hopefully, something will set off your creative juices, and start you on your way.

The following are a few examples of items that we had stored away in our treasure chest of ideas.

Shuck Those PJs

It's unusual for a business establishment to promote itself by stressing the dedication of its retail staff, but such an ad in the *Milwaukee Journal* caught our eye. The Brills ad praised employees who were willing to "shuck those pjs" to get in early for the idea-exchanging monthly sessions. The headline and copy read:

**At 7:30 A.M.
once a month
our associates go
through rain and snow
and gloom to get
together for breakfasting
briefing, brainpicking,
and bellyaching**

> How come? Because we all think it's important to take a minute to sort things out and get perspective and find out what's good, what's bad, and what's new. So we shuck our pj's and wend our way to town for what has become a very important monthly meeting. It's part of the spirit you'll feel when you shop at Brills: an esprit-de-corps that keeps our people enthusiastic and involved and knowledgable. Maybe that's a natural by-product of a store that's been family-owned and family-operated for 60 years. But the Brills family is more than a couple of bigwigs in the front office. It's three generations of wonderful people who've gone more than the distance, year after year, to make sure that everything is the best it can be for you.[3]

When we saw this ad we immediately said, "This is a natural for libraries." It can be adapted to promote the ways employees are learning new skills that will help patrons, or to feature the idea of staff meetings and brainstorming sessions to improve services. The alliteration in the headline is particularly effective and we recommend that adapters try to incorporate it too.

Quick and Easy

Looking for a quick and easy evaluation form to adapt? We found out in La Jolla, California, at the local Yum Yum Donut shop. Their form began as a thank-you to the patron: "Thanks for helping make Yum Yum a more pleasant experience." The form is simple and asks only six questions:

- Were your donuts yummy?
- Was the service friendly?
- Was the shop clean?
- Was the display attractive?
- Was your sale rung up properly?
- Did you receive a sales receipt?

Customers only have to check yes or no for each question. The six questions cover the quality of product, attitude of employee, cleanliness, eye-appeal, and procedures. Space for additional comments is also provided, as well as for date and time, name and address. By dating the visit, the management would be able to trace back personnel on duty at that time.

We collect customer response forms wherever we see them and often learn a new way to structure our own evaluation tools. This aspect of adapting is covered more extensively in chapter 9 on planning and evaluation.

Saying Thanks

Thank-you notes are commonly written by librarians in the course of their professional duties. We saw one used by the Maclean-Hunter Cable Company of Canada that included their own printed thank-you message. On the outside there was an appropriate drawing of television lights with the "Thank-you" in the spotlight. Their inside message was "With sincere appreciation ... thank you for the contribution you have made to community programming." There was also room to add a brief personal message. This is a good idea to adapt because the staff is more likely to use prepared cards. This thank-you is easy to adapt.

Convinced Yet?

You've seen that adapting creatively is an easy task if you learn to look and listen constantly to ideas in all avenues of life. You're probably comfortable with transferring ideas from other libraries to yours, and there are lots of ideas available. But perhaps you still feel that the real challenge is to look outside to see what someone else is doing, and figure out how you can utilize it for your purposes. Therefore, let's examine a few more examples of "business borrowing" to reinforce the concept.

On one of our trips we stayed at a Radisson Hotel. Their newsletter *radisson news* was prominently displayed and had a "take it along" message printed as part of the front page. Putting such an invitation right on the publications instead of on the nearby bulletin board or on a separate sign was easy but effective.

Another idea from the Radisson is their "smiles" incentive program. Each week a member of the hotel management team is a "smile spotter," whose duty is to seek out employees in various departments whose courteous and friendly service is noticeable. The employee is notified immediately and given a cash bonus. Employees wear special buttons promoting the campaign.

This concept could be used with library staff or patrons. With staff the program could be similar to the Radisson's, using spotters and rewards. (If you're in a one-man-band library, give yourself points on your smile days!) Many libraries can't afford cash bonuses, so how about a taffy apple, poster, flower, or even a close parking spot for a week?

To adapt for patrons, try a Smile If You Love the Library campaign, or as an added incentive, Smiling Can Get You Something in Your Library, reinforced by a candy kiss or special bookmark. The potential is there, but it's up to you to use it effectively in your setting.

Don't Touch That Dial

In a Holiday Inn chain we were struck by the sign hanging on a knob of the television set:

Warning: Watching television alone in your room may be hazardous to your health.

The problem: Loneliness, eyestrain, boredom.

The remedy: Come to our cocktail lounge and join in the fun.

A library could use this idea for the basis for a flyer. Again, the format would be the same, a tag punched out to fit on a television knob.

The warning could be edited to "Watching television may be hazardous to your health."

The problem could be changed to "Apathy, eye-strain, loss of muscle tone, boredom, and limited channel choice."

The remedy could be "Come to the library."

Then could follow a description of the vast choices of topics, books, and formats of materials, the countless program options, and most of all the people, librarians and patrons, who'll talk with you, not at you.

Our next idea came from the Golden Bear Restaurant chain. They featured children's menus on placemats, which had a set of clever but faceless characters illustrated on them. Each character had a name and a description of a menu item. For example, Pam Cakes: three big, fluffy pancakes with one strip of bacon or a sausage link. Children could draw in the faces while waiting for their meal.

This idea could be adapted for the library with each face a different department or service. For example, Rhett (or Rheta) Reference: the place to go for answers. Five thousand books filled with over two million pages of information on every topic from abacus to zodiac. Can help with who's who, where's where, when's when, and what's what. Or how about Farrah Fiction: the home of love, hate, fear, anger, and every emotion known to man. Beasts, beauties, and everything in between await on shelves for your reading pleasure.

Also you could produce a doodle placemat for distribution to popular local restaurants (they might pick up the tab) and it could be used by all ages, not just children. A version could be in doctors' and dentists' offices or the local laundromats, anywhere people have to wait. You could also place this item at the circulation desk as a get-acquainted piece.

OVER TO YOU

Now it's your turn. Up until now we have provided the originals and suggested some creative adaptations. We hereby invite you to join the pirating brigade, and issue a challenge to you as well. We have selected a number of items that are part of the American scene. We think they have potential for adaptation for libraries in a wide variety of ways. What kinds of treasure can you find buried here?

- "Caffeine. Never had it. Never will. 7-UP." A recent campaign theme for billboards, television ads, etc.

- Mystery dinner parties. These prepackaged kits contain descriptions of characters involved in a murder. Clues, detective reports, secret letters, and even audiotape reports from the investigating police officer add authenticity. The host and hostess invite friends to come and play characters. Even special printed invitations are also included in these packages. Other commercial spin-offs are the mystery weekend at a resort and the mystery train ride party.

- Cruise mania, especially the "fun" ships.

- Television shows like "St. Elsewhere," "Hill Street Blues," and "LA Law."

- And? Add your own discoveries and try your hand at some creative adapting. If you think you've created a real gem, let us know about it. We'll certify you as worthy of commanding your own pirate ship. Welcome aboard.

NOTES

[1]John Cotton Dana Award citation, Council for Florida Libraries, Fort Lauderdale, Florida, presented by H. W. Wilson Company, 1983.

[2]Teko Wiseman, "Read in – or Take Out!" *Library Insights, Promotion, and Programs* (January 1980): 6-7.

[3]Brills, Inc., advertisement, *Milwaukee Journal*, 14 November 1982, p. 8.

Part II

❊❊❊

NITTY-GRITTY DETAILS

9
How to Design and Judge Public Relations Programs
A Planned Approach

Perhaps it is true that the world is filled with two kinds of people: those who go to the supermarket with a detailed shopping list in hand and those who wing it. The latter may lead a more interesting gastronomical life, but generally the list makers save time and money in the long run, and usually aren't in the midst of preparing for a dinner party when they discover they forgot to purchase an essential ingredient for the "piece de resistance." Granted, some folks are good at making mental shopping lists. We suspect that's also how some libraries function without formal plans for their public relations programs: they're pretty good at planning in their heads. However, we believe that what is currently good will be even better when a more formalized system of designing the library's PR efforts is put in place.

CHANGING OUR ATTITUDES

A variety of possible approaches to public relations planning exist, and it is important to find one that fits your working style, library situation, and the demands that supervisors or governing boards impose. All of the experts seem to agree that planning is essential and it takes time.

Patrick Jackson, a past-president of the Public Relations Society of America, speaks frequently about the need for those charged with PR responsibilities to realize the importance of detailed planning in order to operate in a professional manner. It is critical, according to Jackson, that we change our attitudes about not having enough time to plan. A block of time must be set aside in which planning for the year is done. It is during this planning time that a written document is produced which will guide the PR efforts in the coming year.

Even if you are a "one-man band," you must be willing to manage your time and priorities. Planning is essential if we are ever to solve the basic problem of inadequate public understanding of the library's mission.

Planning must be done at the time that seems appropriate for your own institution. If the library uses annual objective-setting, PR planning probably would come logically at the same time. Because of financial considerations, planning also will need to be tied to annual budget development.

FIRST THINGS FIRST

It is important that a PR plan not exist in isolation. It is critical that the organization's overall plans come first, then the PR plan can be written to support and enrich those plans. Otherwise, PR will not be successful. In other words, first the library's goals and objectives are delineated, and then the public relations design is developed to support and help accomplish those goals and objectives.

Institutions generally go through an evolutionary process in the development of their PR planning system. They usually proceed from less to more planning. In the beginning, or unplanned stage, they are just struggling to survive. Next, they reach a budgeting system stage, where the plan is financially oriented. A third level is the project planning stage when planning efforts are focused on specific projects. In the fourth stage, an annual plan is developed, based on yearly objectives.

Finally, a level is reached where an effort is made to develop long-range plans, with annual plans in place as part of the context of these long-range efforts. These long-range plans are reworked each year as situations change, and they usually take on a strategic character, with an in-depth analysis of possible alternatives.

Useful Yardstick

Many people on the library staff have a stake in the direction of any PR plan. Therefore, they need an opportunity to participate in the PR planning. The easiest way to include them is with a written plan. Another good reason for writing it all down is it is the only way to measure our progress during the year. It serves as our yardstick, showing our progress, our growth, or our lack of success.

Finally, as Patrick Jackson points out, it is the written plan that becomes our freedom device. It allows us to put our time into executing the specifics, since we already know what's on our plate for next week.

Possible Approaches

When we review what has been written about planning for public relations, we find a number of different approaches advocated. Some experts stress a marketing approach, while others urge a system design. We found three-step, four-step, five-step, and even nine-step planning procedures. However, the differences were more often in terminology and ways of outlining a procedure than in the basic principles and steps in PR planning. For our purposes, we have identified four steps:

1. Fact-finding and research.

2. Analysis and selection.

3. Action and communication.

4. Evaluation and recycling.

FACT-FINDING AND RESEARCH

This first step involves identifying problems and consequently goals and objectives. Scott M. Cutlip and Allen H. Center in their book *Effective Public Relations* remark, "Like an iceberg, only a small part of PR is seen above the surface. The part that shows is often taken for the whole—but unseen—research, planning, and evaluation—is more important in the long run."[1]

Those of us to whom the word research is frightening should take comfort in the comment by the great inventor Charles Kettering, "Research is nothing but a state of mind—a friendly, welcoming attitude toward change."[2]

Grid Way

Many PR planners use and recommend variations of a grid system in their approach to planning and decision making. The grid provides a visual representation of the PR program that takes into account two elements, the publics to be targeted and the methods to be employed (see figure 9.1).

The first column in the grid is a listing of the various groups with which the library is or could be involved. It is effective to divide these target groups into two major categories: those that are external and those that are internal to the organization. Examples of external groups might include members of the local business community, service organizations, realtors, senior citizens, parents of elementary school children, etc. Internal groups could include professional library staff, custodial personnel, volunteers, Friends, teachers (for a school media center), etc.

Two internal publics that must appear on all planning grids are the institution's administration and the library's staff. The top management or governing board of the institution must be included for two important reasons. First, we as PR planners need to make them aware of *their* need to know, and second, by including them in our plan, we remind ourselves to be sure to reach them.

The library staff must be included on all planning grids because PR begins at home. It is the employees who will be conveying the library's messages, setting the tone and atmosphere, providing the services, and carrying forward the mission which the institution has identified.

Once you have listed all identified groups on your grid, start the assessment process. Analyze which groups you are presently reaching or attempting to reach. Chart current approaches in the top row of the grid. As part of this assessment, list all of the different methods, projects, and communication tools that are currently part of your efforts. Now you are ready to check off which audiences are reached by which current activity. Most PR practitioners believe that each target audience should be reached by more than one activity or communications effort.

If the planning/assessment grid shows some missing elements, it is then necessary to propose specific activities to complete the program. You may discover that you are aiming most of your communications efforts at only one part of your public. Or you may want to do some housecleaning and clean out what is out-of-style, what the library has outgrown, or what is taking up time and money but is no longer needed or effective.

Librarians seem to have a particularly hard time discontinuing an activity once it has been started. (It must be our preservation instinct.) However, if we want a PR program that is a best seller and not one that is archival, we must weed our ongoing communications efforts as well as our collections. Some may just need a face-lifting, a fresh approach, or a slightly new direction. For a publication, this may be a new look, logo, focus, or distribution method.

PUBLICS \ APPROACHES	Annual Report	Newsletter	Special Programs	Recognitions	Public speaking	"Coffee" talks	Topic "packets"	Press releases	Special events	"Hot line"
Internal: Staff	✓	✓		✓		✓		✓	✓	
Library Board	✓	✓				✓		✓	✓	
Friends		✓		✓					✓	
Custodians		✓		✓						
Volunteers		✓		✓					✓	
External: media	✓	✓						✓	✓	
Businesses	✓	✓	✓		✓		✓			
Service clubs		✓			✓					
Senior Citizens		✓	✓		✓					
Parents		✓	✓							✓
Teachers		✓	✓				✓			✓
Residents	✓	✓						(✓)	✓	
Teens			✓				✓		✓	✓

Fig. 9.1. Planning grid.

Some activities may need major remodeling. Perhaps where you have been relying on informational types of communications (generally those in print format), you may want to switch to interpersonal forms of communication, those which are face-to-face with the intended audience. For example, staff newsletters, though effective in conveying straight news about the library, and its people and programs, will not suffice as the only type of activity for communicating with staff. You also need interpersonal forms of communication. These may be rap sessions with the director, informal visits to all departments by board members, and employee committees that meet regularly with administrative personnel.

When communicating with the public at large, you may have always used informational communications channels—press releases, newsletters, annual reports—but need to look at interpersonal formats as well. Public board meetings can provide an open forum where interested citizens can present concerns, comments, and recommendations. You need to communicate that this type of public input is welcome and not just tolerated.

Advisory committees for various library activities can help guarantee that programs designed for specific segments of the population do, in fact, address a legitimate need or interest of that intended audience. For example, school media centers and college libraries may want permanent student and faculty committees to serve as sounding boards. Geographical advisory committees for public libraries may be your choice if this is the best way to guarantee that the library is meeting the needs of diverse community groups.

TARGET GROUPS

Once you have completed the listing of all possible publics and the assessment of your current efforts, both informational and interpersonal, you are ready to consider whether all of your current target publics will remain on the grid and whether certain approaches need to be changed for these target groups. Then you need to decide who are to be your new priority groups for the next one to three years. In other words, you are starting the preparation of your PR plan, in grid format, for the next year or more.

The next step in completing the planning grid is a consideration of why you are targeting each of these groups. You need to have clearly in mind why each group has been selected as a priority target and also what reaction, attitude, or response is desired from each group. These should be written out and appended to your grid plan. It is not possible to prepare an effective PR plan if you don't know just what it is you are trying to accomplish for each of your target audiences. This is especially true when considering that a central principle in PR is "Different strokes for different folks."

Research Tools

A variety of research tools are available to help library planners find the appropriate approaches for the identified audiences in their PR programs. These same tools can also be used at the evaluation stage to get feedback on your efforts because the planning process is really a cycle which starts with research, fact-finding, and evaluation of current efforts and ends with evaluation of newly executed programs.

Research tools range from a simple questionnaire to a full-scale telephone survey, from an informal count of participants to in-depth focus interviews with scientifically selected sample populations. Whether simple or complex, these research tools provide planners with information upon which to base decisions. As a result, goals and objectives may have to be modified, and alternative approaches considered.

Major efforts to persuade voters, for example, to support a bond issue or rate referendum need to be based on solid research showing current level of voter support, major issues involved, key supporters, and ardent opponents. Only then should a campaign be launched in support of the issue. In the same way, planning for other kinds of communications efforts is best if based on solid information relating to why we are targeting this group, how do they feel or act now, and what do we want them to know or do.

Attitude Assessment

It has been said that three of the most valued words in the English language are "What's your opinion?" Citizens, users, teachers, parents, and residents all like to be asked what they think. Therefore surveys can help pinpoint both information and attitude gaps. In getting ready to conduct a survey, the first step to ask yourself is "What is it I want to know." The question is usually obvious, but the answers aren't always easy to find.

Experts tell us that the biggest mistake in surveying is attempting to accomplish too many things with one survey. By trying to ask too many questions on too many different topics, you will only create confusion.

The best advice is to make a list of what you want to know and then organize those ideas into possible questions. Get others to help you by giving them your list and asking for their opinions and suggestions. Take a second look at your list and select and narrow the items to a single topic of concern.

WHAT IS NEEDED

In planning a survey, it is important to know who to ask and how many respondents will be necessary to make the survey valid. In order to conduct a survey, you will need both human and financial resources. The costs can vary tremendously, depending upon the methods selected for surveying, and whether or not volunteers will be available. The time frame will also be important, especially if a tax referendum is to be based on the results of the survey.

WHO TO SURVEY

Deciding who to interview is directly related to what it is you want to know. Obviously, the sample selected for the survey must be drawn from the group that has the answers to the questions you are seeking.

In order to be reasonably confident that your sample represents accurately the attitudes of the large group, there are specific formulas to be followed. Many resources list tables of reliability for sampling. As an example, it is possible to have a confidence level of 95 percent with a sample of 400 for a group of 20,000, if appropriately and randomly selected.

The list of your total group is called the survey's "universe" or "population." For the community at large, many libraries will find voter lists useful, especially if the survey is related to ascertaining support for bond or tax issues. In some communities, census lists are more complete, but they usually are not updated frequently. The use of phone books is common, but they don't include people with unlisted numbers, and in some areas it will also mean an under representation of minority groups. Consequently, most general population/library/school district surveys rely on voter lists. If you are surveying users, the list of borrowers, students, or faculty served will be the appropriate list.

SELECTING A SAMPLE

For detailed instruction on selecting your survey sample, we recommend you consult a source devoted to surveying. The basic principle is to use a "skip" interval as names are selected from the universe, until the entire sample is selected, based on the sample size needed to establish an acceptable confidence level. For example, every 50th name until 400 are chosen out of a universe of 20,000.

Surveys

Of the three types of surveys commonly conducted, all have advantages and disadvantages. For example, personal interviews allow for the use of complex questions and allow interviewers to probe for answers. Observations of interviewers can also be included and detailed information can be gathered. The person-to-person contact also stimulates a high degree of participation in the survey.

However, there are disadvantages to personal interviews. First of all, the cost to train volunteers or to hire professional interviewers can be prohibitive. Also this technique can be time-consuming and difficult to supervise if vast numbers of interviewers are used. Finally, it is hard to keep consistency between interviewers unless they are highly trained.

MAIL SURVEYS

Surveys by mail are often used because it is possible to distribute them widely at a low cost. Another advantage is they eliminate interviewer bias. It is also possible to reach remote places easily, and respondents can answer them at their leisure. However, they have many disadvantages if they are not limited to a select group with a high degree of commitment to respond. It is difficult to get a high confidence level with mail surveys since the return of mail questionnaires is often very low and opinions are based only on those returned. Often only people with a specific point of view will bother to respond, which will distort the results.

It takes time and money to follow up on mail surveys to guarantee a high return rate. Some places have used postcard reminders and follow-up phone calls, or even mailed a second copy of the survey.

In addition, it is necessary to limit the length of a mail survey to encourage response. There is also the danger that respondents may misinterpret questions and provide unexpected answers. There is also the chance that other people may end up filling out the questionnaire rather than the person to whom it was addressed. Finally, it is usually hard to use a mail survey with complex questions.

PHONE SURVEYS

Telephone surveys are the third format for securing information. They are popular because they are quick, efficient, and generally accurate. They offer the advantage of a wide geographic reach as well as the opportunity for a follow-up phone call for those not reached on the first round. A further advantage is that volunteers can be used after limited training, with a high degree of accuracy and success.

Disadvantages include the fact that usually only listed phone numbers are included although the telephone company can help you establish a random system that would include unlisted numbers if your survey population can be identified with a specific exchange or dialing code. Telephone surveys also need to be limited to specifically defined questions.

THE ART OF ASKING

Through the design of survey questions, you can ask a variety of questions planned to gather a wide variety of types of information. For example, you can ask questions that provide specific information about respondents: "Do you have children who use the school library? Do you have a library card?" Or you can ask multiple choice questions which are easy to tabulate and may give you more specific details such as: "Which of the following services have you made use of in the last six months?" Another type is the rating scale or preference type questions to learn more about the intensity of respondent feeling: "Which services would you rank first, second, and third in priority?"

It is also possible to include questions that call for additional probing on the part of the interviewers: "Why do you like this information source?" Although these questions will provide more information, the results can be difficult to code and interpret.

Again, the choices of questions and question types will depend upon what it is you want to learn through the survey. It is critical that you pretest your questions before you put the survey into use. How do the questions sound? Are they clear to the listener?

VOLUNTEERS TO HELP

It is heartening to know that 20 people can conduct 400 telephone interviews easily in a day or two. It is also reassuring to know that the training for volunteers can be accomplished fairly easily. A five-step process is recommended:

1. It is necessary to go over the questionnaire word for word so that all callers will understand what each question means.

2. Volunteers should practice on each other.

3. Provide standard answers to anticipated questions that will be asked in the process of the phone interviews. Basic questions include those about who is conducting the survey, what the information is to be used for, and whether or not the answers are confidential. Also provide information about the method of follow-up for those homes where no one answers on the first call.

4. It is necessary to provide training on how the survey answer sheets are to be marked for each phone call so that results can be tallied easily and accurately or even machine scored.

5. Have a pretest period with a follow-up session so that volunteers can discuss the results of these initial calls, the problems that arose, etc. Clarification can be made before the actual survey sample is called.

FOR FUTURE REFERENCE

Another advantage of phone surveys is that it is possible to develop a list of the volunteers who are especially talented that could be used in future surveys. The payment of a small stipend might be considered in order to conduct surveys on a regular basis with little fuss and bother.

We mentioned earlier how important it was to include employees on the list of groups to be considered each year in a PR plan. Surveys of employees will help you pinpoint any variances between management's and employee's perceptions. This is also a good way to find out, "How well do we listen?"

Other Research Techniques

We have shown that we are strong advocates of creative adapting: using good ideas from other settings for our work in libraries. The focus group interview is a common marketing research technique used to evaluate what specific groups know or think about a certain service or product. At J. D. Searle Pharmaceuticals they are used at the initial stage of product development to determine if there is an interest in a type of product, to ascertain what the best way to communicate to a potential buyer might be, and to gain insight, information, and direction for the future. Small groups of people, who represent the audience for whom the product or service is intended, are called together for informal but directed discussions. The size is generally 10-12 people, although it may vary from 5 to 20. Trained moderators are used to direct discussions.

The value of focus groups, according to a representative from J. D. Searle, is their timeliness and the opportunity they afford to provide quick responses, immediate feedback, and red flags for potential problems.

Focus groups may be useful when you are contemplating new services or programs. Immediate feedback is one of the advantages to this type of research. Modifications to guarantee success with a target group could be made before the new service and campaign are fully implemented. In order to prepare for future sessions, libraries may want to compile lists of patrons who fit certain profiles to facilitate calling a focus group together.

ANALYSIS AND SELECTION

Once you have completed the surveys, interviews, and other fact-finding research, you are ready to move to the second step, that of planning and programming. This step requires development of possible approaches to attain your stated objectives, followed by analysis and selection. Brainstorming is also strongly recommended in this phase, in order to come up with as many ideas as possible. Remember, it is easier to trim back and to scale down than it is to work with a limited initial list.

Start with a target public. Ask the brainstorming group, "What are all of the ways we can think of to accomplish our stated objective with this public?" This should be based on the why and what you have already spelled out in writing, plus the research you have conducted.

After all ideas have been noted, you are ready for further consideration and development of these approaches. Discuss more specific details for each idea that has been suggested including:

- who would need to be involved
- what would be included
- when would actions be taken
- how would actions be managed
- where would activities take place

The purpose is to look at the parameters and the feasibility of each idea in terms of manpower, facilities, budget, and timing. Discussion is the best way to explore ideas in these terms.

Don't be too quick to reject an idea because of a perceived limitation in staff or funding if there is agreement that it has great potential for reaching one of your objectives for a target audience. These are the kinds of projects that require creative efforts in looking for alternate ways to get the expertise or funding required. Many of the J. C. Dana award winners have been able to overcome apparent barriers by looking for nontraditional solutions when faced with such problems.

Selection Criteria

Now you are ready to consider the selection criteria to be used in making a decision on which ideas will be developed for the PR plan. Each library will need to establish their own selection criteria, but some criteria are fairly universal:

- expected level of success in achieving the objective
- cost effectiveness, i.e., cost per target person
- total cost
- timing
- staff availability and expertise
- avoidance of untoward consequences
- risk
- ability to maintain over time if appropriate
- policy and probable level of acceptance by staff, management, and library or school board
- negative or positive impact on other programs

After you have gone through each proposed approach and considered them in the light of the selection criteria, you should have an excellent sense of which ones will fly, which ones will need some creative thinking efforts to make them feasible, and which ones do not measure up.

Now your PR plan is taking shape. You have selected your target publics and you have done research to establish why each group should be selected and what action or response is desired from each. You have brainstormed ideas that might be considered, and weighed them against your selection criteria.

As you move from this level of planning toward anticipated action, it is imperative that management provide a commitment of support and participation. Planners must have an idea what the minimum level must be for this administrative support. Without it you're going to have a most difficult time pulling off your plan, and are probably doomed to failure. Get decision-makers involved early and get their commitment before you start.

Writing the program means actually spelling out the details on proposed projects and activities. It is crucial that others in the library are kept informed during this stage, with an opportunity to add their input.

What is needed is an action program, a translation of your selected strategy—who you are targeting and how you will reach them—into a specific set of actions, including which person will perform each one, and when that action will be completed.

Once you have reached decisions on what projects and activities will be implemented, it is tempting to consider the analysis and selection task complete. But what must follow in the post-decision phase is the preparation of a logistics document to facilitate the plan.

PERT Charting

One method often used is the construction of a PERT (Program Evaluation and Review Technique) Chart. The central concept in PERT planning is that it deals with events rather than tasks. An *event* is described as "... an action, activity, or occurrence that can be observed and that takes place at one point in time."[3] This is in contrast to tasks, which may occupy a span of time.

For example, cataloging of new reference materials by technical services staff is a task, whereas completion of cataloging of new reference materials by technical services staff is an event since one can observe the final item being processed. The difference makes it possible to pinpoint the completion of essential steps in preparing a plan.

The first step in PERT is to list each event in the proposed project or programming. Then a linear diagram is constructed to show the sequence of events, like a computer program flow chart, to indicate which events must occur before others.

Stech and Ratcliffe in *Working in Groups* recommend following these four steps in PERT chart construction:

Step One: Write down the first event on a large sheet of paper or chalkboard.

Step Two: Write down the events that will follow the first event and draw lines with arrowheads to show the sequence.

Step Three: Some events may lead to two or more other events, and some events may be preceded by two or more other events. Identify such cases with appropriate lines and arrows.

Step Four: Continue writing down events that must occur in sequence until the project can be completed.

The result is a diagram showing what events must occur in what sequence in order to implement the plan. PERT chart planning is only as good as your ability to forecast what will be required in order to complete the job.

It is also imperative to work backward in time from the final event in order to guarantee that you don't run out of time. You have to know how much lead time each event will require in order to complete a project smoothly.

ACTION AND COMMUNICATION

Step number three is the main thrust of your program as you target your specific messages and projects to specific audiences to achieve your identified results.

The principle of pretesting, especially of materials to be used, is an important one. Through pretesting, you can detect possible backlash effects or lack of clarity in messages prepared for the intended audience.

As plans are put into motion, it is important that you monitor progress. There is nothing wrong with mid-course corrections if it is obvious that changes will increase your chances for success. As you monitor "What is happening?" and "Why is it happening?" it may be obvious that corrective action is called for. So ask yourself, "What should we do about it?" and act.

Never proceed with your action plan under the assumption that it is written in stone. Perhaps your timetable needs revision or your budget needs revamping. Perhaps personnel assignments need adjustment or your communication approaches need enhancement. Only you can make these decisions, but don't be afraid to decide on a change if that change will increase your chances for success.

EVALUATION AND RECYCLING

The fourth step in the planning process focuses on judging the results of your efforts. This step really leads full circle, back to fact-finding through feedback. Cutlip and Center remark, "Evaluation is the common sense of learning from experience. We ask ourselves, 'What did we get for what we spent – in time and effort as well as dollars.' "[4]

Several different approaches can be taken at the start of your evaluation. For example, you might consider the degree of implementation of your plan, the degree to which the program goals were achieved, and the degree to which the outcomes have been attained. In terms of evaluation, there are ten possible questions to ask:

1. Was there adequate planning?
2. Did others understand the job to be done?
3. Did all groups cooperate?
4. How could results have been made more effective?
5. Did you reach all pertinent audiences?
6. Did you receive desired publicity before, during, and after?
7. Could you have made better provisions for unforeseen circumstances?
8. Were you within budget?
9. Did you have provisions for measuring results?
10. Can you identify steps to improve in the future?

In 1920 Evart G. Routzahn told attendees at a national PR conference, "put yourself and your methods through the third degree so that you will be able to untangle the lessons to be applied to the next project."[5] That advice is still valid today.

The evaluation stage is the time to employ a variety of post-testing and evaluative tools. Which ones you choose will depend upon what objectives and methods were incorporated in your plan. For example, you may want to measure impact by calculating the percentage of the target audience you reached. Or you may want to calculate the audience response. The ultimate test is the results obtained.

That Bucket of Eels

When American Telephone and Telegraph (AT&T) launched a concerted program of PR efforts in the 1970s, one executive compared measuring public relations to trying to measure a bucket full of eels. There is a dilemma in trying to measure responses of people in purely statistical and numerical terms. Because they have shades of opinions and responses, it is inappropriate to try to measure one overall response or opinion. The solution, as conceived by AT&T, was not even to make an attempt to measure a single vague question such as "How's our PR?" or "What do you think of the telephone company?" Instead, AT&T broke activities down into small units and measured specific activities one by one. This is exactly what we suggest for your evaluation. Take each element, objective, or activity in your plan and consider it separately.

There are some other approaches and methods used by American business that you may find helpful in your approach to evaluation. If you are distributing a newsletter to the community and your list is growing ever larger, you may want to do what controlled circulation magazines do from time to time. Annually a response is requested from anyone who wishes to remain on the list. In the same way libraries can request a response from those who wish to continue to receive their newsletter. Requests received by patrons to be retained can be the actual evaluation measure of the value the patrons placed on the publication. This technique might be most appropriate following a major mailing campaign which covered the entire community.

Feedback? Ask Them

The managements of many institutions are always concerned about customers who leave unhappy with service and yet do not complain. To overcome this lack of feedback, the Hyatt Hotel in Minneapolis has a standard phone inquiry at 4 p.m. each day to all guests in the hotel. Although not all guests are reached, a sufficient number are contacted to make the effort worthwhile. Each guest is asked, "Is everything all right with the room, service, etc.?" The direct contact allows individuals to register complaints while the management can still do something about them. This is a good solution to guests who will not bother to complain, but will leave the hotel unhappy and not return.

Libraries can adapt this technique easily. The simple way to get feedback from a target group is to ask them. For example, if one of the goals for the year has been to increase the quality of service at the circulation desk, it would be easy to take a random sample survey of patrons who checked out materials during a particular shift—call them to ask if the staff was courteous, efficient, etc. The same could be done for parents of children enrolled in summer programs, or patrons leaving the reference area. If it is obvious to the patron that your questions are nonthreatening and designed to guarantee good library service, the responses will be honest.

How to Listen

The best examples of evaluation as PR are the customer response forms used by the national hotel and motel chains. Howard Johnson's has an outside message of "Who listens to you?" The inside catch line is, "If it's not your mother, it must be Howard Johnson's!" This message is clear: Howard Johnson's is willing to listen. Guests are encouraged to fill out the response form and send it off to the corporate president in the postage-paid envelope.

You should collect and examine the various customer response forms used by corporate America. These companies hire experts to keep their questionnaires simple, clear, and non-ambiguous. Creative adapting is easy if you have a file of samples on hand when you are ready to prepare patron response forms for the library. These work well for evaluations of library programs, special events, etc.

And where do we go from here? We recycle back to step one, fact-finding and research, using the results of our evaluation efforts to start the planning process again.

WORTH IT? YES, INDEED

Is it all worthwhile? There seems to be a unanimous yes to this query. There are three key reasons for libraries to develop a planned program for PR: first, such a plan will help the library in attracting and serving its clients; second, such a plan will help in attracting financial support for the institution; and third, a PR plan can help to stimulate the employees of the library.

Sometimes the final factor is not considered, but job satisfaction is indeed improved by a public relations plan, not only because one of the target audiences should always be the employees, but because, through a plan, there will be an enhanced sense of direction and mission for everyone connected with the library. In other words, a game plan helps all staff members feel that they are on the same team—and it's a winning one.

NOTES

[1]Scott M. Cutlip, Allen H. Center, and Glen M. Broom, *Effective Public Relations*, 6th ed. (Englewood Cliffs, N.J.: Prentice-Hall, Inc., 1985), 200.

[2]Charles Kettering, quoted in Cutlip, 202.

[3]Ernest Stech and Sharon A. Ratcliffe, *Working in Groups* (Skokie, Ill.: National Textbook Company, 1976), 176.

[4]Cutlip, 307.

[5]Ibid., 295.

10

How to Communicate "Live"

Mastering Public Speaking

There comes a time when many of us realize that there are a lot of things we didn't learn in library school that we need to know to be effective in practical application. One area we feel is particularly overlooked is the librarian's role as a public speaker – a vocal ambassador who brings a bit of library lore to those who want, or need, to hear it.

Most of us have no problems dealing with our assorted publics on a one-to-one basis. We can do it with ease in the library or out in the community. Talking about library services, resources, programs, and problems with those who wish to hear is natural, even if we're in the bank or the grocery store. But, for some reason, when those same individuals are gathered in groups, many of us begin to doubt our ability to be the public spokesperson for the topics we handle so well in individual situations. We not only ignore the potential in creating these situations, we even avoid them when they occur naturally.

We lose confidence and convince ourselves "They don't really want to hear us." We assume someone else is more interesting or more authoritative than we are. And, at the same time, when some major issue like a referendum or a censorship question forces us to the public podium, we wonder why we lack speaking confidence.

Ironically enough, this avoidance is perpetuated by us, the same people who conduct excellent booktalks, who delight children with our storytelling, and who vocally and enthusiastically represent our library's concerns at board meetings, all clear examples of public speaking. But, because these situations are job related, we choose not to regard them as public speaking. Let's be clear about one thing: anytime we're speaking outside of the privacy of our own home, we're in a public speaking situation, regardless of the subject we're presenting or the age of the audience.

Why do we librarians ignore and avoid opportunities to represent our libraries vocally to the public? Could it be that librarians ignore the more formalized public speaking role, and the positive results associated with it, because they feel ill-equipped to deal with it?

We propose that understanding a few basic concepts about public speaking and learning some tricks of the trade will help many librarians to speak up, loudly and frequently, for their libraries.

TRIAL BY FIRE

The first principle that must be accepted is that there is no substitute for experience. Trial by fire is the only way to become an accomplished speaker. Thinking about it, writing about it, even preparing a speech is not the equivalent of doing it.

But making speeches can be done in small and sequential steps until you feel confident enough to tackle nearly any public speaking situation.

To begin, you need to consider what situation would be least threatening. A short presentation on a popular service, or a new program or a topic specific and appropriate for a friendly group would probably allow you to be comfortable. It would also demonstrate to the group involved that the library is a place which cares about them, and the librarian is the type of individual who is concerned about their needs and interests. The best way to find this comfortable start is simply to analyze your own areas of interest and to identify those groups with whom you would feel most welcome.

Once a group is identified and a subject is determined, it's simply a matter of seeing if the two match. If not, work until they do mesh into both a group and a topic that make sense for each other. If that seems impossible, then you must either change the topic you have in mind, or the group you choose to approach.

When the two finally match, and you can honestly say "I could talk to x about y," contact someone in that group and offer your services as a speaker. It is best to start small, requesting perhaps 10 minutes. If the group is hesitant, it's easy to "sweeten the pot." For example the group can be invited to come to the library for their next meeting. Or, if it's a small group, offer to bring refreshments. It's bribery, but it'll probably work. If there is still hesitancy, it's time to get a little pushy. Such persistence can be done subtly – "I really feel it's important to tell the Lions about our new collection of large print books." Or, you can be upfront and honest: "I don't mean to be bold, but I am working on improving my skills as a public speaker, and I would feel better if I could begin with your group. Everyone has always been so warm, so supportive that I, well, I just could use your assistance." What hard-hearted person could resist such sincerity?

Either approach, if done honestly with an air of concern, should produce the desired result – an opportunity to speak, in public, in what might be regarded as a nonjob related situation since it's out of the library, and not with a pre-identified patron group.

At this point, you must recognize the major points to be considered in library speech making:

1. Know specifically the audience, the topic, the physical facilities, and the time constraints.

2. Prepare extensively an outline, notecards, and tricks or props, and practice.

3. Present your speech dynamically with enthusiasm, confidence, accuracy, and warmth.

4. Evaluate thoroughly your reactions as well as theirs.

Armed with these concepts, an effective speech is not only possible, but probable.

One thing you must identify before a speaking engagement can be successful is the parameters. You must carefully analyze exactly who the audience is, what topic is to be presented (in the mind of the audience), what the room is like, and how long you are expected to speak.

THE AUDIENCE

We've already indicated that for your first encounter it is best to set your own topic and time limit. "I just need 10 minutes to talk about our new reference sets in Business Services." We have also urged that the audience selected be a group with whom you are comfortable. Nevertheless, it is still wise to doublecheck with your group contact so that no one has any surprises for you. And, if you are responding to a request for a speech, rather than setting up your own situation, all these details must be checked out even more carefully.

In knowing your audience, it is not enough to know why they are gathered. Naturally, it is helpful to know that it's the Rotary or the Mothers Club for Plainview School or the Society for the Preservation of Red Squirrels in the Wild. But more details about the group are also important. You might, for example, ask for a membership brochure, which would spell out in detail what the group's purpose is, who is encouraged to join, how frequently they meet, what amount of money they're willing to pay to be members, and other pertinent information.

Other questions to ask should include: How many speakers has the group heard before? Who have they been? (There's a lot more pressure on you if they listen to speakers every meeting, and if the ones they've heard are the best in the area.) Has this particular topic been covered? If so, when and in what detail? How many members are anticipated for this gathering? Who is likely to attend in terms of age, sex, and specific interests?

For example, you may know that the local chamber of commerce consists of those individuals with business interests in town. It may well be that the majority are owners of small, one-person businesses. But, it could well be that these are exactly the people who cannot make it to the quarterly luncheon. Rather, the luncheon crowd may be composed of the bankers, realtors, and the PR people from the larger corporations of the area. Under these circumstances, a carefully prepared speech designed for the group you are anticipating will not be appropriate for the specific individuals who are actually there. Consequently, a thorough check is wise. It helps to be a member of the group. Then you are totally familiar with who is involved and who would be in attendance, besides having the advantage of being "one of our own."

Getting to Know Them

Most of the specific knowledge we have mentioned so far is something you can gather in advance. But, there's yet another way to prepare for your audience right before you speak, which is especially helpful if you don't know the group very well. We observed one speaker add to his knowledge of his audience so that he would get a better response. He stood at the entrance to the room and greeted his audience as they arrived. He introduced himself, asked each person's name, and their relationship to the meeting. He engaged in polite and warm small talk. Therefore, when he began to speak, he had a couple of advantages. He knew a little bit about several members of the audience and managed to find ways to fit that knowledge into his speech: "This item may be of particular interest to Harvey because he was telling me before the meeting that he has three red squirrels living in his oak tree."

Secondly, because each person had an opportunity to meet him, many in the audience felt a sense of rapport and were receptive to what he had to say. And, finally, he had learned a little bit about his audience. He could see their ages, sense their attitudes, and assess their attentiveness for this topic. He had heard about their jobs, their concerns and, perhaps, bits of history related to the group or the occasion.

We watched another speaker, a politician, use this same tactic during a luncheon meeting where he was the keynote speaker. Since the head table was served first, he ate sparingly, and then wandered among all the other tables and introduced himself to each person. By the time he spoke, everyone felt he had singled them out and they were totally receptive to his message.

The Topic

If the speech has been initiated by you, you have probably chosen the topic. But, if someone has called and asked for someone from the library to speak about a particular issue or service, you have to be sure what the caller wants. Is he or she seeking an overview of the service? Specific references available? A history of how the service came into being? Is it a controversial service? Is the group seeking an explanation for its existence? Would handouts be appropriate to help demonstrate the topic? Should such materials be distributed beforehand? Placed at the table or on the chairs? Given out only to interested people after the program?

And, it's quite possible that the library or a library service might not be the topic at all. It just might be a subject you are very interested in, capable of talking about, or willing to share, like your trip to Africa or to the Library of Congress. Naturally, you can, and probably should, tie the topic into the library somehow, most logically by mentioning sources people can use for follow-up information. Look at the recent television specials that have been doing exactly this, using a 30-second spot after the program to identify additional sources for reading.

A librarian need not "talk library" to be an interesting, informative ambassador for the library. A brief presentation on any topic of mutual interest can still be a PR boon if it is known the presentor is a librarian.

The Illinois Library Association (ILA) realized this fact several years ago when the members designed an outreach program entitled Librarians to the People. The idea was to offer civic and community groups, as well as state organizations, an opportunity to hear a speaker at relatively little cost. The speakers were all librarians. The interested organization indicated to ILA what topic they wanted, and when and where they wished to have a speaker. The ILA then attempted to fulfill the request with a librarian in the area. The only commitment on the part of the group requesting the speaker was to pay expenses if a long trip, meals, or overnight stays were necessary, and to publicize the fact that the speaker was a librarian obtained through the project.

This successful idea is quite adaptable on the local level. Many local community groups want programs but can't afford speakers. Knowing someone from the library can and will help them out is an excellent PR bonus. Surveying the library staff to determine hobby and interest areas could be a first step in establishing a library speakers' bureau for your community.

As another option, it may be worthwhile to keep a few topics and staff members as "instant replay" for groups that find themselves in trouble with program ideas or last minute speaker cancellations. Our local groups were truly ecstatic to find the library had a few "canned" presentations which could be made available to groups on very short notice. Some of these were "live"; most were audiovisual, but all had a librarian involved in the presentation so that the group could see another example of their library in action.

THE PHYSICAL LAYOUT

The physical facility should also be looked over as far ahead of the actual speaking engagement as possible. If this is a local meeting, there should surely be an opportunity to visit the room to see how large it is, what the lighting is like, where outlets are if audiovisual equipment is to be used, what the shape of the room is, and how it will be arranged that day.

Further questions can be asked of the contact person: What will be the specific setup of the room on the day in question? Will there be a podium? A dais (in the event of a meal function)? What will be the exact arrangement of the tables and/or chairs?

There are other details you need to know: Will there be aisles? Will someone be introducing you? Will you introduce yourself? We prefer the latter as sometimes the introducer will take up too much of your presentation time. Also an introduction will sometimes make it seem that you should walk on water and the audience is going to be disturbed if you don't. And, it always seems warmer, friendlier, more sincere when you greet people and introduce yourself.

It is also important to know if you will be seated at the front or in the audience. Are you to be there for the entire function or are you expected to arrive at a specific time? Are there certain procedures to be followed, such as addressing officers in a particular way? In short, what is the agenda and what are the procedures? The more you know, the more you will fit in with the group, and the better you both will feel.

If you are planning to use audiovisual equipment, there are other questions that need to be answered. Where are the outlets? Where are the lights? Will the group provide the equipment? Must you bring your own? If so, will a cart for projection, a screen, and an extension cord be available? Are there three-prong outlets for your cord?

The details are myriad and sometimes picky, but often they are critical to the way a speech is accepted.

TIME CONSTRAINTS

If this is a first speech and you have set the time limit, it is vital to adhere to the time established. No one appreciates being told they will hear a 10-minute presentation that is still dragging on after 20 minutes, even if the speaker is good. People set their inner clocks in anticipation and resent their mental alarm being ignored.

It is also critical that your contact is keenly aware of the time limits you are anticipating. It is awkward to prepare a 10-minute presentation and then be asked to make it 30 because the group has decided to make you their entire program.

Along this line there are other details to check out: What time of day is the presentation? What is the format for the day? Where do you appear on the program? What is preceding and what is following? Is there another speaker? What are the chances he or she might have a conflict or a travel problem? It's smart to prepare a few extra minutes in the event the other speaker cannot attend at the last minute. This is an especially good idea if the weather is poor or the other speaker is someone like the mayor who may be suddenly called to other duties.

Such preparation might panic the librarian who is undertaking a first crack at public speaking, but, if the remarks are prepared in advance so they'll be well-presented, the group will be grateful and impressed.

PREPARE EXTENSIVELY

It is difficult to describe exactly how to prepare a speech. Each one of us develops our own "modus operandi," our own unique way of preparation which is perfect for us and awkward for another. We can only suggest how we do it and urge you to adapt and adopt according to whatever seems comfortable and usable for your style.

Any speech, regardless of length, topic, or intended group, should be approached seriously. Even if the topic has been presented before and the material is already prepared, it is a good idea to review it and perhaps update it or change it around a bit. Sometimes this revision is good not only to give the audience a revised perspective but also to refresh yourself so the words do not seem too programmed.

Let us assume, however, that this is a first time speech. The ways to begin can vary depending on the topic, the occasion, and your mood. Sometimes it is best to begin with a clever title, which will become the hook on which to hang all remarks.

Sometimes a particular anecdote, quotation, or statistic is significant and should be included in the first few moments of the speech. If this item truly sums up the speech, then the rest of the speech somehow seems to flow from the incorporation of this information.

Sometimes we begin with the basic work that eventually has to be done anyway—digging, searching, and gathering of supportive information. But, most typically, we start with the ultimate question which must be answered before we can give a successful presentation: What is my purpose? What do I hope to accomplish with this speech? Why am I here? If the speech is at the request of someone else, we may ask them what their purpose is, what they are hoping our speech will accomplish for their group.

No presentation can be truly effective until you come to grips with what you want to accomplish. Maybe we just want people to feel good about the library. Maybe you want them to realize there are a lot of sources available to them. Maybe we want them to focus on specific resources useful to their situation. Maybe we want them to become part of our undertaking by volunteering time or money or services to the library. Maybe we want them to walk in the door and check out some materials, or attend a specific program. Whatever it is, there should be an ultimate goal we can focus on, which in turn should direct and shape our remarks.

MAIN AND SUB POINTS

Once it is established what it is that we want to accomplish, the next step is to make a list of the main points to be made in the speech which will help us towards that goal. Actually writing out these points focuses our attention on what needs to be said.

The way to write these out can vary. They can be listed in the traditional outline form we learned in our high school English class. Then we start filling in under each main point the subpoints we want to make. Or we may list each point on a separate 3-by-5-inch card and then start listing subpoints on other cards and physically arranging them to see how our speech is starting to shape up.

One trick which aids in this visualization is to utilize 3-by-5-inch cards of assorted colors. The main points can each be placed on a different color card. The subpoints, sudden ideas, statistics, quotations—anything related to that major point—can be placed on the same color card. By spreading these out, we can quickly see if one area is receiving too much attention, another too little, or if a change in major points needs to be made.

Ready for Research

After main points and subcategories have emerged, we begin to see what research we need to do. The areas that have ideas but no substance are researched to get that substance.

Sometimes we make a list of all the sources we need to investigate. For example, we may need to analyze what materials the library has in a particular area that will be helpful to a certain group. Or, we may need to do some reading on a particular subject so that we can speak with authority.

Exactly what we must look at, what resources we must use, or what areas we need to review are dependent on the topic of the presentation. But, everything that will be mentioned should be checked and double-checked to be sure it is accurate. It is not only inaccurate, it is embarassing to tell people that specific resources are available only to have them discover there is limited, or no, circulation of the items. Or to urge them to attend a certain program or activity and then let them discover they need advance reservations. The cautious speaker makes a list of what needs to be checked and researched, follows through on this list, and is sure the results are written down so there is no slipup during the speech.

Our preparation is greatly assisted if we look for items that can spice up a speech. Significant quotations, an anecdote, or other bits and pieces can help a speech. Whenever we hear a potentially useful story, find an article with interesting information, or note another speaker who uses a technique that's especially relevant, we write it down, make a copy, or clip it, to keep that information available to us for later use. This system demands our constant attention to thinking ahead, but it is highly effective. Our files are filled with newspaper articles, cartoons, scribbled stories, statistics, anything and everything that attracts us and might someday be useful in a presentation. Some of it will never be useful, but it's there if we want it.

GETTING ORGANIZED

Once the research is done, the material gathered, and the outline created, the next step is organizing it for actual presentation. Here again the techniques vary. When we made our first speeches, we wrote out the entire speech since it helped us get all our ideas out, allowed us to edit ourselves, and gave us something to practice with for timing. We occasionally still write out a speech, especially if it's a new topic, a somewhat unfamiliar area, or one which is really critical to us. But, this method can be awkward. A fully written speech is tempting to use in the presentation. Such use is deadly. We've all witnessed a speaker who begins to read the text, and reading aloud is boring to almost any group. Another problem is that paper is noisy. If there's a microphone, the shuffling of papers, no matter how carefully, carries and sounds like an elephant crashing in the bush. If there's a slight breeze, papers blow about, sometimes getting out of order. In short, the paper speech just doesn't work.

We recommend the use of notecards, which we believe are the only way to prepare a speech. We have experimented with different sizes, with different colors, with cards on spiral holders, and loose cards and have found 5-by-8-inch cards are most effective. We can write large enough to easily see our comments and they are much harder to lose than the smaller cards. There are spiral notecard booklets that can be used. But we like loose cards because they can be shifted and reorganized.

We usually organize our cards by main points, identifying each point with a large Roman numeral which we then place on every card that relates to that point. Then we put all the cards with the same Roman number in one pile and arrange them in the order we anticipate using in presentation. Once we have established that order, we then write Arabic numerals or capital letters on the cards to keep them in exact order of presentation within that major point. (See figure 10.1.)

If we use transparencies, or other audiovisual materials, we highlight the card at the point where we want to direct attention to the audiovisual component. Notecards allow us to arrange them as we go and rearrange whenever we wish. Of course, we organize our total speech on paper and then transfer it to notecards.

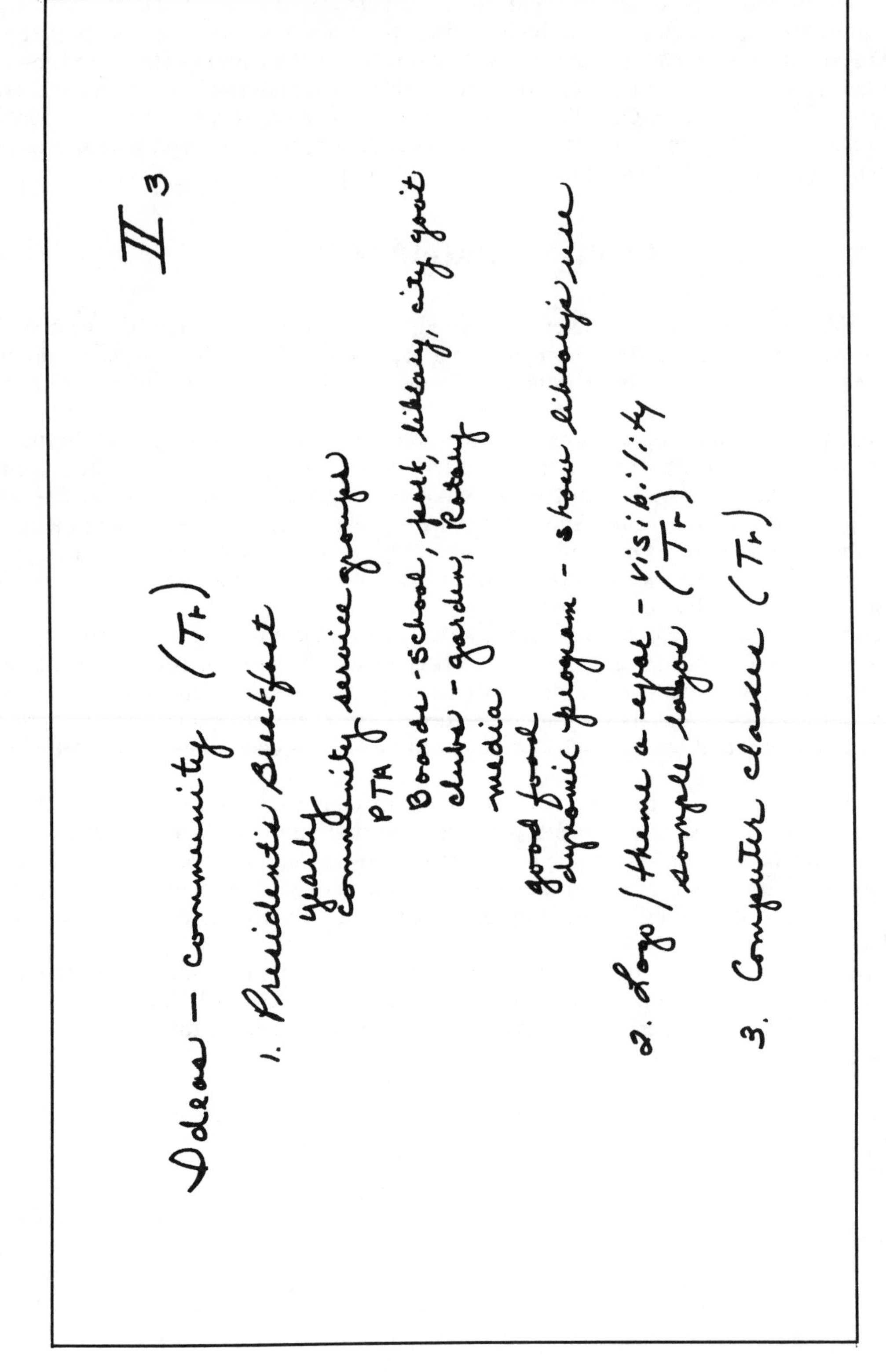

Fig. 10.1. Notecard marked for transparencies.

TRICKS OR PROPS

During our first few speeches we discovered a problem which is not unique to us: While speaking, we are plagued with what to do with our hands. This simple problem is exacerbated when we remember what we've seen other speakers do. Some speakers hold or perpetually adjust the microphone. Others use dramatic gestures, flinging their arms hither and yon with all the zest of a melodramatic actor. Some tuck their hands into their pockets, thus looking rumpled in spite of neat clothes. Some fold their hands behind them, a gesture which inevitably causes them to develop what we call the "Tower of Pisa Sway." Some fiddle with their hair, jewelry, glasses, anything and everything until the audience is so distracted that they have no idea what the speaker is saying.

However, it is possible to use your hands effectively in a speech, keeping them occupied so they add to rather than distract from the speech. Speakers who know how to use their hands often use notecards to organize their remarks. Such a practice not only assists the organization of the speech, it frees the speaker's hands for more important things, like using visual aids.

Visual Assistants

Visual aids can add impact to your presentation. Not only do they keep your hands occupied, but they assist your audience, giving them something to focus on, something their eyes can use to reinforce what their ears have heard.

The most typical use of visual aids in a speech is in a demonstration. A sample of such a speech on the library level would be to demonstrate book repair, audiovisual equipment operation, or the new computer check-out system. Such topics, while perhaps routine, are of vital interest to more groups than librarians realize. But, such a speech is also limited in terms of the size group that can comfortably see what's happening. Checking out your group's size in advance will let you know if this approach is practical.

Another simple visual aid is the poster or bulletin board. A series of posters or changing bulletin board elements during a speech can effectively highlight a presentation. Naturally, such graphics must be large enough, bold enough, and clear enough for the entire group to see and to link to the elements of the speech. Simple backgrounds and graphics are best for this visual aid. For example, an uncluttered chart, like a line chart showing a steady or dramatic increase in circulation, reference requests, new borrowers, or new population will more effectively illustrate the situation than a recitation of statistics.

When the group is simply too large for such graphics to be usable, it's time to switch to audiovisual equipment. The overhead projector offers potential too seldom tapped by speakers. Transparencies made in advance can be projected while you point, highlight, or circle selected elements. Or, you can write on the overhead surface while talking, thus focusing the audience's attention on whatever points you're trying to make. The overhead is easy to use and, while extremely useful for large groups, can also be effective in smaller groups. Its overall effect is increased if you remember the key points of good visuals—size, color, clarity, and simplicity. Other techniques with the overhead include overlays, transparencies of different colors, and polarizing motion, a technique often used in science presentations.

Another advantage of the overhead is it can be used in a fully lighted room allowing your audience to take notes, and you to see faces. After it's initially set up and focused, there is no further need to do anything except turn it off and on as you change transparencies, a cardinal rule in using an overhead. An audience finds it disconcerting to view a glaring white screen behind the speaker. It is equally disconcerting to view one transparency while the speaker has shifted to another point but apparently doesn't have a visual to illustrate it.

The overhead is an excellent aid, allowing you to control the pace, the selection, and the emphasis of your speech. By organizing the transparencies in the order in which you wish to present them, you will find that your speech gains added punch. We rarely create a speech without adding transparencies. We may utilize cartoons, catchwords, or other bold graphic components (see figure 10.2) but we are always rewarded by an audience that comments on the transparencies and how much they helped in the understanding of our major points. Sometimes we even paperclip our notecards to the transparencies, using them, in essence, as an organizer for the speech. Then, with a separate notecard for the introduction and conclusion, the whole speech is pulled together around the visual components. Suggestions on how to create transparencies can be found in chapter 12.

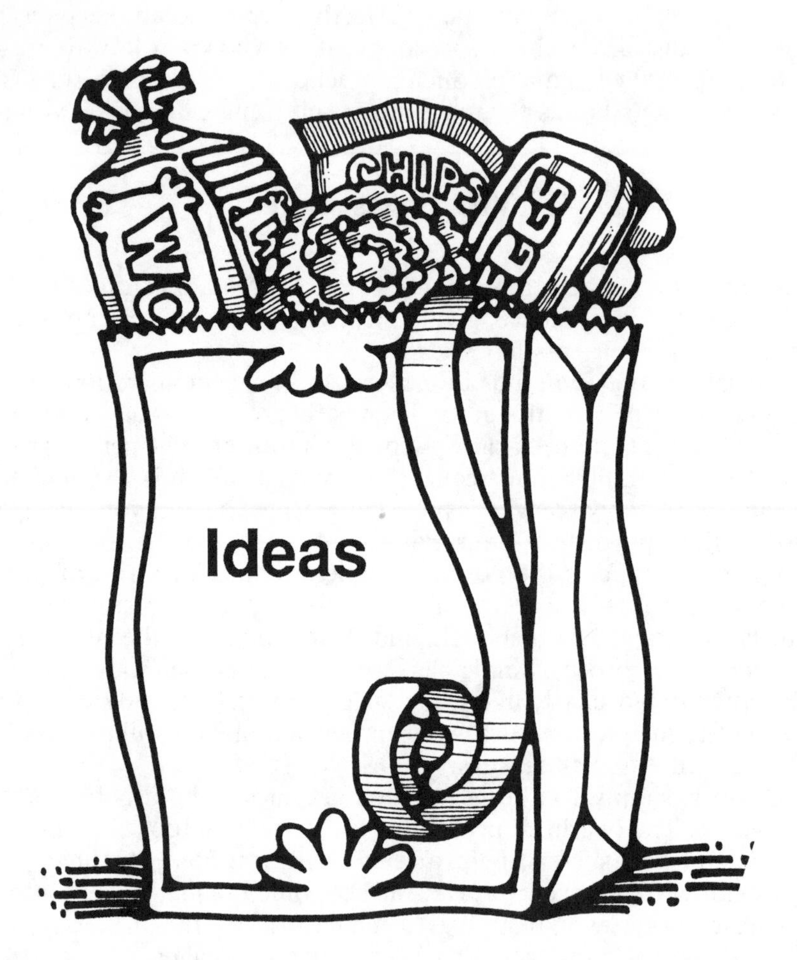

Fig. 10.2. Transparency master.

Yet Another

Another visual assistant is the slide projector. While the room needs to be slightly darker than when using an overhead, the slide projector still offers a visual element which can be easily seen by a large group, can be referred to, and can be totally controlled by the speaker. Just in case the light is not variable enough for your use, a small flashlight permits reading your remarks in the dark. Slides are especially useful to illustrate places, persons, and activities the audience needs to know for your speech. For example, projecting slides of library programs or facilities at a community group's meeting might entice them to a visit.

In using slides, there are basic rules to follow. The speaker must be sure the slides are focused, large enough to see, and related to the topic at hand. It is also a good idea to utilize a remote control unit so you can operate the slides from a comfortable distance.

There are other potential visual aids, including filmstrips, motion pictures, and videotapes, but many of these require detailed planning to prepare and should not be chosen by beginning speakers. They also bring limitations in terms of room lighting and/or the number of individuals who can effectively see them.

PRACTICE

We cannot imagine anyone attempting to give a speech without first practicing it. As you become more adept at making speeches, you will probably need less practice—you will reach a point where you know exactly what aspects you need to go over. However, you will always need to work on parts of the speech in advance in order to get it together so it works out best for your audience.

We have found practice allows us to time our speech, to work our visual aids naturally into the speech, and to identify those portions of our presentation that need rewriting because they are awkward or difficult to fit in with the rest of our remarks. Only by going through the speech, exactly as you anticipate giving it, can you get both the timing and the pacing right.

It is especially helpful if you can practice with a video camera and recorder. This device may be threatening, but there is no better way to see exactly how you'll look and hear how you'll sound. You can catch any annoying mannerisms that may interfere with your speech and detect any awkward speech patterns you'd rather not use.

If access to a video camera is limited, or if the whole idea is just too threatening to you, then use an audiotape recorder. Listen to your pace. Do you rush too much? Do you talk too slowly? Listen to your pitch. Is your voice high with excitement? So low it can hardly be picked up? Then work on lowering or raising the pitch. It can be done; all you need to do is work at it and let the tape recorder help. When we first started doing "character" storyhours, we were convinced we could never change our voices. But, thanks to the tape recorder and several sessions of work, we can now find a perfect voice for characters ranging from a wizened old wizard to a cackling witch to a lovely queen.

The tape recorder can also tip you off if you're using slang, jargon, or flippant remarks. It lets you hear if your tone is warm or cold, or if you sound sincerely friendly or phony. But, it cannot indicate how you look while giving your speech. If a video recorder is not available, give your presentation before a colleague, a spouse, or a child. Let them tell you how you look or what seems right or what seems awkward. If you can't stand the thought of anyone watching you practice, then watch yourself in a mirror. Notice if you glance up and make eye contact with yourself. Notice your posture. Do you sprawl on a lectern? Do you slouch? What is your general appearance?

It is also essential that you practice with any audiovisual devices you may use. Get used to holding up any posters or working with a bulletin board. If you're going to use a projector, practice with it, especially in terms of how it fits in with your remarks. It's hard enough to give a speech without worrying about when to turn on and off the projector.

Finally, it's a good idea to practice how you'll look that day. Go through your wardrobe. Decide in advance what you will wear when the day comes so the outfit will be ready rather than at the cleaners. Remember, how you dress will depend on whom you talk to and when (checking will help out here). Also remember the type of impression you want to make.

SHOW TIME

Once you've thought, researched, prepared, organized, and practiced, there's nothing left to do but do it. Many times you'll find out that it's really not nearly as bad as you had anticipated it might be. But your success still is up to you. Your presentation must be done with warmth, enthusiasm, accuracy and confidence. If you present yourself as having these characteristics, that's the way you'll be seen. If you've prepared thoroughly, you should have confidence. Chances are no one there knows as much about the topic as you do, so you should feel at ease. During the first few speeches, this feeling will be hard to attain. It will become easier as you become more accomplished. But there will always be times when you will have a little stagefright, and a need for someone to give you a little boost.

Under these circumstances, learn to be your own booster. Develop little tricks that'll make you comfortable. It may be the clothes you choose to wear. For our first few speeches, we always bought something special to wear, to carry, or to have on hand, telling ourselves, "You only get this because of the great speech you're going to give." You may find a good luck charm you'll want to carry. Perhaps you'll give yourself a little perk like a boutonniere for your lapel or a bouquet for your office.

Greeting people before the speech, as mentioned earlier, also can loosen you up and let you see that some of your audience are nice people. Then, while giving the speech, you can find these friendly faces and focus on them for your remarks. We try to find one friendly face in the first two rows and just talk to that person for the first few paragraphs.

We also try to "psych" ourselves up before a speech. What will do it depends on you. Maybe it's a walk around the block, a sip of cola (caffeine truly helps some people), or just a quiet moment to yourself to think of something nice. We've found that getting to the room early, checking out how everything is set up, testing and focusing audiovisual equipment and just getting set begins to build our excitement and we're ready to go.

SO, HOW'D IT GO?

Once your speech is over, there is a tendency to just get away and forget it. Naturally, the louder and longer the audience applauds, the less likely you are to do this. But, perhaps there's no applause because it's not that type of meeting. Or perhaps, there is polite appause of a moderate nature. Remember, the Gettysburg Address wasn't recognized as great at the time it was given. Rather than judging yourself on the basis of immediate reaction, it is best to try to be objective and find out if you accomplished what you set out to do.

Develop an evaluation form that you can pass out to the audience, or, if that seems inappropriate, that you can give to the individual who contacted you. Design this form with four or five questions, all related to the purpose of your speech. Include such things as: Was the speaker prepared? Did the speaker seem to know the topic well? Include the specific items that relate to what you were trying to do. If you want a truly objective evaluation, use an even-numbered rating scale since it forces people to choose towards the positive or negative side. If you want to feel good, use an odd-numbered rating scale so people can choose the middle road.

Listen to questions that people ask after your speech. It's another good indication of whether they were listening. Watch the audience while you're speaking. Are they paying attention? Do they seem interested?

Don't ignore the delayed reaction syndrome. Perhaps you get no immediate response from your audience, but a week later you see one of them in the library for the first time. Or, perhaps one of them approaches you in the store or post office and thanks you for coming. All these responses are good. However, you can't expect everyone to come to the library as soon as you finish speaking.

And what about you? How did you feel during the speech? Afterward? If you didn't get booed, have fruits and vegetables thrown at you, or have a hook come out of nowhere to jerk you away, you probably did just fine. Remember, don't be too hard on yourself. You might want to tape record the speech to see how well you did. Or you just may want to go on "gut reaction." Whatever you decide, however you feel, do it again and again until you become a natural.

11

How to Communicate in Print

Write, Write—Right!

The format we all use most frequently to communicate with our public is the printed word. We create posters, flyers, brochures, bookmarks, newsletters, annual reports, press releases and, as the King of Siam would say "et cetera, et cetera, et cetera." This proliferation of print is handed out at the circulation desk, distributed anywhere three or more may gather, entrusted to postal carriers, and otherwise given away at every opportunity.

This common method of getting out our message is typical, normal, healthy, beneficial, and frustrating. Many of us don't like to write, don't write well, can't think visually, or exhibit other traits which block the flow of ink. When we consider the daily bombardment our average patron faces in flyers, junk mail, and literature, it becomes even more difficult to figure out how our piece is going to capture their attention. We need to concentrate on doing our best job, following basic principles of good publications, and being alert to what seems to appeal to our patrons.

RULES ARE RULES

The first rule is that we cannot operate in a vacuum. We can't just charge ahead with what we like and pay no heed to what is going on around us. We can't perpetuate the same thing over and over because it's familiar or it's the "way we've always done it." Being aware of current events, of current trends, of the world as it is helps us develop a style that is appealing and a message that lets our public know we, too, are part of their world.

Today's society lives in the fast lane. Technological changes, cultural overlaps, and an attitude of "use it and lose it" abound. A reflection of the current attitude is that nearly everything is disposable. We are not a society that wants to spend a great deal of time on any one thing. Therefore, our printed messages should be as brief as possible. If a short article will say it, that's enough. If a paragraph will say it, don't use an article. If a sentence will say it, don't waste ink on a paragraph. And if it can be summed up in a word, forget the sentence.

Take a tip from current advertising, which analyzes their target population. Advertising agencies develop profiles of what their group likes and dislikes, what they eat, how they dress, what they tend to buy, how they spend their leisure time, and what jobs they hold. Librarians can do the same thing by seriously and earnestly analyzing their target group. Don't assume, for example, that young mothers haven't changed much, or that your flyer for them may be a waste of time and money.

Young mothers, as an example, have changed. They are older as a group than they were a few years ago, they have fewer children, they are more inclined to work, and many of them are single parents. Knowing these demographics and being aware of how true they are in your community changes the way you appeal to them as compared to an appeal of 15, 10 or even 5 years ago. This kind of knowledge helps you develop a mindset appropriate to writing something for a particular group. It also indicates again the time constraints many of our social groups operate under today because of ever-expanding interests and pursuits.

Looking at our population in general, it is interesting to see we are getting older and becoming more conservative. Also recent studies have shown young people in the office tend to work longer hours, to spend more time on the job, and to demand less leisure time. For younger members of the work force, work is becoming more intermingled with avocational interests. Therefore, if you create publications, you owe it to your public to read and to be aware of their world and their interests.

BASIC ELEMENTS OF PUBLICATIONS

Beyond this basic element of knowing your audience there are other rules, principles, procedures, and hints to keep in mind. Let's examine a few of these and then look in detail at two common publications, the annual report and the newsletter.

Some of these elements are simply housekeeping type chores to help keep your files in order, to assist in establishing a history of your publication efforts, and to aid in avoiding a common problem, cloning your efforts. If you date all your publications, regardless of what they are, you can see what you've done and avoid needless repetition. You can also see how you've changed over time. And you will know how long ago you highlighted a particular service, feature, or program. One copy of everything you print should be in your files with the date of its distribution indicated. Therefore, if you don't want to date a flyer because it may limit its usage (a correct way of thinking), at least you will know exactly how old the piece is.

It is also critical that every printed piece bear the name of your library, as well as its address and phone number. Even in a small town where everyone knows who you are and where you are, it doesn't hurt to say it again. Have you seen advertising which doesn't mention the name of the product, even when you can see what it is? Would McDonald's leave their name off their building, hoping that you will know what their golden arches represent? You don't know that your publication won't end up outside your city limits.

Simple, Simple, Simple

A common, often used, often stated, sincerely meant rule holds true: keep it simple. It is not only dangerous, it is self defeating to make your publication too complicated. Whatever the document is, mixed type faces, type sizes, colors, busy visuals, a collage of images, and a potpourri of words can turn off the very people you want to reach. Remember, nearly everyone you're trying to reach is busy; they want things simple, easy to read, and easy to understand. Otherwise the publication either hits the waste can or, equally deadly, goes on that stack to "get to later."

Writing should be short, simple, and lively. Verbs are great because they sing of action, capture attention, and encourage reading. At least 10 percent of your writing should consist of verbs – aggressive ones, not overworked forms of to be. Don't use "the meeting was productive." Use "the meeting generated many strong ideas." They say the same thing, but one is worth reading. Don't change verbs to nouns. Don't use "consideration was given to." Use "the board debated doing ________" or "the board considered the question."

We also urge use of adverbs and adjectives, but don't get carried away. These forms of speech add color, character, and clarity. That's why they exist. But if you get too enamored with them, the sentence may ramble on. Reading your writing then becomes too involved and too time-consuming, and the message gets lost.

Considering the art of writing in general, simplicity is again the key. Paragraphs should be indented. Businesses may use block style writing, but most people are used to indented paragraphs and they *are* easier to read. Also they help indicate content shift.

It's also a good idea to check the readability of your writing. School teachers do this all the time when they consider texts and other materials for different students. You can do the same thing with Gunning's fog index:

1. Take a 100-word sample of your writing.

2. Calculate the average number of words per sentence. If your 100-word segment stops short of a complete sentence, then go over 100 words to the end of the sentence for this step. You can calculate the average words per sentence by dividing the number of words by the number of sentences.

3. Add the number of three or more syllabled words from the first 100 words to the number you obtained in step 2.

4. Multiply the final figures obtained in steps 2 and 3 by 0.4. This is the grade level. Most Americans read on the ninth grade level (and it's falling). Also, most people prefer to read just below their level, especially for nonrequired reading.

People and Visual Appeal

Appeal to readers through "people type" elements, like descriptions of emotion, mention of people's names, quotations, and consequences of actions. Writing which reflects human interests is appealing rather than dry and devoid of the qualities that make us the living, breathing, thinking creatures we are.

A few hints for the visual aspect of publications includes:

- Type superimposed over visuals – photographs or drawings – signals that the message in type is unimportant, because it is not easily readable.

- Reverse type (white on black) is effective only in small segments. Beyond that it becomes difficult to read.

- Red or black headlines seem more effective in attracting the reader's eye than other colors. This principle applies more, however, to newsletters and other longer pieces than to flyers or short pieces where a different color combination may be used for effect.

- Other guidelines for type sizes and styles are shown in figures 11.1 and 11.2.

ALL-CAP HEADLINES ARE HARD TO READ. TYPE A PARAGRAPH IN UPPER CASE, AND YOU'LL SEE WHAT WE MEAN.

Headlines In Upper And Lower Style Are Easier To Read. So, This Has Been The Standard For Some Time.

Downstyle headlines, like this, are the easiest to read. They're also easier to write and set. This style is becoming more popular.

Bold face is good for subheads or sideheads.

Italic face is for emphasis. But be careful; too much of it is hard to read.

Fig. 11.1. Heads and typefaces.

Headlines that are 14 point whisper.

24 point headlines talk.

36 point headlines shout.

48 point screams.

Fig. 11.2. Type sizes.

When we consider the visual aspect in our publications, we still should keep simplicity in mind. For one thing, simplicity in color lowers our cost. One color of ink is cheaper to reproduce than using two or more colors. Remember, you can achieve a two-color look by shading. A light gray background (shaded black ink) with black letters on it looks like two colors, but it's one ink and that's what you pay for.

Color use should be approached with an eye on readability. It may seem flashy to use orange ink on tan paper, but the readers may have trouble reading it. The eye works best with maximum contrast. "Hot" colors should be used cautiously and infrequently. An example of what not to do is a library that regularly publishes combinations like purple ink on chartreuse paper and blue ink on florescent paper. They're trying to communicate they're with it, but what they're really saying is they don't care if their patrons can read the pieces or not.

The Picture Part

Pictures are worth a thousand words. Hasty readers will grasp the information from a photo and ignore the article. Effective pictures show action. Other consideration for pictures include:

- Pictures placed at "cutesy" angles often turn off a reader.
- Photographs appeal more when in rectangular rather than square shapes.
- Thumbnail photos, little ones indented in the first paragraph, increase readership of a column. Notice how many newspapers utilize this method with regular columnists.
- Captions under pictures are a must. Misunderstanding often results from no explanation.
- Photographs should reflect quality. Human interest and action shots in good focus with good balance and lighting make you look good. Photos that are fuzzy, too dark, or too light should simply be eliminated.
- No photo is better than a poor photo.
- Closeup photos are better than ones which look as if they were shot from across a football field.

When You Produce

In terms of production of any piece, check carefully for typographical errors. Let the individual who provided the information read for content and meaning. You check for accuracy and try to find someone to check you. We have a tendency to read what we think we wrote rather than what we did write. (One of the saddest instances of this problem was a library which did an annual report on which they spent a lot of time and, for their budget, a lot of money. It was their first effort, and they wanted to make a big impression on the community. They did. When the ________ *Pubic Library* report came out, everyone wanted to see it, but the embarrassment of the library staff lingered on for a long time.)

It is also essential to obtain cost estimates for each publication. If you have an established printer or if you print in-house, these estimates may not apply. But you still might check around to see if someone else can print your publication for less money. Just remember, price variation sometimes also indicates quality variation. Try to determine why one price may be considerably lower. It may be the printer has some down time and is eager for business. It may be some element, like typesetting or paste-up wasn't considered. Or it may be a different paper stock was used in the bid, one which might not be acceptable to you.

Develop a specifications sheet for each publication if you're using an out-of-house printer (see figure 11.3). If you can anticipate a year's publications efforts, or even six months, you might get a price break from the printer, because he sees ongoing business.

Monitor the full production process for each publication. Assuming someone knows what they're doing can spell disaster. If publications are your responsibility, you are going to be more concerned than others. A simple telephone call to see how things are going will put your mind at ease and may inspire someone who slacked off a bit on the job. Even the most reliable printers, typesetters, or layout artists can get preoccupied with another job, experience spring fever, or develop a personal problem which gets in the way.

There are lots of other considerations, but the ones we've mentioned are among the more basic.

THE NEWSLETTER

Being the one responsible for the newsletter is a consuming, unending task which often requires being writer, editor, photographer, artist, layout specialist, and, occasionally, printer and delivery person. A recent survey of nearly 100 library newsletter editors revealed some statistical data about library editors. Only 5 percent of the editors were employed full time, yet 63 percent wrote over 25 percent of the copy for the newsletter. Two-thirds spent over 10 percent of their time on the newsletter, while the other third spent over 25 percent of their time in this task. In terms of working hours, 56 percent spent 21 hours or more per issue, and 28 percent spent over 36 hours per issue.

This survey dramatically illustrates:

1. Newsletters are important enough to libraries to demand a large amount of staff time.

2. A great amount of professional time is siphoned from other duties to tend to this task.

3. Although many editors are not technically employed full time in this position, they spend a considerable amount of time doing it.

The problem is how to efficiently, effectively handle a newsletter, giving it quality without sacrificing other responsibilities. The answer is you don't. You recognize that if you want a good newsletter, you have to sacrifice something to give it the proper time. The initial start-up of the newsletter may well be the biggest expenditure of total staff involvement per issue. But, the nitty-gritty routine operation does take time. The time factor needs to be recognized and, where possible, built into a staff member's assigned duties rather than added on.

Specifications for LIPP

Job Title: **LIPP**-- a newsletter (See sample)

Quantity: 10,000 every other month (6 times per year)

Size: 8 1/2 x 11 inches

Number of pages: 12

Binding: stapled, center

Stock: standard white 60 lb. offset (other suggestions should be so noted on bid quotation)

Ink: Black--red on pre-printed cover

Halftones/Artwork: camera-ready art utilized regularly; halftones occasionally. Sizing of art work (blow-ups, reductions) in most issues

Composition: typesetting and paste-up to be done by client (us) May have occasional need for typesetting

Proofs: Not needed in normal operation

Schedule: Prefer 3-5 day turn-around time for any typesetting
1 week for printing, collating, stapling,
additional 3 days for labeling, mailing

Copy return: All paste-ups, extra issues and art work to be returned to client after printing of each issue.

Special instructions: Occasionally, "overprinting" is done for special projects

Additional information, contact: Ann Tuggle, phone:

Fig. 11.3. Sample specification sheet.

Written Policy

Another problem for the newsletter editor revolves around control. It is essential to develop a written editorial policy, approved by the administration, that the editor can follow. It is also necessary to identify to whom the editor is to report and the exact amount of editorial control to be exercised. Being responsible for the editing but consistently countermanded by other people is a serious disadvantage for an editor. The editor must have the final authority for content while using others as a sounding board. If an editor goes too far afield, it is then time for a reprimand, a process of remediation, and/or a different editor. Until such time, the editor should be trusted by those who have given him or her the responsibility.

The editorial policy must include a purpose statement for the newsletter. The statement should clearly define why the newsletter exists. The purpose should be developed on the basis of what type of information the publication will carry and what type of reaction is desired from the reader. Is the newsletter to inform, influence action, inspire, educate, or entertain? Decide what's to be done and write it down for all concerned. Better yet, have all concerned help develop the purpose. And remember, it may be feasible to have several newsletters, published for different groups at different times for different purposes in different manners.

Crucial Issues

The crucial elements of your newsletter's success, once you have policy and purpose defined, are in the areas of production, content, graphics, and delivery. You can reproduce by office techniques like the stencil or spirit master (both nearly obsolete) or photoduplicator. Or you can use more professional methods like the letterpress or the offset. None of these methods is right or wrong. Some look better but cost more. The choice must depend on your budget, circulation, and purpose. If you have a sizable readership, the more professional techniques may actually cost less per unit than the in-house methods, especially if staff time is calculated as part of the cost.

We have encountered situations where hiring one person to perform all duties – writing, editing, photography, layout and pasteup – was considerably cheaper than paying for each of these tasks to be done individually. All too often, these duties get parcelled out and viewed in isolation so their real cost isn't realized.

You can use a typewriter for the copy or have it typeset. Typesetting costs more, but it often uses less space, thus saving paper costs. Typesetting also offers flexibility of type size and style. Typesetting is easy to read, better looking, appears more professional, and offers an easy way to develop headlines.

The typewriter, however, renders an air of timeliness and sometimes assures critics that you're not wasting money (although the hours you or a secretary spend typing should be included in the cost). Also, when using a typewriter, what you see is what you get. There's no waiting for the copy to come back from the typesetter to find what length each article is. Unfortunately, a typewriter, even with the varied elements of some models, rarely has a type size big enough for headlines. Therefore, you must use press-on letters, transfer letters, or lettering generated by the Kroy or Gestefont type systems.

There is another alternative. Many computer systems offer word processing which has features much like those you get with typesetting. Some, when combined with the right printer, give the same quality appearance as typeset copy. It is worth investigating to find a printshop which may have on hand a printer which is compatible with your computer. Then, you could type the copy, save it to disc, and take it to the print shop where it could be printed out on the appropriate electronic printer. With the right program, you could even format the publication on the computer.

Publishers of electronic publishing software, as well as some graphic houses, offer information and workshops on the various desktop publishing options. Call various computer firms or watch for announcements in local papers and professional literature to investigate this new development for publications.

The Heart of the Matter

The content of your newsletter is really the heart of its success. The best produced, best-looking newsletter will fail if it has nothing to say. On the other hand, a highly readable one, even if it's not so attractive, will become popular with its audience.

First of all, accept that the newsletter is for your readers, not your ego. You may think you have the greatest thoughts and opinions in the world, but your readers probably don't care. Package the newsletter in a "you" approach. The reader often doesn't want to be "we" or "us," so direct your content in terms of benefits to the reader. What's really in it for him or her?

One newsletter expert goes so far as to state that you should stress things so that they'll make a difference to the reader, especially items that increase power or money, or save time or money. He also encourages you to appeal to what he sees as basic human interests: avarice, greed, fear, and profit. You need not go that far, but there is a grain of truth in the remark. The readers must be convinced that reading your copy is worth their time because there will be something of benefit for them.

Your content should revolve around the seven C's of writing: certainty, concern, creativeness, character, completeness, clarity, and conciseness. Plunge in with confidence yet individualize your approach to get that "you" feeling. Try to visualize the reader as you write and direct your copy to that individual. Use short sentences, an active voice, and strong words so your copy has a distinctive character. Reread everything you write and edit it. Force yourself to cut some of your prose by deleting excessive words.

Work on developing alluring leads to articles, especially feature articles. Don't use the same type of approach in every feature. Use timely anecdotes, pithy, pertinent quotes, vivid descriptions, smooth transitions, and memorable endings. The reader should enjoy reading your newsletter. There should be no doubt in his or her mind when an article is finished.

There is no magical method to ensure development of good writing. You should take some creative and expository writing classes, and practice, practice, practice. Criticize your own work. You also have to recognize that if you just don't have the writing knack, you need to enlist the assistance of someone who does, either a fellow staff member, board member, trustee, friend, teacher, or student. Someone has to do the writing, and it's up to you to find that someone.

A Matter of Style

Once content is written, there comes the problem of layout, design, and graphics. The purpose of the layout is to make your piece readable, attractive, and eye-catching. Once again, simplicity is the key. Use one dominant feature. Use white space (space without copy or graphics) liberally. White space allows the eye to rest, an important consideration in retaining readers.

Use big headlines to draw the eye to important articles, but don't overwhelm the page and don't create a collage of assorted type faces and photos which convey a grocery ad appearance. Use color purposefully and boldly, but don't overdo it. Intense color is hard on the eye, and color should highlight, not overwhelm.

Plan each page, considering the page opposite it. If one is heavy on copy, perhaps the other should be light but not so light that it looks like you worked hard on one and didn't have anything left for the other. Focus the reader's eye where you want it. Draw the eye with white space, headlines, subheads, and graphics.

Break up heavy copy with these same elements. Shorten your column width so the eye can rest. A column over 25 picas, about 3½ inches, can tire the eye. Use as many as five columns on a page, depending on your page and type size. Experiment until you find a style you like and stick with it as your established identity. Read other publications, even the highly circulated magazines, to watch for layouts that appeal to you. Clip or photocopy them and add them to your files for inspiration and ideas.

Who's This?

Establish your library's identity on page one. The top of the page should indicate whose publication this is. The eye enters at upper left, so that's the best spot for this important information. Make your newsletter's name, your library's name, and your logo specific and simple. Be sure your nameplace is bold, reflective of today's style, and distinctly your own. It's also wise to develop a logo that's easily enlarged or reduced and adaptable to colors. Then use it consistently on all publications.

Even though your front page always carries your identity, logo, and an appearance that are consistent and recognizable, there should be a freshness in every issue so your reader doesn't think he or she has already read it. Accomplish this appearance by retaining the nameplate but rearranging articles, headlines, and graphics. Your front page should also have a sense of immediacy, a simplified terseness which says "read me now" but still retains warmth and a light touch. Your readers will probably be browsing through your newsletter, perhaps over coffee or a sandwich, and you want to appeal to that type of usage. You will convey, graphically, to the reader "I care about you, so I'm not going to take up your valuable time with nonessential details."

Try to establish a certain style that is uniquely yours. The style becomes comforting to the reader. Your newsletter becomes like a familiar friend who changes clothes but remains the same good old pal. You determine that style. You decide if you reflect a touch of class, a touch of down on the farm, or just that personal touch. Your nameplate, column width, type style and size, layout pattern, paper stock, ink color, and writing style all influence your overall style. If the paper stock is flimsy, your library may be perceived as such. If the appearance is too expensive, your library may be perceived as wasting money.

Other Considerations

Smoother, glossier papers reproduce photographs better but cost more. Newsprint stock seems inexpensive but it actually costs about the same as a better stock of paper. Colored stock is distinctive but can be hard to read. Textured paper is rich-looking but reproduces photos poorly. You can add a classy look at a reasonable cost by using contrasting color just for your nameplate and printing a year's supply in advance. The stock will be held for issues of your newsletter as they come in, with the remainder of the publication printed in regular black ink.

Many newsletters include regular features, which highlight ongoing services and are often appreciated by readers. These features become old friends. Certain departments, like reference or the children's section; certain services, like homebound or senior citizens; or regular programs, like films of the month, are natural regular features. But, these columns need to be reviewed periodically so they don't become houseguests who have overstayed their welcome.

One regular feature in most newsletters that is dull and tedious but required is the director's column. Usually labeled "from the top" or "from the director's desk," this feature is often the worst thing in the newsletter. However, it should be the best. It should reflect the administrator's views on what is happening. One newsletter that handles this feature beautifully uses the same graphic each time, while the headline changes according to the topic. The director uses the space to talk about new services or new issues in the community. He also writes about issues that concern him, as a librarian, and sometimes makes controversial or contemplative statements which readers respond to. Other times he rambles on in a delightful fashion about something he's seen or read, almost in the manner of a cracker barrel philosopher. This type of director is a real asset to your newsletter.

Another regular feature in many newsletters is a feedback section. Some merely allot space for "If you have something to tell us, write it here." Unfortunately this portion is often on the back page by the mailing label and the patron who wants to state something, without being identified, is immediately stymied. Other newsletters use graphics to ask readers what they like, dislike, miss, or whatever.

A final consideration for your newsletter is distribution. For most libraries, the distribution is by mail. Check with the post office to identify slow times of the month when a nonfirst class publication will get speedy handling. If you mail it at the same time all the bills are sent, you won't receive any priority. Usually before the 28th of the month and after the fifth are good times. If you are part of a newsletter, like part of a school district newsletter, or if you are cooperating with another agency, like the park district, you may have no say in when the piece gets mailed.

Another aspect of distribution is the mailing list. Some libraries mail to card holders only. They believe this system reaches the people who use the library and are interested in it. Some libraries advertise in a local paper that the newsletter is available and send it to those who respond. In the first case you never reach the nonuser; in the second you avoid the nonreader or the person who doesn't subscribe to that particular paper.

Other libraries make arrangements to get lists from the local city government or arrange for inserts in local newspaper-styled advertisers which are delivered free to every home. Still others use a postal patron – local label and contact everyone in the community. The choice is yours and should reflect your purpose and budget.

So, How Was It?

Whatever you decide, the final concern that needs to be addressed is evaluation. Give yourself time to get the newsletter established in the public's mind. Don't make a decision about continuing or discontinuing after just one or two issues. You might include a feedback form. Suggest you're trying to find out who wants this newsletter and include a coupon or form the reader can fill out and return to continue to receive the publication. But do try to find out what people think. Ask individuals who come into the library. You could hand out questionnaires at the desk, but we recommend a more direct approach.

Set aside a day, an hour once a week, or some other scheduled time which varies so you don't encounter the same people over and over. During this time, seek out patrons and ask them questions. Do you read our newsletter? Here's a sample. Are you familiar with it? Do you receive it? If you read it, what parts do you read? Is there something you don't look at? Why? If you're doing a newsletter in a school or business situation, go to the staff lounge or cafeteria and ask people there how they feel.

To find out the response from nonlibrary users, do your informal canvas at the post office, local bank, or grocery store. Check with those in charge first so they know who you are and what you're doing (this is also a good opportunity for a little PR). Another way to get a response is to arrange for random phone calls in the community. This same method will work at the school level, but it's smart to check with the principal or superintendent before you make the calls. If you lack time, structure the questions and send out volunteers. At least you'll get an idea of what's happening when that newsletter arrives. Then you can make decisions and appropriate changes.

Your newsletter reflects your library. To some people, it's the only library contact they have. Make it worth their time, and make them curious about coming in to meet the people who create it.

ANNUAL REPORTS

Annual reports, unlike the newsletter, are not a regular occurrence during the year. Like Christmas, they come once a year and, like Christmas, they can be anticipated or ignored. The cycle for the annual report is your choice. It can be at the end of the calendar year, fiscal year, school year, or whenever you want to issue it.

There can also be different kinds of annual reports. Surely the administration wants some type of "what happened this year" account. That report reflects whatever kind of information in whatever fashion your administration wants. Sometimes there's a report to the staff. It may be statistical, as well as narrative.

Either of these reports may be written or oral or both. Reports to administration, and often to staff, emphasize facts and figures with an indication of what these figures prove about the value of the library's service. This businesslike, professional approach naturally pleases an administrator. Administrators like to know what's been done with an allotted budget, whom that budget affected, and how. Frequently such a report includes an evaluation of services and/or positions.

The problem comes when those reports are lifted verbatim or near verbatim and issued to an unsuspecting public who wonder "why in the world am I getting this?" If an annual report is going to go public, it needs to be approached with the same care as the newsletter. Much of the information in an administrative/staff report is not adaptable, nor should it be, to the general public.

We Did It, Guys!

The annual report to the public is a public relations tool. It is a chance for the library to shout "Look what we did!" Naturally, the public is interested in how their dollars were spent. But they don't have the same perspective as the administration and should not be treated the same way. They need assurance that their support of your library is a worthwhile activity. And if they are not active supporters and users, they need to wonder what they're missing and be encouraged to get in on the action.

The same principles just mentioned apply in a school or college situation. Faculty members like to know exactly what types of funds the library has had and how the library has used those dollars for the maximum benefit of students and staff. Alumni and the general public in the community are equally curious about the value and activities of the library. Why not tell them?

People react to most things by what they feel, so an annual report to the public should be people oriented: it should incorporate pictures of people using services. Figures and facts that may be necessary should be presented in simple visuals like graphs. A pie chart of how each library dollar breaks down in service terms or stick figures which represent circulation statistics are far clearer to the public than rows and rows of numbers. (Unless you admit you're trying to dazzle them with statistics, which often backfires with the general public.)

The report should relate to people's interests, needs, and everyday lives. There should be a touch of humor, a bit of emotion, and a dab of cleverness to breathe life into what could be a stale document. The trick is not to go too far, not to fall from the solid grounds of ingenuity into the pits of kitsch. Such problems can be avoided if the primary purpose of the report is to show people they have a great library, designed and working for them.

Occasionally a library will issue what seems to be the same report year after year. They change the color and, of course, the content, but it looks like the same old document. These libraries either:

1. Got a compliment on a report format several years back and assume public taste doesn't change that much.

2. Have convinced themselves it is professional to have a series of reports which look the same.

3. Hate doing the report, have found one method they can handle, and just give it the old instant replay every year.

In any case they should change their style or drop the report. Nothing annoys people more than waste, which is what unread, unattractive, and unidentifiable reports are.

Dollar for Dollar

A key factor in issuing any report is the cost. Dismissing a clerk to pay for the report is not a recommended move. On the other hand, a quick and dirty ditto which leaves purple tracks is not exactly a PR plus. What is spent depends on the budget and the community.

The budget may not change, but the community is another matter. If taxes have recently soared, if there are scandals about frills at taxpayers' expense, it is not the time to issue a slick, breathtaking report that seems expensive. Rather, it may be the time to issue something more conservative that emphasizes the bargains available from library service. If the community prides itself on quality, a cut-rate report printed in the basement of a friendly neighbor may rankle even the staunchest of library supporters. An attractive piece that subtly states quality might be a wiser plan.

The solution lies both in the library staff's awareness of its public and its ingenuity to get good quality at reasonable prices. One way is to obtain sponsors who'll be credited within the document for helping to underwrite the cost. Another trick is to create a solid report which looks less expensive than it is. A mini-newspaper which is a special edition from the library can be typeset, have superb photos, and clear graphics. It can fit all the criteria for a good report, cost the same as a slicker version, and look less expensive and please the penny watchers. This is also an opportunity to use the assorted desktop publishing options available, an especially attractive option for schools and colleges which may already have access to computers.

The same factors that apply to all good publications apply to annual reports, but a few additional elements should be noted. Continuity is critical. Develop a theme and stick to it. Don't let it become a gimmick for the cover that doesn't relate anywhere else in the document. Keep things organized. Repeat issues and conclusions which are important. Relate costs to services. Help people translate their dollars into assistance for them and their fellow community members.

End with a positive, forward look. People don't want to hear that their library is an endangered species because of lack of funding. They want to believe there is hope and are skeptical about supporting something that seems to want to depress them. Former ALA President Russell Shank put it succinctly: We point with pride, view with alarm, and then ask for more money. Our patrons are weary of that routine. Surely we should indicate if we are not keeping up to standards, but there are ways to state it that are positive rather than negative. It is the old "is the glass half empty or half full" philosophy. Keep it part way full and you can inspire people to help fill it. Indicate it's half way empty and individuals may feel it's a hopeless situation.

If you take the time and trouble to do an annual report, get it to everyone. Mailing it may be too expensive or it may get lost in all the other mail that comes into the home, including your newsletter. Try different distribution points. Hand it out in the library, advertise its availability in the paper, put it in doctors' and dentists' offices, stuff it in grocery bags (some stores will help out), or drop a pile at the car dealers. In the school, hit every mailbox and pepper the counters, department offices, teachers' lounge, and the cafeteria. Distribute it to the PTA and the school board, as well as the president of every civic group.

Some Examples

While these examples were not selected from Dana award winners, they effectively illustrate the principles we have itemized. The Prince Georges County Memorial Library System in Hyattsville, Maryland, published an annual review which was a bookmark with a removable calendar. The back side of the pocket calendar listed library phone numbers. The bookmark highlighted key points of the year. A few years after this report, Prince Georges expanded into an 8½-by-11-inch format in perforated sections to be torn off and used. One piece was a Where To Find It – a quick Dewey guide to general subjects, arranged A-Z in a bookmark size. Another bookmark, slightly shorter in length, was filled on one side with reference phone numbers of county services and on the other side, again with the list of library phone numbers. The very top portion was a commentary on system highlights, emphasizing new and expanded services as well as the contributions of volunteers. There was a brief review of the budget and budget sources. The majority of the document was a library card application form, self-addressed, which could be filled out, folded, and mailed to the library. (See figure 11.4.)

Fairfax County Library in Springfield, Virginia, used a thrice-folded 8½-by-14-inch document centered around the theme "Moving Ahead" (see figure 11.5). A Mileage Chart rendered a statistical analysis of three years in circulation, collection, number of borrowers, transactions, volunteer hours, staff, and space. Below was a simple graphic of the number of people served by the library. The Mileposts section itemized numbers and types of materials available. The Distance Covered section indicated years of library service. A Road Map showed where all branches were located. The reverse side listed the library services beneath Itinerary. Indications of new services and facilities were shown, plus a quick chart of expenditures and revenues. An indication of the library's place among other southern public libraries in terms of budget and circulation was given. And, finally, there was a list of supervisors and trustees.

FY 85 ANNUAL REPORT

What's in it for you? Lots more than last year! During fiscal year 1985 your Prince George's County Memorial Library System was able to add to our long list of services and improve some others. Here are some highlights from the 1985 fiscal year. The remainder of our branch libraries went on-line during FY '85 completing our automated circulation project begun in 1981. Each of our full service, community and neighborhood branch libraries now uses our central computer for faster, more accurate circulation of materials, obtaining up-to-date information about the resources of all 21 branch libraries and for filling your requests for high demand items.

The popular video cassette loan service was expanded by adding browsing collections to our branch libraries in Bowie, Laurel, Oxon Hill and Surratts-Clinton. We began circulating compact audio discs from our Hyattsville Branch Library, the first such service in the metropolitan area. A new special collection, the Parent-Child Room, which promotes children's reading, parenting and reading aloud to children was established and is also located in the Hyattsville Branch. The Magruder Branch Library was moved to new quarters on the first floor of the Hyattsville City Building on Jefferson Street. Patrons there now have increased parking and easier access to the branch's facilities. Our former Division for the Visually and Physically Handicapped has become the "Talking Book Center." Its services remain the same

Quick Reference Phone Numbers

Fire; Police; Rescue	911(V/TDD)
Child Abuse	699-8605
P.G. County Hotline	577-4866; 577-0577(TDD)
Poison Control	800-492-2414
Psychiatric Services	322-2606
Sexual Assault	341-4942
Spouse Abuse	864-9101
Animal Control	336-3221
Consumer Protection	952-4700
County Council	952-3700
County Executive	952-4131
Handicapped Services	952-3210;627-3352 (TDD)
Health Department	386-0300; 773-8717 (TDD)
Job Information	952-3408
Landlord/Tenant	952-3200
Voter Registration	627-2814
Women's Commission	952-3383
Legal Aid	445-0200
MVA	350-9770
SENIOR CITIZENS	699-2670; 699-2845 (TDD)
Energy Assistance	699-2660
Cooperative Extension	953-3313
Human Relations	952-3070

LIBRARY CARD APPLICATION FORM

DATE ____________

Prince George's County Memorial Library System

Have you ever applied for a Prince George's County library card before? Yes ____ No ____

PLEASE PRINT: One letter or number in each space. Skip one space between requested information.

FIRST NAME　MIDDLE INITIAL　LAST NAME

NUMBER　STREET　APT. NO.

CITY　STATE　ZIP

TELEPHONE NO.　COUNTY (EXCEPT PRINCE GEORGE'S)

STATE　DRIVER'S LICENSE NO. OR MVA AGE OF MAJORITY CARD ID NO.

IF UNDER 16 YEARS OF AGE LIST PARENT'S NAME

FIRST NAME　MIDDLE INITIAL　LAST NAME

PERMANENT ADDRESS IF DIFFERENT FROM ABOVE

NUMBER　STREET　APT. NO.

CITY　STATE　ZIP

FOR LIBRARY USE ONLY

APATID (PA)

ID (PZ)　NEW

PATCAT　P

AGENCY　-

SCAT

ICATOR

STATUS

DELREA ____________

ADDATA ____________

TO BE NUMBERED ☐　RENUMBER COMPLETED ☐

OLD ID ____________

NEW ID ____________

OVERDUE MATERIALS ☐ YES ☐ NO

CHANGE OF NAME/ADDRESS ☐

WHERE TO FIND IT

USE THIS QUICK DEWEY DECIMAL REFERENCE GUIDE TO LOCATE SUBJECTS OF GENERAL INTEREST

Accounting	657
airplanes	629
appliance repair	643.6,621.3
astronomy	520's
auto repair	629.2
Biology	574
birds	598.2
black studies	322-323
boats & boating	623.8, 797.1
business	650's
Camping	796.54
carpentry	694
chess	794.1
civil rights	323.4
coins	737.4
cookbooks	641.5
crafts	745
Dance	792, 793
dictionaries	423
diets	613.2, 641.4
diseases	616
drawing	741
Ecology	574.5, 301.3
education	370-378
electricity	537, 621.3
etiquette	395
Films	791.43
fish	597, 639.34
folklore	398.2
furniture	684, 749
Games	793, 795
gardening	635
genealogy	929
geography	910's
geology	550's
guns	623.44
Health	613
history	930-999
holidays	394
home repairs	643
Indians, American	970
insects	595.7
interior decoration	747
investments	332.6
Language	400's
law	340
literature	800's

Fig. 11.4. Multipurpose annual report. Reprinted with permission of Prince Georges County Memorial Library System, Hyattsville, Maryland.

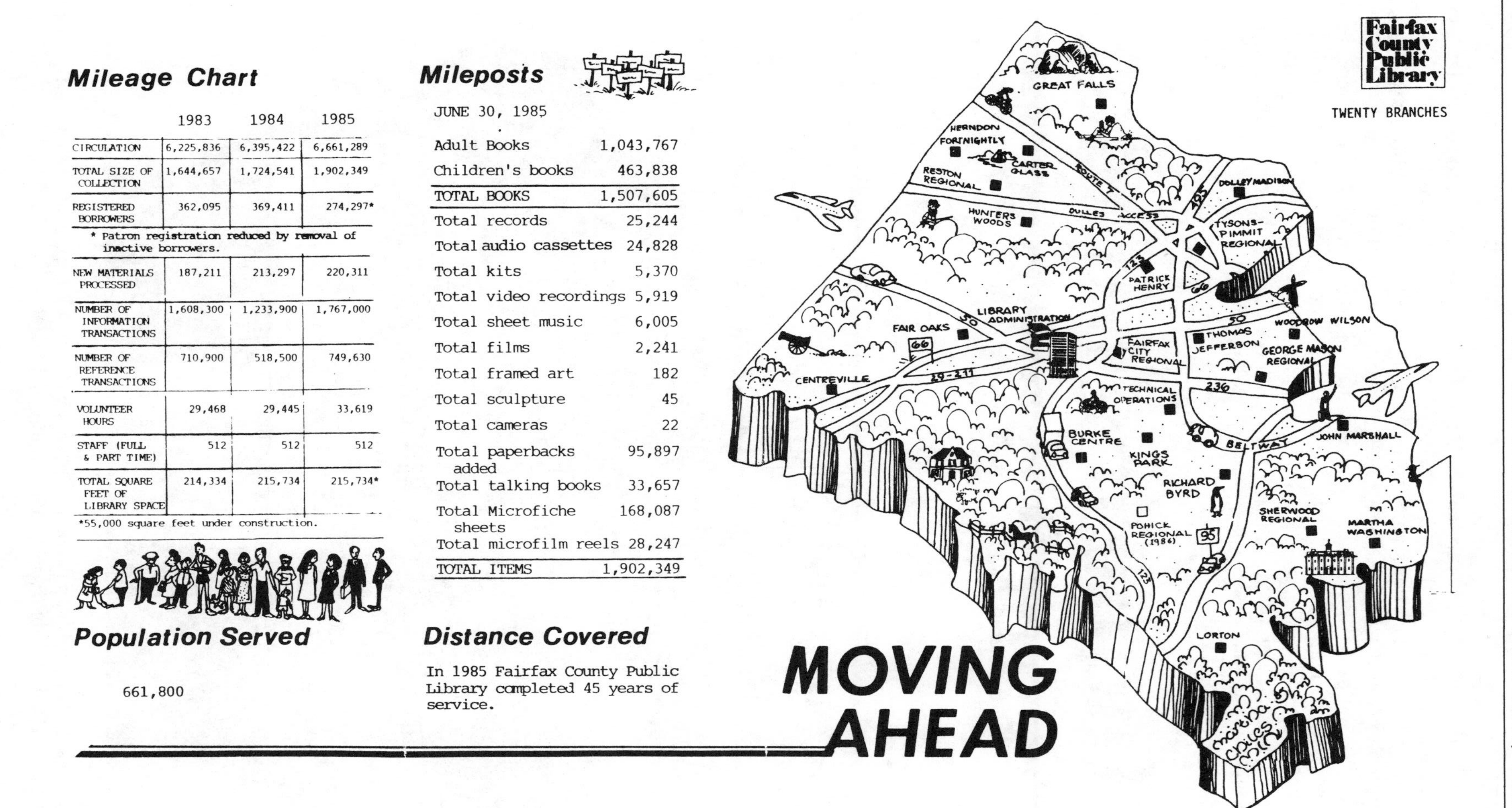

Mileage Chart

	1983	1984	1985
CIRCULATION	6,225,836	6,395,422	6,661,289
TOTAL SIZE OF COLLECTION	1,644,657	1,724,541	1,902,349
REGISTERED BORROWERS	362,095	369,411	274,297*
* Patron registration reduced by removal of inactive borrowers.			
NEW MATERIALS PROCESSED	187,211	213,297	220,311
NUMBER OF INFORMATION TRANSACTIONS	1,608,300	1,233,900	1,767,000
NUMBER OF REFERENCE TRANSACTIONS	710,900	518,500	749,630
VOLUNTEER HOURS	29,468	29,445	33,619
STAFF (FULL & PART TIME)	512	512	512
TOTAL SQUARE FEET OF LIBRARY SPACE	214,334	215,734	215,734*

*55,000 square feet under construction.

Population Served

661,800

Mileposts

JUNE 30, 1985

Adult Books	1,043,767
Children's books	463,838
TOTAL BOOKS	1,507,605
Total records	25,244
Total audio cassettes	24,828
Total kits	5,370
Total video recordings	5,919
Total sheet music	6,005
Total films	2,241
Total framed art	182
Total sculpture	45
Total cameras	22
Total paperbacks added	95,897
Total talking books	33,657
Total Microfiche sheets	168,087
Total microfilm reels	28,247
TOTAL ITEMS	1,902,349

Distance Covered

In 1985 Fairfax County Public Library completed 45 years of service.

Fairfax County Public Library

TWENTY BRANCHES

MOVING AHEAD

Fig. 11.5. Library on the move. Reprinted with permission of Fairfax County Public Library, Fairfax, Virginia.

Memphis Shelby County (Tennessee) Public Library and Information Center utilized a newspaper appearance. The report had a "teaser" cover which unfolded into the annual report done in a newspaper style. The newspaper was entitled "The Annual Report" (see figure 11.6). Black and white photos illustrated the headline feature: a change in library directors. The article immediately below the photos indicated problems and progress of the year. There were other short articles about National Library Week, special events, the planning progress for the library, materials, services, bargains purchased by tax dollars, the top reading list, special anniversaries, exhibits and even awards won by the library's logo. The reverse side continued the informal style and listed administrators and quick summaries of statistics.

Inquiring Minds Want To Know...

Fig. 11.6. *The Times*, an annual report in newspaper style. Reprinted with permission of Memphis-Shelby County Library and Information Center, Memphis, Tennessee.

The Providence (Rhode Island) Public Library produced an annual report which looked like a magazine. A black and white photo on the cover showed a young woman eagerly using the card catalog (see figure 11.7). The inside offered excellent photographs of library staff, administration, and users, all in action in the library. A president's letter summarized major accomplishments while the director's review looked over the entire year. There were summaries of various departments and pages devoted to the branches. A summary of statewide services, a statistical overview, a financial chart, and a letter from a certified public accountant that the report represents fairly the financial picture of the library were included. The final pages named library financial supporters, as well as committees for all library functions. It was attractive and thorough.

On the school scene, the Washington Middle School in Aurora, Illinois, used an annual report modeled after the U.S. government. Each year the librarian issued a "State of the Center" message. The document was produced at school, using a typewriter and the ditto machine. It was stapled inside a construction paper cover. An accompanying letter explained the purpose of the report and encouraged anyone with questions to contact the librarian. The contents included statistics on budget, circulation, student visits, class usage, and other pertinent data. One section dealt with the new things tried that were successful. Another tackled the area of "things that didn't work out as planned." A third portion offered a futuristic view of "what we'd like to try next year." The report was placed in every teacher's mailbox, sent to the administration, both at the building and district level, and mailed to every board member and PTA officer.

In Illinois, one of the reactions to the public cry for accountability in education is the yearly issuance of a school "report card" wherein each district indicates its test scores, number of students graduating, and other statistical information. Additional summarative data may be included at the school's option. This is a natural document for including a report about the importance and services of the library media center.

Fig. 11.7. Emphasis on people. Reprinted with permission of Providence Public Library, Providence, Rhode Island.

The Tulsa City County Library issued one report as a deck of cards (see figure 11.8). There were 52 cards in two red and two black suits. There were two jokers and an explanatory card. The suits were library logos, film reels, books, and records. Each card highlighted a library service, statistic, usage pattern, department, branch, program, or special event. The deck was attractive and sturdy.

Fig. 11.8. Deal out an annual report. Reprinted with permission of Tulsa City-County Library, Tulsa, Oklahoma.

The Edmonton Public Library featured a cascade of events in one of their annual reports. Included were Library Lovers Day, a pioneer costumes parade, a stagecoach and antique car parade, most lovable patrons awards, and a celebrity bookstacking contest. Other, more serious, views of services and history of the library were included, but the tone was definitely bright.

The Denver Public Library shocked its patrons in 1980. Inside the envelope mailed to each patron was a note: "Our 1980 Annual Report is NOT enclosed." The letter continued to explain about what was inside, a discarded microfiche. The narrative explained the similarities between the library's year's efforts and a microfiche—both reduce costs, both do more with less, and both make better use of available space. But microfiche, as evidenced by its presence, can be discarded when it has out lived its usefulness, while the library must go on because it cannot be reproduced. An attached card allowed the recipient to obtain a copy of the actual annual report, if so desired, either on microfiche or in a regular printed format.

The Elk Grove Village library used a catchy gimmick, a modified income tax report form which ended up in a "refund" to each taxpayer of over $1,400 for his or her library tax expenditure of just over $26 (see figure 11.9).

An annual report will not be a joy forever. It may not even be a thing of beauty, but if you try to view it from your public's perspective, it may at least get a reading. The key thing is to approach it as an opportunity to communicate with your public in yet another format. A positive, upbeat, enthusiastic report can do wonders to let people know you're there.

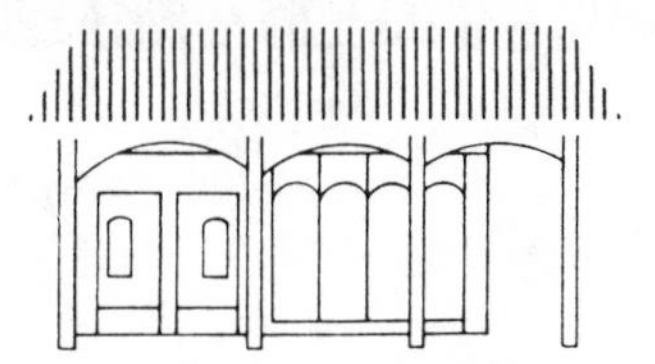

Highlights

Elk Grove Village Public Library — Winter - Spring 1981

LIBRARY SAVES COMMUNITY OVER $1 MILLION!

1040L Library Annual Report Form 1979-80

Use IRS Label. Otherwise please print or type.

Your first name and initial (if joint return also give spouse name and initial)	Last Name	Telephone Numbers
Elk Grove Village Public	Library	439-0447

Present home address (Number and street including apartment number on rural route): 101 Kennedy Blvd.

City, town or post office, State and ZIP code: Elk Grove Village, IL 60007 — Your occupation: Information, Education, Recreation

Filing Status — Check Only One Box.			
1		Academic Library	
2	X	Public Library	
3		School Library	
4		Special Library	

Hours of Service: Monday-Thursday 9-9; Friday-Saturday 9-5; Sunday (September-2nd wk. June) 1-5; Sunday (summer) Closed

Exemptions (Always check the box labeled Yourself. Check other boxes if they apply)
- 5a [X] ADMINISTRATOR — [ ] 65 or over — [ ] Blind
- b [ ] ADMINISTRATIVE ASSISTANT — [ ] 65 or over — [ ] Blind
- Enter number of boxes checked on 5a and b ► 1

c

Other dependents (1) Name	(2) Relationship	(3) Number of months lived in your home?	(4) Service	(5) Dependent's Circulation
K. Satzke, T. Paglia, K. Fleming, R. Fleming, D. Greaves, N. Klyber, M. Norwood	Board of Directors	12	Policy makers	More than 252 volunteers hrs.
5 Dept. Heads, 4 Professional Lib., 11 Tech., 11 Library Assts., 9 Lib. Clerks, 13 Pages	Staff	12	Ref. circulation, Book Proc., Information, Bldg. & Maint., Shelving	68 hrs/week

Enter number of other dependents ► 60

Add numbers entered in boxes above ► 61

(6) Total Number of Exemptions claimed.

Please Attach Copy D of Forms W-2 Here

	Line	Community Saving	Income
7. Tax income	7		$907,247.28
8. Income from fines	8		12,920.61
8a. Other income (donations, etc.)	8a		31,401.84
9. Adjusted gross income	9		951,569.93
10. Total library tax withheld per homeowner	10		26.22
11. 114,777 books were loaned during 1979-80. At an average retail price of $13.00 the community saved	11	1,492,101.00	
12. 19,869 paperbacks were loaned during 1979-80. At an average retail price of $3.00 the community saved	12	59,607.00	
13. The public borrowed 8,013 magazines. At an average price of $1.50 the community saved	13	12,019.50	
14. In 1979-80, 96,401 children's books and paperbacks were borrowed. At an average cost of $8.00 per book and $1.50 per paperback, the community saved	14	731,571.00	

15. Did the library provide other services during 1979-80? — 15
- (X) records and cassettes
- (X) programs for children and adults
- (X) 8 mm films
- (X) displays
- (X) art prints, sculpture
- (X) toys, games, puzzles

Attach Payment Here

16. How much did these services save the community? — 16: 88,674.50

17. What other services were offered to the community? — 17

Copy machine, newspapers,telephone directories, business services, college catalogs, projectors, cassette players, meeting rooms, teleray computer, pattern books.

Please Sign Here

18. What was the total community saving? (Add lines 11-17) — 18: 2,383,973.00

19. What was the cost of library services in 1979-80? — 19: 951,569.93

20. Refund (Subtract line 19 from 18) REFUND — 20: $1,432,403.07

During 1980, the undersigned library will provide more services to the community:

► Elk Grove Village Public Library

Fig. 11.9. Return on investment. Reprinted with permission of Elk Grove Village Public Library, Elk Grove Village, Illinois.

12
How to Communicate with Images
Seeing Is Believing

One thing we've learned in our years of concern about public relations is that the publicity aspect of PR has changed through time. Once the print medium, ads, brochures, flyers, reports, and newspaper articles, seemed to be sufficient to communicate the library's message to the majority of the people. But times have changed. We are living in an electronic age. People have become accustomed to obtaining information from a variety of sources which include radio, television, and computers. Our patrons are sophisticated, and while they do not necessarily expect us to use these electronic means, they are responsive when we do.

ON THE BRIGHT SIDE

An audiovisual production—a slide show, videotape, or series of transparencies—is one way to make your work, your ideas, your creation come to life before an audience. Patrons, regardless of the type of library, enjoy seeing their library on the screen, whether as part of a special program or on their television. They like seeing scenes and people they recognize; they relish anticipating who or what will appear next, and they appreciate knowing that what they see is what they get.

The Possibilities

Let us consider the possibilities of the audiovisual medium as a communication vehicle. First, it is flexible. You can reach groups of varying sizes. Equipment for individual viewers can be set up in a small space and programs played repeatedly to one or to several persons. Or, depending on the format selected, the presentation can be shown to a group in an area ranging from a small room to a large auditorium.

Second, a picture does carry considerably more weight than words, whether on an audiotape or in a brochure. Patrons find it especially helpful if they can see what you mean. Slide and video are real; they represent circumstances that actually exist; they give viewers a means for identification. Such realism is especially important if you're trying to reach an audience who are not library users. Show them what they're missing to pique their interest.

Audiovisual methods can be personal. If you're presenting the information, controlling it manually, narrating as you go, you are the pivotal factor. If you record an accompanying audio track, the narrator's voice may be familiar to the audience, providing a personal linkage. And familiar sites in the community are definitely a personalized experience which is not part of normal audiovisual viewing via the television tube. The personal touch also comes through in the way you convey your message, the humor, the compassion, the gimmick, the little bits of you injected into your program.

The audience usually appreciates your efforts. Most patrons don't expect you to create such a production, so they are delighted when you do. Nearly everyone in your audience will be an amateur (at best) in photography, so they'll recognize this is an extra task you've undertaken. And, they'll be especially pleased if they are stars in your production.

Keeping It Simple

When we make a presentation, when we incorporate a program into our services, when we want to capture people's attention, we consider what audiovisual possibilities there are. We will share our experiences with you, but be warned in advance—we are keeping things relatively simple. Entire books are devoted to how to create any one of the mediums we're going to discuss. Therefore, we will be giving only an overview which will help you understand what is involved in this type of production and what kinds of issues and steps you need to consider. You will not, at the conclusion of this chapter, be an expert at using any one of these audiovisual methods. But, you will be probably be a lot more confident about trying these techniques.

We also are not assuming you have a full-time audiovisual staff member simply for production, an audio studio, a television studio, or a complete photographic lab at your immediate disposal. If you do, great; you are probably already doing most of the things we'll mention. But this chapter is for those of you who wish to incorporate audiovisual components in an intelligent fashion in your public relations program and do not have the advantages we've cited.

The J. C. Dana award winners we previewed in part I often had effective audiovisual components. Certainly, their graphics, in both print and audiovisual formats, were creative and professional. Frequently, the library did have professional staff for audiovisual production, either as part of the library staff or hired for the specific project mentioned. But, other winners, especially schools and small to medium-sized libraries, developed their materials themselves. They discovered that audiovisual elements attract attention, communicate effectively, and impart a different image of the library from that conveyed through print only.

Use It or You'll Lose It

No audiovisual element is effective if it is poorly designed, poorly created, and poorly presented. Patrons may be delighted by our efforts to reach them in this format, but they will have the same ho-hum reaction to obviously amateur efforts as they do to home movies. This negative attitude can be avoided by adhering to some basic principles in utilization of any audiovisual format.

Examples of poor audiovisual presentations include:

- A presenter fussing and fumbling for switches on a machine he or she has never tried to use before, while the audience sits, literally, in the dark.
- Slides that are shown upside down or out of focus because they haven't been viewed beforehand.
- A visual (regardless of format) which has lettering too small for anyone to see.
- A glaring, blank screen because no one has inserted a dark slide to signal the end of the presentation, or has simply turned off the machine when the presentation is finished.
- An obscure visual, which someone has obviously selected with great care but which means nothing to the audience.
- A number of images presented in either a dizzying time sequence or a collage of multiple images, all supposedly representing relevant things which are incomprehensible.

Such errors are common and typical of those unfamiliar with or intimidated by audiovisual production and/or equipment. But, overcoming these problems is a simple process which leads us to our Must List.

Must List

You *must* learn about equipment and practice with it before using it. As we consider each of three different visual formats, we will alert you to the specific things you need to remember in working with each one.

You *must* have a reason to use audiovisual. Granted, a great deal of the time it is simply for effect. But you need to understand what the effect is you're seeking in order to find it. Audiovisual components should make your information clearer or more identifiable. They can either focus on important points or they can simply be clues that your audience can use for later recall. They may be guides or markers for various parts of your presentation or program. But they *must* have a reason for being used. What is the basic purpose? What are the major points you wish to make? Are there special features you wish to highlight? Do you have all the necessary information on hand? In some ways, you could approach this issue in much the same way you approach a speech, as outlined in chapter 10.

Whatever the visual created, whether transparency, slide, or video, it should be bold, simple, clear, easy-on-the-eyes, and part of the entire presentation. A gimmick visual used alone is seldom effective because the audience is too busy trying to figure out why it's there to appreciate the unique sense of humor that created it. Inside jokes belong inside, not in a presentation to the public. We had empathy for a presenter at a national conference who discovered halfway through her slide presentation that a staff member had jokingly inserted a slide of a Playboy playmate to break the monotony and refocus the audience's attention. The slide had the desired effect. The audience perked up, and wondered if they had seen what they had seen. But the presenter became so disoriented, she had difficulty in returning to the content, and the audience was so preoccupied they didn't really listen to her either.

One way to avoid this situation is to be sure each visual relates to the overall theme developed for the presentation. You *must* plan the total audiovisual format to fit the total purpose. No visual should be created until the entire project is planned, with a script, a storyboard, a list of pictures, or whatever it takes to know exactly where you're going to start and where you're going to finish.

More Musts

Inevitably, planning points out that you must allow time to develop effective audiovisual presentations. The first time through, you will begin to understand the advantage of allowing plenty of time. As you become more accustomed to developing audiovisual materials, your time element naturally shortens. What then develops is an attitude that you can create a quick but still effective audiovisual program, but it is always critical to allow enough time to create the best possible presentation. Once you've experienced success with audiovisual, once your patrons recognize you have the ability to do something creative and meaningful with this technique, you owe it to them to consistently give it your best efforts, partly by allowing a proper time factor.

One additional aspect of time—you *must* adhere to the schedule you've worked out for planning and producing the audiovisual components. We recommend you create a time line and stick to it. In chapter 9 we mentioned the PERT system and the backward planning sequence. These methods are equally appropriate here.

Another must is a part of every aspect of public relations—you *must* consider your target audience in creating any audiovisual presentation. Without knowing who it is you wish to appeal to, how can you know if you've reached them? Consider if your audience is staff members, other librarians, your board, a specific group of patrons, children, faculty, businessmen, senior citizens, or any other specific group.

It is also best if you limit your target audience. You may be tempted to combine several possible audiences, which can be done in moderation for groups that are somewhat compatible. However, you have to analyze your audience. You have to consider what they like and dislike, what is appropriate for their age, location, and interests. What may captivate the library nonuser could be insulting to the library professional. An emphasis on financing might really interest the administration, but totally perplex the everyday patron.

TRANSPARENCIES

Looking at specific formats will help give you the information and confidence you need to begin incorporating audiovisual materials into your PR program. The simplest format is transparencies, pieces of acetate film, usually in a size roughly 8 by 10 inches, which are projected via an overhead projector. They can be created by writing directly on them with specially designed markers, or they can be created by using an infrared copy machine designed for that purpose. (Other copy machines will also create transparencies; just check the machine's manual to find out.) Either method can be effective, but we feel the copy machine technique offers more variety and yields more pleasing results.

When making a presentation, we frequently punctuate our remarks by using transparencies. Sometimes the transparency is a cartoon which draws attention to the main point we are making. For example, if we're discussing negative behavior, we might project a cartoon of a rebellious child blowing up a stack of books in which *Gone With the Wind* is one obvious title. Or, if we're discussing statistics and facts, we might use a bar graph or other simple chart.

We have found effective graphics in the clip art books which are available. Simply cutting the art, photocopying it, and feeding it through the copy machines mentioned earlier produces a highly usable result. Adding appropriate (but limited) text can be done by hand lettering or by using other lettering techniques. For example, a large type typewriter, the "Orator" element on an IBM Selectric typewriter, a Gestefont or Kroy type lettering machine, or the Alphaline system can all produce pleasing results.

Transparency films are constantly being developed which offer unique special effects. In addition to the typical black image on clear film, there are assorted color films and reverse image films. Also available are films which offer four-color reproduction. These must be created on special copy machines developed for color reproduction.

Whatever film you decide upon, be sure you keep graphics simple and that you allow at least a 1-inch margin all the way around the edges. Center the graphic component and add text below it, or place it off center with the text to the side. Compose the intended transparency on a plain sheet of paper first, adjust it, change it, then create the final product. You will find the more often you create transparencies, the more you will experiment with placement.

If you are using only text in your transparency, keep it large and simple. A few words will convey more than crammed words. Include indenting to highlight main and subpoints.

You can add color to black and white transparencies by using markers (preferably permanent ones) or by using special adhesive films. Another effective technique is to use overlays to build on your visuals. In this process you simply create a base, or basic, transparency and add components by flipping one or more overlays on top of the base. If you wish to keep things together, attach the base to a transparency frame and then tape each additional overlay to one of the four sides. This procedure limits you to five total projections, the base and four overlays.

It is also effective to reveal your transparency a bit at a time, section by section or line by line, using a piece of paper to cover items until you're ready to show them. This requires no extra preparation and is a good way of holding the audience's attention and of pacing your presentation.

And After You Create It

Once effective transparencies are created, the next critical element is proper use of the equipment. The overhead projector should be positioned in the front of the room, preferably using a corner screen (see figure 12.1). This placement permits ease of use for you and good viewing for your audience. If you have no choice but to use a centrally placed screen (which is the typical arrangement in most rooms), be sure the screen is high enough for the audience to view easily and, more importantly, that you will not be blocking the view. To avoid blocking the image, sit next to the projector while using it, or move about frequently enough to give everyone a chance to view the screen. We find it most effective to sit next to a low table or cart. In this setup, we are out of the way, we can still project our voice so that the content is easily followed, and, if we occasionally stand to emphasize or expand a point, it carries more impact than if we've been standing all along.

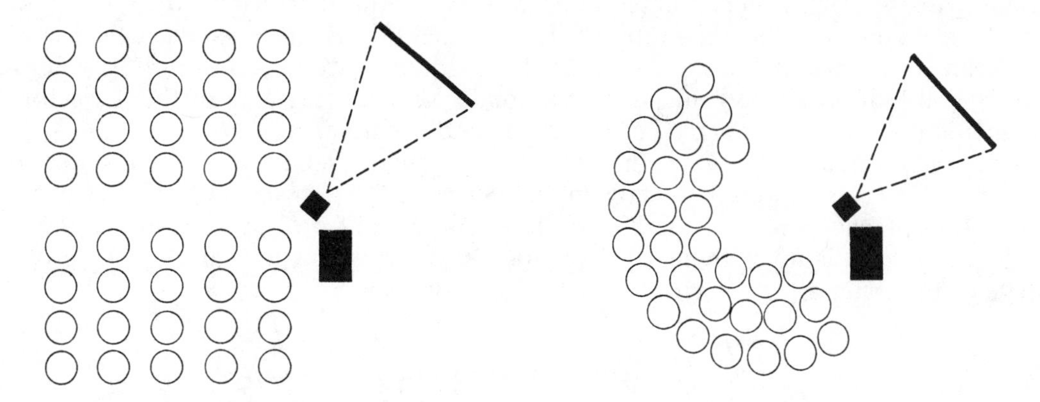

Fig. 12.1. Projector placement.

Once equipment is placed, check it out, even if you've used the projector before. Place a visual on the stage (see figure 12.2), turn the projector on and move the machine forward or backward from the screen until the projected image fills the screen. Remember, the farther away from the screen the machine is, the larger the image. If the image falls above or below the screen, tilt the head of the projector until the image is where you want it. If the image has a "keystoning" problem, where the image is wider at the top than the bottom, correct it by tilting the top of the screen forward.

Focus the projector to get a crisp, easy-to-see visual component. Remember, you face the audience, the visual faces you, and the projector projects behind you. Walk to the extreme side, front, and back perimeters of your audience's space to see how they'll be able to see. Notice where on the stage you have to place the transparency to get it to fill the screen the way you want. Once you determine that, you need not readjust each transparency.

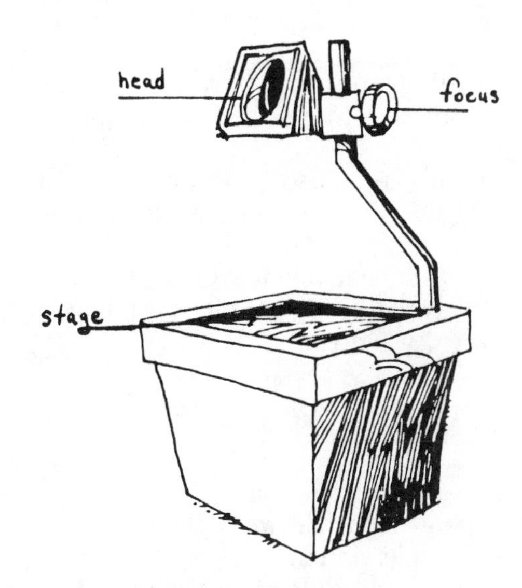

Fig. 12.2. Overhead projector.

Getting Set

If you haven't already done so, arrange all your transparencies in the order in which you'll use them with the first one on top. You might separate each with a sheet of paper, especially if you haven't used a transparency frame. The acetates tend to stick together without the frame. (See chapter 10 for some hints on using notecards with the transparencies.)

If you have an adequately sized table or cart, you can place the transparencies on one side of the projector, show them, then set them on the other side, thus maintaining both their order and a sense of flow. You can go left to right, or vice versa, whatever is comfortable for you. While this may seem like a small point, it helps make a smoother presentation and avoids awkward shuffling and searching.

You might also place a small pointer on or near the overhead projector; then, if you wish to emphasize something, you have the tool handy. A pencil or any other similar device is a good pointer. Remember, since the image is projected behind you, you need not turn to point to the image or to check on it. Using your hand or a pointer on the stage area of the projector is far more dramatic than standing in front of the screen and pointing.

If you plan to underline, circle, or write during your presentation, have a water soluble marker handy. You can then mark directly on the transparency and wipe it off later. You can also cover your transparency with a clear sheet of acetate and mark on it, protecting your original. You could also keep a damp cloth handy (like those magic wipes) so you can clear the projector's glass stage or the transparency itself.

And Another Thing

When you use the machine during a speech, turn it off between transparencies. It is more effective to have the machine project your visual at the exact moment you want it. Then turn the projector off, remove that visual, and position the next one. This action directs audience attention to the visual element when you want it and redirects attention back to you when you want it there.

You will find the overhead offers several advantages:

- It allows you to face your audience.
- It is used in a fully lighted room so you can see faces and your audience can take notes.
- It can be simply operated by anyone.
- It can be paced by you. You control the rate, the selection, the emphasis. You can linger or speed up as you see fit.
- It can be used with any size audience. Your only limitation is screen size, and you can always use a white or light colored wall.
- It is relatively inexpensive. The equipment and supplies are fairly affordable and, if not available in your library, might be borrowed from another library, a school, or a community center.

SLIDES

The next format we shall consider is that of slides, specifically slide shows. Creating a slide show is not as simple as taking a few shots, throwing the slides in a tray, and flipping the advance button. A good slide show requires the must list we mentioned earlier in this chapter.

One of the biggest errors made by would-be presentors is the classic "I have a few slides I took of ________, so I think I'll make a slide show." While there are occasions when you'll take slides before developing an idea for a slide show, you usually have the idea before the slides. If you do have some slides that may fit some presentation, you still need to approach things from the correct perspective.

On a sheet of paper identify the primary audience and any secondary one(s). Then write down your purpose. In a brief outline, write out the major points, the things you feel would be of interest or importance to your audience. Try to put these points in order with subpoints. Then indicate any visual elements you think will be needed to effectively illustrate the points.

Once you have this rough outline written down, you are ready to proceed with the hard part, the script. Script development is not an easy task, but it is easier to approach if the concept is developed first. We recommend having a nearly finished script before continuing on to the visual portion. You can be thinking about the visual as you develop the script, but concentrate on the message first. You may leave a few rough spots, a few areas you'll want to rewrite or rework, but be fairly comfortable with the content of the script before you begin to worry about taking pictures.

One good way to test your script is to read it aloud, or better yet tape it so you can hear it. It's amazing how often a script that *reads* well *sounds* poor. Time your script. If it's too long, cut it. It's highly doubtful that it will be too short, for slide shows should be 5-15 minutes in length, definitely not more than 20 minutes.

Think Visual

Once you've tested and finalized the script, develop specific ideas for the slides. You can write them into the script across from the portion you wish to illustrate. To develop the visual aspect means thinking through exactly what you want the audience to see. Sometimes you have several ideas for one part; sometimes you have none. Begin to schedule the photo sessions for those areas where you know what you want. You can always pick up the other portions later. As a guide, you should plan at least 6 to 10 slides per minute of script.

Creating the visual component for a slide show is an activity that is fun and frustrating. Stories about lens caps left on, film not catching, cameras not loaded, faulty camera batteries, and poor lighting are bound to spark fear in the beginner. Yet most problems in taking pictures can be avoided by preplanning. If you know in advance what types of pictures you'll take, you can schedule shots, obtain permission (if release forms are necessary), purchase the proper film for the available light, and, in general, prepare yourself for the task ahead.

Cameras come in a range of sizes, shapes, and prices. Instant-style cameras, which use cartridge film, have most controls preset. You simply sight and shoot. These cameras do need care when focusing because the picture you see is slightly different from the one the camera records. The slides from such cameras are square, and if they are mixed with those of the rectangle format, the results are not pleasing to the eye. So, decide on one format and stick to it.

The 35mm automatics usually have a finer lens which will require focusing but have preset exposure controls. These cameras produce rectangle slides and may or may not record exactly what you see. A "through-the-lens" metering camera allows you to see an approximate idea of the way the completed photo will turn out.

Both cameras, the Instamatics and the 35mm automatics, are excellent for beginners and/or those who don't want to get really involved with photography. The slide quality is usually good and the cameras are relatively trouble-free and simple to operate.

35mm Work

The single-lens reflex 35mm camera is the most expensive and involved camera of those which can be used for slides. However, it is the one we prefer because of its flexibility and accuracy. It also produces rectangle slides and is relatively simple to learn to use. Frequently these cameras have both preset and manual light meters, giving the photographer even greater flexibility.

It is possible that you'll need assistance in providing proper additional lighting for some slides. In this case, you may need a flash cube, flash bulbs, electronic flash, or photo flood lights. All have their advantages. Which you choose is your preference, according to your camera's features and limitations. Another device for low-light situations or shots where it is necessary to steady the camera is a tripod. Mounting the camera on this stand eliminates jiggling, especially at low shutter speeds. When the shutter will be open for a long interval and the camera might be jarred, a cable release is often used. The cable release is also necessary if you are doing copystand work, which we'll describe later.

An assortment of lens and special effects filters can be adapted to a 35mm camera. The most useful ones are the standard 50 or 55mm lens and the 135mm telephoto lens. You may wish to consider a 28mm wide angle lens for shots in close quarters in the library.

Basically you can use Kodachrome, Ektachrome, or assorted "housebrand" films. Kodachrome has good color but a lower ASA (film speed) so it's best used in daylight. Ektachrome offers slightly flatter color but has the versatility of a range of ASA, including a high one which allows you to work in some low light situations without a flash. We have found the 400 ASA film, however, is about as high as we want to go. The new 1000 ASA is often too grainy for an effective presentation.

Housebrands like those at discount stores are worth investigating. They are cheaper and the quality is not drastically reduced. However, the processing is usually by mail and takes longer than brand names at local photo stores. Sometimes, if you anticipate buying a lot of film, you can frequently get a good discount from a local photo store, especially if you indicate the purpose.

To become truly adept with photographic equipment, it is best to take a photography course, read books on the topic, or talk to a knowledgeable individual at a local camera store. Asking questions to help decide which camera and what attachments will work for you and then experimenting with that equipment is the only sure way to become comfortable with photography.

Factors in Photography

Two crucial factors in taking pictures are knowing exactly what you're trying to express, and second, scheduling shots in advance to allow plenty of time to get what you want. It's a good idea to allow time for processing after the shots are taken and to allow time for "retakes" in the event what you got isn't what you wanted. If you are uncertain about what the shot should be, you'll waste film shooting things you won't use. If you try to rush yourself and your subject, you'll end up with a picture that will have to be retaken because of a movement or other minor problems that wouldn't have occurred if you had taken time.

To take better-than-average pictures, you need to be both creative and alert. Vary your camera angles and distances. If you're shooting the card catalog, don't show the whole unit. Open a drawer, use a good close-up lens, and concentrate on a single card. Or back off and have someone use the card catalog. Don't shoot everything from 15 feet, eye level. Stand on a chair, kneel on the floor, or get very close. Don't back off so far that you lose a focal point – it's disastrous to watch a slide show in which the presentor states "If you look very closely in the lower left corner, you'll see ________." Many judges for slide presentations recommend an emphasis on close-up shots.

Be careful, however, that you don't become so enamored with being different that none of your shots fit together and viewers are taken repeatedly from the top of a building to the bottom of a pit. Be careful that you don't become trite in your picture selection or overly artistic in expressing a concept.

You can also use a different lens or add a filter. Filters offer soft focus, assorted colors, split image, or other special effects. Again, don't become so attracted to a special effects lens that you overdo it. We once viewed a slide show in which the photographer overused a fisheye lens. It was strange and difficult to watch.

Another trick is to be alert: watch what you're doing and be aware of what's happening. When you look in the viewfinder, be sure your subject is where you want it. Look at the background to avoid clutter or ridiculous situations. Make sure there's no plant "growing" out of your subject's head. Check for cracks, tears in posters, or other unsightly problems. Offices are especially prone to embarrassing background clutter. On the other hand, an office that doesn't look lived in or used is equally uninteresting.

It's also important to note any people in the background and to be aware of what they're doing. Youngsters can offer some especially interesting gestures which will spoil the photo. Be fair to your models and allow them to adjust their appearance so they're comfortable. If they blink, move, or are disarranged by a wayward breeze, retake the shot. If they appear awkward or uncomfortable, give them a chance to relax. It is a good idea to take a shot while they're posed, and then another immediately following, while they're still in position but more relaxed.

Another good idea is to try at least two or three shots for each visual you want. Professionals often shoot at a ratio of 10 takes for each shot used. Unfortunately, many of us cannot use that much film because of budget limitations. Until you become better, you'll be surprised how many "perfect" shots are somehow less than you expected when you see them developed. If all else fails and the slide has a salvageable part but is not usable in its entirety, purchase slide masks or mounts which cover the offending portion. It is possible to get masks in various shapes and figures to either mask problem slides or to create a nice effect.

The more you practice, the better you'll feel about your work and the less time you'll take. Soon you'll be an old hand, ready and willing to "have camera, will travel."

Graphically Speaking

An integral part of most slide shows is the graphics, those slides which carry out the underlying theme; provide the titles, subtitles, and credits; or illustrate the abstract ideas in the script. Usually, the graphic slides relate directly to the overall concept with which the designer of the slide show began, and they can be critical in turning what might be an average slide show into a dazzling success. Of most importance is the unifying quality which well thought-out graphics can provide. Certainly, graphics that are related directly to the theme and purpose of the presentation help to make its message remembered long after the last credit is projected.

The following examples will illuminate what we mean. One audiovisual presentation with which we were involved had as its message "The Library Is People." Throughout the program, simple one-color paperdoll cutouts were part of the main title and sectional title slides, thus reinforcing the message with visual symbols.

Abstract lines, color, and shape can also be effective. The slide show "Once Over Lightly," provided a quick overview of the components of a school media program. A student designed sectional title graphics which used parallel cut out curves of construction paper in four analagous colors. Bold, white lettering set down to follow the cut out curve line completed each graphic.

In a slide show indicating the various components of a special education program within the school district, jigsaw puzzle shapes represented each element. When the pieces were all placed together, they created the total program for the district.

Additional good sources for an effective starting point are contemporary movies and television commercials, creatively adapted to your purpose. Superman can become Media Man. Burger King's *Have It Your Way* can promote the multiplicity of services available to individual patrons. We've seen takeoffs on *Star Wars*, *Close Encounters*, *Raiders of the Lost Ark*, and *Tarzan*.

Other shows have used growing seeds which develop into blooming plants to present the history of growth of a library. We've seen a news show format used with on the street type interviews with patrons about services. And we've seen a takeoff on Inspector Clouseau as he pink-panthered his way about a library, trying to find out what made it so popular.

Sometimes you can use real objects to set up still life scenes for your graphic slides. We have used globes, straw hats, toy trucks, flags, and ship models as tangible symbols of themes studied in a special history program: diplomacy, politics, business, nativism, and mobility. The slide program was for parent orientation to promote an understanding of a new U.S. history course.

A three-ring circus approach can be carried out with old-fashioned circus posters. Appropriate lettering can be placed on acetate sheets and laid on top of posters or pictures and the slide taken without damaging the original in any way. White ceramic letters, available in photography stores, can also be placed on top of existing illustrations to create effective title slides with a three-dimensional effect. Other possibilities include record album covers of popular groups about a show for young adult services, Mother Goose illustrations for children's services, or memo forms or business cards for business services.

Whatever technique is selected, it is critical that the lettering look professional. Most of us are not capable of producing professional hand lettering, although if you have access to such individuals, use them. For most of us, transfer letters or other mechanically produced letters are strongly recommended. We are particularly fond of the Leteron machine, which is easy to use, creates good-looking results, and offers a variety of type sizes and fonts, as well as colors.

Certainly, the style of the lettering should match the mood of the slide show and the message it conveys. You don't have to be an artist to produce appropriate graphic slides, but it does help if you have an artistic eye for color, line, and balance.

The Copystand Plan

Copy work is often a good way to prepare slides for a presentation, especially the graphic type slides we've just discussed. Copies of lettering, photos, brochures, graphs, charts, and other material can be transferred to a slide through the use of copystand photography. The essential principle in copystand work is that the camera is placed on a special holder or "copystand" and is equipped with a lens or lens attachment that allows focusing for closeup work. Equipment for copystand work includes:

- Any 35mm camera with closeup rings or a closeup (macro) lens.
- A copystand from the wide variety of models available, ranging from simple to complex.
- A bracket to hold the camera in a horizontal position so that the lens faces down toward a table surface.
- An adjusting mechanism which allows the camera to be moved up and down easily.
- Lights, usually attached, to provide a source of illumination.

As previously noted, many copystands come with lights attached. Photo-floodlights on separate stands can also be employed, but require some experimentation in placement to avoid shadows or "hot spots." A built-in camera lightmeter or a separate lightmeter will be necessary to determine appropriate exposure levels. The use of a "gray card" to set exposures on very white or very dark originals is highly recommended.

Because of the flexibility in a movable copystand, it is possible to do copy work of material in a full range of sizes. The critical factor in preparing materials is to remember the standard ratio for 35mm slides, which is two to three. Materials selected for copying or graphic masters prepared locally should conform to this ratio. Good sizes to work with are 6 by 9 inches or 8 by 12 inches. Again, masks may be necessary to eliminate unwanted portions of originals.

Another warning: be careful of fingers, jewelry, camera straps, or long hair getting into the frame area while you are activating the shutter. Beautiful shots can be ruined by an unseen thumb or forefinger.

The flexibility of a 35mm camera and a movable copystand make this approach most useful over the long haul. If you already own a 35mm camera, it is logical to try it for copy work. But remember, some knowledge of photography, exposure, lighting, and camera operation is imperative in order to expect consistently successful results. Equipment costs can be fairly steep for an initial investment, particularly if a 35mm camera is not already owned, but can represent a good long-term investment.

The Next Voice You Hear

It is now time to consider creating the audio portion of a slide presentation. One option is to narrate the slide show while it is being shown, but a truly effective slide presentation is one which is prerecorded. The narration is consistent, it always says the same thing the same way. You are free to troubleshoot, the message has a more professional tone, and, if you have the proper equipment, you don't even have to be present for the show to go on.

In creating a tape, the choice of a narrator is critical. It is important that the person selected has a voice that is easy to listen to. We recommend trying voice tests on tape and listening to them before making a choice. Some of us have flat monotonous voices, while others sound like potential successors to Walter Cronkite. If you can find a professional, so much the better. We know of some libraries that have talked local radio or television personalities into narrating a slide show. It is also possible to use patrons as narrators. However, a word of caution is in order: If you decide to use children, don't overuse them. Selected segments, narrated by children, would be better than an entire program, even if the program is on children's services. "Little voices" can become wearing very quickly.

A musical background is also important. The easiest method is to start with music, fade it out as you begin the voice narration, and bring the volume back up at the end of the presentation. Naturally, the musical selections chosen must also match the mood of your slide show. There's no substitution for listening to lots of possibilities and trying them out while you narrate the script or view the slides to see if the music fits the mood. If there are natural transitions in your script, you may want to change the music also. For segments with little or no narration, music is a good filler.

Annoying pops, crackles, and snaps in a tape are often caused by improper microphone handling and use. An inexpensive microphone stand is most useful and highly recommended. In its place, you can use the place-on-the-pillow routine. Microphones are meant to pick up sound, and hard surfaces vibrate, causing unwelcome additions to your tape, so the pillow is a logical, inexpensive way out. Using a microphone stand also eliminates noise interference caused by simply holding the microphone.

To help your narrator, be sure the script pages are clearly numbered but not fastened together. Sliding the pages quietly aside avoids a rattling noise which occurs when papers are stapled together. We often read a page, then quietly push it to the side, not worrying about where it goes.

It is possible to create an acceptable audiotape, with a musical background, by using a microphone with a cassette player, picking up sounds from a phonograph or second tape recorder located in the background. We have used a speaker situated directly behind us as we speak and controlled by an extra pair of hands to fade volume up and down when necessary.

Audio Assistance

A better product can be obtained through the use of a simple mixer, into which sounds from a phonograph or cassette player, as well as microphone, can be balanced. A simple mixer usually has three input connections with three separate volume controls. Therefore, you can mix or balance sounds from three different sources and feed this balanced sound directly into any cassette tape recorder. This process eliminates trying to pick up music from a phonograph or tape player through a microphone, since connections to the mixer are made with patch cords. It also means that you control the various volumes on the mixer without jumping from volume control to volume control on various machines. A monitoring headset, connected to your master tape recorder, allows you to listen to, control, and vary the mixing sound as it is being recorded.

There's no harm in experimenting with your audio track. Fortunately, audiotapes can be erased and reused. New tapes, even good quality ones, are fairly inexpensive so trying varieties of music, different voices, and sound effects is not costly.

A final masterful step to your production is synchronizing the tape. This term, in application to audiotapes, means placing inaudible tone signals on the tape which trigger the slide projector to advance to the next slide automatically. With the tape in cassette format, the audio (voice and/or music) is first recorded in final form. Then the inaudible tone signals are recorded, basically on the other side of the tape, by using a cassette recorder that is especially equipped for such synchronization. The actual process consists of listening to the tape and pressing a sync-record button at each point where a slide change is desired.

Careful planning of where slide changes should be placed must be made in advance. Then, a couple of careful rehearsals with manual advancing of the slides is a good idea. Finally, the "sync" is completed with a well-marked script that shows the exact position of each desired signal. If mistakes are made, it is possible to remove extra pulses and add omitted ones, but it is much easier to do it right the first time.

The beauty of synchronized presentations is that they play the same way every time. Slides change exactly as the creator envisioned, and you don't even have to be in attendance when they are presented. The sync recorders are needed for playback, as well as recording. They are available through audiovisual equipment dealers and can sometimes be rented. In addition, some slide/cassette previewers have the potential for sync recording built into them.

Some Final Words

A final word about slide shows seems in order. They are more expensive to produce than the transparency presentation discussed earlier. Thus, local resources should be tapped for both talent and funding. Money should be budgeted for duplication of the product if you do not wish to loan out the original, and there's a good chance you'd get loan requests. The chances go up if it is a synchronized show.

If you do loan your program, package it carefully, include easy-to-follow directions for setting it up, or better yet, send a representative with it. Insure the program for its replacement cost if it is mailed.

Include an evaluation form or rating sheet whenever the program is used so that you have a good idea how well it is being received. Ask questions related to content, message, graphics, audio, narrator, and photography. You should also use an evaluation form for in-house showings.

When you are taking your show on the road prepare an emergency kit. Even if someone has promised to provide equipment, bring along a few often-overlooked extras. Pack an extension cord, preferably one with three outlets, and a remote cord to fit the type of projector you're using or to link the projector to the cassette sync recorder. Include a three-prong adapter, an extra projector lamp, a small flashlight, and a marked copy of the script. Then, if there's a problem with sync equipment, you can still present the show with the lights off.

Never present any slide show until you've checked out the setup of the equipment and tested it thoroughly. We like arriving early enough to prefocus our presentation, rearrange chairs if we don't like the way they're placed, and preset the volume on our tape player. We also find a good spot to sit where we can troubleshoot.

VIDEO

A final audiovisual method that carries great impact is video. As librarians we have discovered that there are only 24 hours in a day, seven days in a week, no matter how we try to stretch it. We can honestly be in only one place at one time, no matter how hard we try to clone ourselves. We have learned there is a limit to what we can do, and it's impossible to be everything to everyone. Still, a stubborn streak in us subconsciously refuses to accept all this, and we keep plugging away, trying to change the inevitable, accomplish the impossible, and spread ourselves thinner than the laws of physics will allow.

With this in mind, we stumbled upon one way to actually do what everyone said couldn't be done: we found a technique that allows us to repeat ourselves, to be in several spots simultaneously, and to give the exact message the same way every single time. We uncovered the magic, the mystery, and, occasionally, the misery, of videotaping.

We realize that for some, video presents some serious problems:

- What if I have no equipment?
- If I can obtain equipment, then what will I do with it?
- If I have someone who'll handle the operating end, how do I approach the creative part?
- How do I know my patrons will react well to this idea?

Obviously, we can't solve all these problems but we can get you off to a good start. First of all, as with all projects, you need to identify what you want to do and who you want to reach. Is this viewing strictly in-house? Is it for staff or patrons? Will you cablecast it? If so, who's your primary target? Remember, the beauty of cablecasting is narrowcasting—beaming a specific message to a specific group—the opposite of broadcasting, which is for the masses. Are you trying to motivate, to inform, or to entertain? Or all three at once? Do you have one main theme, with perhaps a couple of related themes of lesser importance? Once you know what you want to do and who you want to reach, you can start to struggle with the specifics. Since most of us become anxious about the equipment, let's deal with that first. In addition, working with the equipment and finding out it's not so threatening is sometimes a great impetus to get on with the project.

If you're interested in cablecasting, you've pretty much defined your equipment as ¾-inch U-matic video cassette. There are some franchise areas which deal with ½-inch VHS or Beta, but ¾ inch has become the industry standard. This format gives excellent quality, has color, can be duplicated as is or duplicated "down" to ½ inch without losing quality.

If you're thinking of something in-house, you have more options – ½-inch VHS or Beta or ¾-inch U-matic, or even the new ¼-inch and 8mm formats. It all depends on the equipment you own or have access to. Most libraries own VHS or Beta if they own video equipment as do most consumers (possible sources to borrow equipment for the production). Therefore, we'll concentrate on in-house ½-inch production. Since most libraries with their own units generally have VHS, we'll use that term in the remaining of our discussion, but the same principles apply to Beta and in many cases, to most other formats as well.

Video Basics

Many libraries own recorders to playback prerecorded tapes. Some own a compatible video camera. If you have the recorder but not the camera, find out what it would cost to add the camera. Or, find out if a patron, local school, area library, fire department, police department, or other group has a camera which is compatible. If you're not sure what is needed, ask a dealer for the video recorder.

If you do own the camera, practice with it, or identify someone who'll do your camera work and have them practice with it. Learn how to move the camera smoothly on pans (side to side sweeps, not swoops), zooms (tight in, wide out), and tilts (up and down). Most moves should be slow and graceful, not quick and wild. There may be occasions when you utilize quick moves for effect but normally steady is the right technique.

If you don't have a tripod for the camera, get one. Buy it, borrow it, but use it. While many of the VHS oriented cameras are light enough to hold on your shoulder, they get heavy quick. The new all-in-one recorder/camera units sometimes are lighter, but they too can begin to feel heavy when you work with them for a while. And the camera will recognize your fatigue before you do. There'll be slight wobbles in the picture noticeable in the video playback which will signal you were tired. Take no chances. Use a tripod.

It's also best if your camera has a remote control. That way neither you nor an assistant has to keep running to punch the VCR on and off when you shoot. The all-in-one units have this feature since the VCR is part of the total unit, but these units also sometimes use smaller than usual cassettes. The format of the tape is ½ inch but the size of the tape is different, sometimes limiting the amount of time on the tape.

Many of today's cameras have all kinds of special effects – built-in character generators for superimposing titles over video, fade controls, automatic white balance, automatic iris, etc. Each of these has a distinctive advantage, but check out how the effect works and what it looks like before you plan to use it. We personally like automatic white balance and iris settings since they eliminate two major problems areas, color control and light/dark settings.

Check Things Out

Let's stop and take stock. You'll need a camera compatible with your VCR, a VCR, a tripod, a video cable from camera to VCR, and a microphone with any necessary cables. Most cameras designed for VHS units have built-in mikes, which solve your audio problem. Many are also equipped to handle remote mikes and some of them will accept lavalier mikes which can be clipped on the actors with the cords hidden. However, if you use more than one mike, you'll also need a mixer box like the one used for slide shows mentioned earlier. You'll also need extension cords so you have some freedom from walls. And don't forget the videotapes.

There are many VCRs which are battery operated, highly portable types you can take in the field. They are wonderful units to work with, lighter and far less cumbersome than the bigger models. But, their batteries have a limited life. Some batteries will operate the unit for only 20 minutes until they're dead. Such a brief span may be extremely difficult for your project. You'll either need to find a unit which has stronger, longer batteries, resign yourself to carrying lots of batteries around, plan your shooting in locations which have power, carry long extension cords, or use a combination of all these possibilities. Our solution depends entirely on what we're trying to do. If we want an outside shot, we go for either longer lasting or more batteries, or we carry 200 feet of electric cords. In truth, we haven't found a spot we want to shoot that we can't get power to in that distance.

Suppose you know what you need, but you don't have any or all of the equipment. If you're missing the camera, try borrowing or inquire about renting one, probably from the company who sold you your VCR. They may even cooperate by providing an operator or making a special deal in the hopes you'll buy the camera or in exchange for a credit in your production.

Go for It

We suggest buying the equipment. Organize a special fund raiser if you've no funds in the regular budget. Sometimes specific items get a good response from the public, especially with a catchy slogan: "Improve the library's outlook; help us buy a video camera" or "The better to see you with—help us buy a video camera." You'll find a way if you want to and think about it hard enough. Also, there's the option of cooperative buying with another group.

Once you've got the equipment issue determined and you know the limitations for your project, you must begin to work out exactly what you plan to do. You've probably given this some thought and bounced your idea off a few other heads to get some initial reactions and better direction.

One of the best ways to develop the content of the production is to organize a brainstorming session. We believe involving others is one of the most productive ways to obtain valuable ideas. Involve those individuals who'll present as many perspectives as possible for your project—staff, patrons, friends, etc. A common mistake is to use only staff to develop a program that's intended for the general public. Why not ask someone from the general public?

Invite your selected people to a meeting. Be certain each one knows why he or she is being included in this initial meeting. Many people are willing to give ideas if they know no additional time commitment is expected from them. Who knows? They might get excited enough to volunteer to help out.

Prepare an environment that is casual, relaxed, and conducive to voicing ideas. Choose a time that will let everyone be as fresh as possible. The last thing at the end of a workday, right before dinner, is *not* the best time. A lunch break, a coffee break in the morning, or, perhaps a "start your day with an idea" meeting are all possibilities. But, if the end of the day is the only time, make the best of it. Make it a break; have fresh fruit on hand, it's refreshing and special. Encourage everyone to stretch or walk first to "get out the workday kinks." It sounds crazy, but that's the tone of the meeting you want to set to get those creative juices surging.

Begin the meeting by being sure everyone knows everyone. You decide if it's best to let them introduce themselves or if you want to do it yourself. Then tell those gathered what you hope to accomplish. Fantasize a bit, express your ideal image of the final product and what you want it to accomplish. When you've visualized the ultimate, then analyze exactly who is to be the primary target for this video endeavor.

If you're like most beginners, you'll want it to be all things to all people. You'll want to hit as many groups as possible to get the most out of your money. Such a production would be like a February bulletin board with Cupid shooting arrows at Washington and Lincoln who were ignoring their wives to read books, the real "love" of their lives. Such shotgun targeting is not as effective as it is limiting.

Discuss all possible viewers. Urge the group to reach a consensus on a primary audience. You can have a couple of secondary audiences, but your production will be better if you gear it toward one group and organize your planning primarily in terms of that group.

The Message Is the Medium?

Once you've identified the target audience, which will be determined partially by considering your means of distribution (in-house or cablecast), you're ready to deal with the message. Keep the audience in mind during this next session by writing who they are on a blackboard, overhead, a large sheet of paper, anything you can keep visually before you and your brainstormers.

You now remind your group what the ultimate goal is: we want more usage of our business collection, we want to increase the usage of the reference collection, or we hope to bring in more volunteers. Focus on what you want viewers to know or to feel at the end of the viewing. Using that as a springboard, ask for suggestions on what to include to accomplish your purpose.

Listen to every idea, encourage interaction, take notes. Let one person expand another's idea. Use a blackboard or tape large sheets to the wall so everyone can see what ideas are being generated. If the group won't mind, audiotape the session for later review so no ideas get lost.

Encourage all participants to identify anything they feel is relevant to the purpose. Pull ideas out of them. Don't let anyone you felt was valuable enough to include sit there without giving you something. Listen for patterns, common ideas, repetitions. Tune in to those who are especially vocal about a certain point or area. If you have people who are representative of your target group, be closely attentive to their suggestions.

When you honestly feel the group has given you all the ideas about what to say in the program that they can, change the topic. Ask them to identify a gimmick, a technique that sells them on a product or service. Ask them to think of something catchy they've seen on television or in a magazine or newspaper that got their attention. Jot down these ideas to help you consider an approach for the program.

During this entire session your role is basically to be a catalyst/listener/recorder. Avoid evaluating or you'll turn off your idea source. The total time spent on the meeting depends on how much time you and the group have. When you sense it is time to end the meeting, do so by thanking everyone for their input and assuring them that you will continue to communicate with anyone interested. Put the ball in their court, find out who's likely to keep on going and who just wanted to give some input and get out. This is also a good way to begin to identify future workers.

Then give yourself at least one full day of time to mull over the ideas. Let the ideas rest in the back of your brain. But don't give yourself more than two days or the freshness of the meeting will fade.

After your day off pull out your notes, your tape, whatever you have from the meeting and review everything. Try to find some uninterrupted time so you can give it full creative attention. You decide when and where, but make this time enough of a priority so it is as uninterrupted as possible.

Look everything over carefully and begin to pull things together according to the major areas that seem to merge and relate. Is anything missing? Add it in. What's superfluous? Take it out. Does any area need clarification? Call someone from the group and doublecheck what they heard. Does any logical order seem evident? If so, begin to develop it. If not, charge on anyway.

You will automatically know that certain things follow or precede other things. Number them that way and develop an outline of all those informational items you want to include within the content of your presentation.

Decision Time

Now you can make your first big decision. As you look over the outline, note the items to be included and contemplate possible order. How will you proceed with writing the script? You *can* do the whole thing yourself; you *can* delegate it to someone else and let them bring it back to you; or you *can* deal out portions to others and incorporate these pieces when they are returned. The right approach is the one with which *you* are comfortable.

We've used all three approaches. Each one has been right in a particular situation. We have written the entire script. If you've never tried that before, begin as if you are writing an essay about your program's topic. Pretend it's for publication in a magazine your target audience might read (not a professional journal). However, if that is hard for you because they read *Time* and you can't write like *Time*, then write as if it's for your library newsletter.

After rereading and editing your "article," give it to someone from your target group to read. They can quickly point out confusing terminology, information they already know that's needlessly repeated, or things that are too sketchy and in need of further explanation.

If you take option two and delegate the script to someone else, you have three possibilities: a volunteer, a paid consultant, or a staff member who may have no choice. We have often been hired to perform this service for a client. We ask to be provided with information which includes:

- the target audience
- the ultimate purpose of the program
- an outline of the content
- detailed information about the content (from brochures, manuals, guides, whatever the library may have)

Armed with this information, a script writer can get a better feel for what is desired. Upon completion of the script draft, meet in person or over the phone and work through changes together.

A volunteer or a staff member doing the script should have this same information and follow this same procedure. However, since this person is not receiving compensation for the endeavor, a great deal more persuasion may be in order to get the product you want. Paramount to the decision about who will write it in this case is an understanding of who has interest in the project and who has a talent for writing.

Divide and Conquer

The third possibility, dividing the script into segments, yields interesting results, actually great ones if handled right. For example, if you are featuring different services or departments, you might ask those who head these departments to write that portion of the script, even if they weren't involved in the brainstorming. If you're in a small library where you are in charge of nearly everything, why not delegate sections to patrons who particularly know or like or use that area of service? You then coordinate all the information when they return it, developing the theme you've chosen, fitting the material in, and giving it an overall flow and tone.

We have frequently run into this third way of script development in libraries with few funds for audiovisual production, or no staff for such activity. One tape we worked on not only used staff members to write the sections but also used them as on-camera talent to introduce the area and narrate the section about it. By using this technique of divided authorship, you have the job of developing the introduction, the conclusion, and the transitional pieces of the script. You also have the awkward problem of dealing with a staff member who may be a poor writer. To avoid a confrontation, let everyone know up front that you are the editor and will have final say in the script's wording.

Once you have a rough script together, it is a good idea, if possible, to reconvene part of the brainstorm group. This second gathering should be small. Hand out copies of the script in advance, let everyone read it and ask their opinions about it. Specify you aren't interested in little details, like typos, but in content, flow, intent, tone. Listen, take notes, but don't let them believe the whole group is now going to rewrite the final product. They are a sounding board only.

Breathe Life

Once you've received their input, reviewed their suggestions, and revised the script, it's time to breathe life into it. Video is a medium that is quite real, it is audio and visual. Just as you would with a slide/tape script, record this script and listen to it. Concentrate not on your voice but on what the script is saying. Close your eyes, visualize what could be happening on screen while the narrator or characters talk. Imagine those scenes that could happen with no one talking, with musical interludes and appropriate shots. In short, dream a little and begin to see your production. How does your script sound? If you're like most beginners, it will sound stilted, like it was written to be read not heard. Revise it. Simplify your words. Determine if parts could be handed over to "actors" to ad-lib.

Once you've listened to your script and revised it (again), it's time to see it. To help you organize things appropriately, divide your script into two headings with roughly one-third for video and two-thirds for audio. Under the audio part, type out your script, doublespaced. Leave an extra line between each scene change. (A scene change means each time you change what would be on the screen during the audio.) If you have portions where there'll be things happening in the video while the audio remains the same (like a musical interlude) just write down the audio once – MUSIC – and write out all the visual changes. (See figure 12.3.) Video scripts can also be divided into three sections: video, camera, and audio. Since we are looking at simple, one-camera production work, we keep it simple, adding camera directions to the video portion once we know what we want.

This script will look strange to you if you've never done one before. Separating the audio and video is, at first, difficult, but it helps you understand not only how your script sounds, but how it will look. This script version, when finished, should also be shared with someone for input. If you have an audiovisual "expert" available, use them. You can talk to a local school audiovisual person, a local cable television staff member, a patron who plays around with video, or the local photographer, anyone who thinks visually.

We've found this is a critical time to involve a consultant, either a professional audiovisual person or a good professional friend. It's the opportune moment to talk about the treatment, to consider the way the entire piece will look, to evaluate the length of the finished piece, and to begin planning how to proceed from here.

It may seem that the script planning and writing takes a long time. But this is a point where time is well spent, where haste can waste the results of the final product. This is where you deal with what you want to convey. This is the skeleton, the frame that supports everything else. If it's poorly done, nothing will hold together effectively in the final version. Therefore, take time to define your message, to be sure your purpose is clear, and to assure that you are reaching your intended audience in a manner they will both understand and pay attention to.

VIDEO	AUDIO
Logo (close)	Up music: traveling harmonica (10 sec.)
	Narrator: On Track with Service is a series of four programs to acquaint you with different types of libraries in our community.
Elementary school (medium shot)	Today's program features the services of an elementary school Library Media Center, or LMC. Down music: fade
Close-ups of kids working in LMC (at least 5)	Voice Over: I think I can. I think I can. I think I can. I think I can; I think I can; I think I can; I think I can........
Close up of book Little Engine	Narrator: Most of us remember the little engine that could, a tiny locomotive that could accomplish the nearly impossible because it thought it could.
Kids working in classroom (wide shot)	Our schools foster the same belief about our youngsters. Children today can do nearly ANYTHING if they think they can.
Kids working in LMC (wide out; slow zoom in)	And one area in our schools where children are encouraged to reach beyond themselves...to tackle the impossible...is in our Library Media Centers.
Media specialist with a group of kids (medium)	Voice over: I chose the library media field because I believe it is one area where students can really be all that they can be. I encourage young people to pursue individual interests as far as they can go.
MS (close) talking to camera	Today's students aren't satisfied with answers from the teachers as easily as they were when I was in school. They are really eager to find information on their own, and I'm eager to help them.
MS and student (medium shot)	MS: Hi Bob. What are you looking for today? Bob: I saw a neat thing on tv last night, Mrs. Smith. There were these big ants that ate up everything. And these guys kept trying to stop em, burning em and stuff. They had to drown em! Are there REALLY ants like that? MS: There may not be ants quite that super, Bob, but I know that there are some very strange species. Want to

Fig. 12.3. Video script.

What's the Gimmick?

It is also time to review the second part of the initial brainstorm session: the part where you asked people to identify the gimmicks and techniques that caught their eye. Are any of them appropriate and adaptable to your video production? Do you want outer space visitors, talking books, bizarre characters, balloons, or anything else you haven't thought about until now? Do you have a specific theme, a title, a mood, a piece of music, something you want to use at the beginning, the end, or between parts of the piece?

Concentrate on this area. It is possible there's a totally adaptable idea just waiting from a movie, television show, current event, commercial, or other source. Your purpose is an overriding factor. If you're planning a serious documentary, drop the gimmicks.

But let's say you do want a light touch. What could you do? For example, several years ago we saw an excellent introduction to the Learning Resource Center (LRC) produced by the William Rainey Harper Community College Audiovisual Department in Palatine, Illinois. The tape was a takeoff on the movie *Saturday Night Fever*. The hero went out, dressed in his best, to the LRC. He was "king" because he knew everything about using the resources in the facility. Aspirants to his title and clingers-on wanting his attention listened to what he had to say and watched what he had to show them. The piece ended with dancing in the stacks and disco music. It is one of the best targeted pieces we've ever seen. We cannot imagine a single community college student (the intended audience) who wouldn't watch it and learn about the LRC in the process.

Another tape, which served as a public service announcement (PSA) on local television, was a takeoff on those television hard-sell ads for audiotapes and cassettes seen on late night television. With music droning in the background, the narrator spieled off the names of title after title, breathlessly giving a short blurb such as "read the amorous interaction of the lovely Scarlet and the dashing Rhett." The titles of book after book rolled by while the camera simply scanned the shelves. "Act soon," urged the off-camera voice. "These books are available for an unlimited time only at absolutely no cost at your public library." Clark County Library in Las Vegas, Nevada, which developed this clever spot, has frequently let their imaginations roam to sell their library services.

It is *essential* to think about theme, tone, mood, treatment, and gimmick at this point, if you haven't already done so, because it controls how you put your tape together. If you start taping and then consider techniques or theme, you will find yourself reshooting pieces and using up extra time.

Setting the Scenes

Now, it's time to consider production. First of all, analyze your script to determine exactly what's needed. We've found dividing the script into scenes is helpful since it lets us deal with smaller segments, which helps us pay attention to more of those nitty-gritty details (see figure 12.4). (We define a scene as a consistent setting, staging, on camera. Change of place equals change of scene.)

Marking for scenes is simple. Just mark scene 1 or scene 2 and draw a line across the end of that portion. We usually use a colored pen so we can quickly find scene changes.

We also make a chart to guide us. Our chart keeps track of what's involved in all different areas. It allows us to see what's needed, where we can get it, when we need it, and if we took care of arranging for it. It also allows us to identify the audio or video portion, and when and where the scene will be shot. (See figure 12.5.)

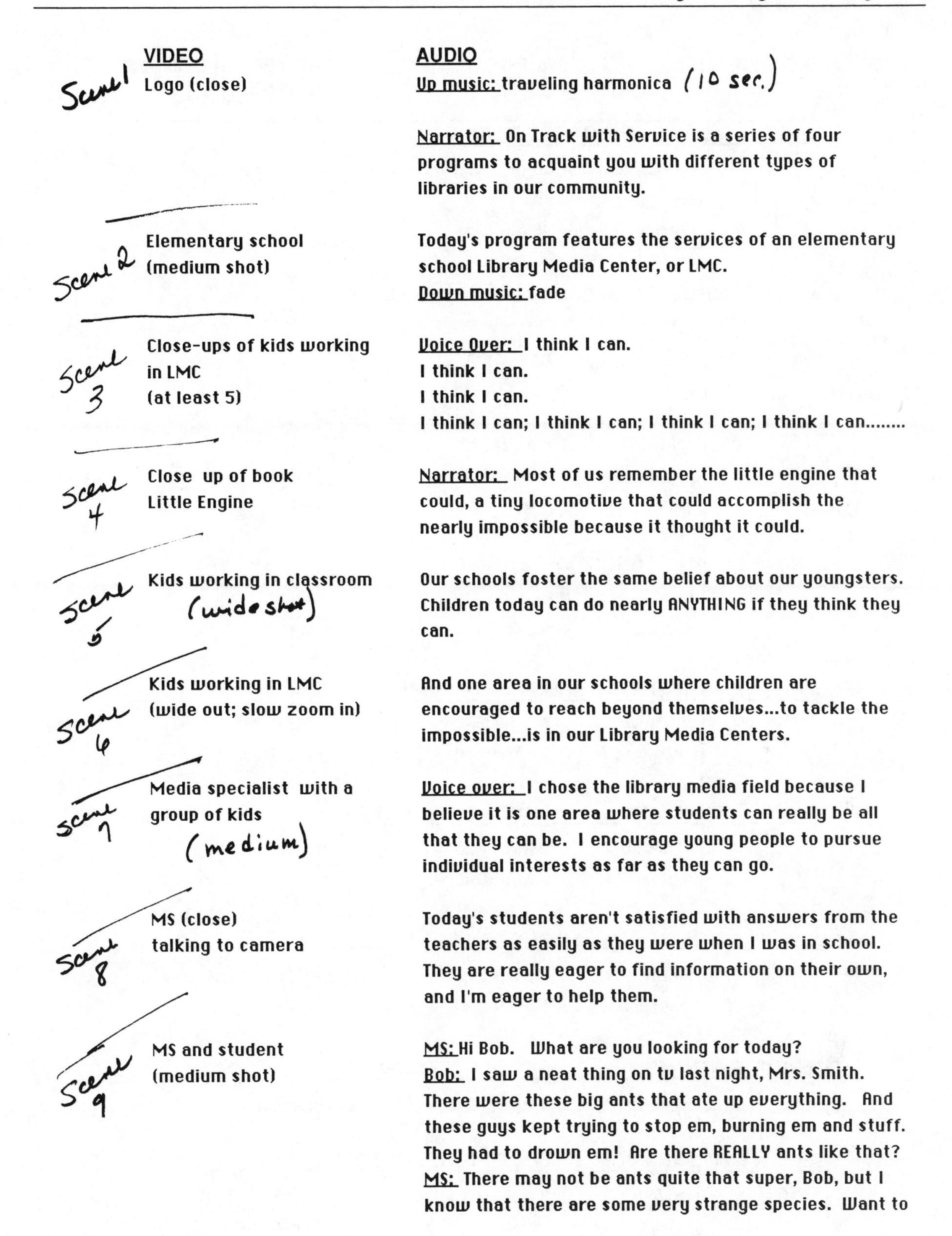

	VIDEO	AUDIO
Scene 1	Logo (close)	Up music: traveling harmonica (10 sec.) Narrator: On Track with Service is a series of four programs to acquaint you with different types of libraries in our community.
Scene 2	Elementary school (medium shot)	Today's program features the services of an elementary school Library Media Center, or LMC. Down music: fade
Scene 3	Close-ups of kids working in LMC (at least 5)	Voice Over: I think I can. I think I can. I think I can. I think I can; I think I can; I think I can; I think I can........
Scene 4	Close up of book Little Engine	Narrator: Most of us remember the little engine that could, a tiny locomotive that could accomplish the nearly impossible because it thought it could.
Scene 5	Kids working in classroom (wide shot)	Our schools foster the same belief about our youngsters. Children today can do nearly ANYTHING if they think they can.
Scene 6	Kids working in LMC (wide out; slow zoom in)	And one area in our schools where children are encouraged to reach beyond themselves...to tackle the impossible...is in our Library Media Centers.
Scene 7	Media specialist with a group of kids (medium)	Voice over: I chose the library media field because I believe it is one area where students can really be all that they can be. I encourage young people to pursue individual interests as far as they can go.
Scene 8	MS (close) talking to camera	Today's students aren't satisfied with answers from the teachers as easily as they were when I was in school. They are really eager to find information on their own, and I'm eager to help them.
Scene 9	MS and student (medium shot)	MS: Hi Bob. What are you looking for today? Bob: I saw a neat thing on tv last night, Mrs. Smith. There were these big ants that ate up everything. And these guys kept trying to stop em, burning em and stuff. They had to drown em! Are there REALLY ants like that? MS: There may not be ants quite that super, Bob, but I know that there are some very strange species. Want to

Fig. 12.4. Script by scenes.

AUDIO	VIDEO	ITEM	SOURCE	DATE NEEDED	PROGRESS
SCENE 1: Logo			**SHOOT DATE: JUNE 2**		
X		cassette tape	library collection	6/1	✓
	X	logo	artist	6/1	✓
X		narrator	Joe Simpson	6/1	✓
SCENE 2: Elementary School			**SHOOT DATE: JUNE 3**		
	X	school	Burckle elementary	6/3	
X		narrator	Joe Simpson	6/1	
SCENE 3: LMC			**SHOOT DATE: MAY 25**		
	X	students(5)	Burckle LMC	5/25	✓ X
	X	media spec.	Burckle LMC	5/25	✓ X
X		voice	Bob Kruzich	6/1	✓ X
SCENE 4: BOOK			**SHOOT DATE: JUNE 1**		
	X	book	library collection	5/30	
X		narrator	Joe Simpson	6/1	
SCENE 5: KIDS IN CLASS			**SHOOT DATE: MAY 25**		
	X	classroom	Burckle Elem--Dunn	5/25	✓ X
X		narrator	Joe Simpson	6/1	✓ X
SCENE 6: KIDS IN LMC			**SHOOT DATE: MAY 25**		
	X	kids in lmc	Burckle lmc	5/25	✓ X
X		Smith(ms)	Burckle lmc	5/25	✓ X
SCENE 7: SMITH, MS			**SHOOT DATE: MAY 25**		
X	X	Smith(ms)	Burckle lmc	5/25	✓ X
	X	students	Burckle lmc	5/25	✓ X
SCENE 8: SMITH, MS			**SHOOT DATE: MAY 25**		
X	X	Smith(ms)	Burckle lmc	5/25	✓ X
SCENE 9: SMITH AND BOB			**SHOOT DATE: MAY 25**		
X	X	student	Bob Ritter(with book)	5/25	✓ X

Fig. 12.5. Production chart.

The audio and video parts refer to whether the needed item, which includes talent, is going to be on the audio or video track, or both. The item is everything we need for the scene. The source is where we will find that item or, in the case of talent, who the talent is. The date needed is the time we want to have that item in hand or, in the case of talent, the day we want them available. The progress is how we keep track of finding, contacting, and returning items. We sometimes mark a check (√) when we have located the item and an X when we have finished with it.

It's possible to add columns or to divide columns. For example, if the talent needs costuming and a script in advance, we could create subheads under source for script and costume. Or, we could make a new column—talent—and deal with those elements there. How the chart is constructed is up to each of us and may vary from production to production. It's merely a way to organize all the bits that need to come together.

Once we list everything and once we've checked on everything needed, then we set a target shooting date which we write in on the chart. If a rehearsal is needed, we indicate that date. We frequently batch scenes for final shootings, doing all exteriors, for example, on the same day, and all of one department, floor, or wing on another day. We try not to shoot everything in one day. By taking our time we do a better job. By not pushing, we avoid fatigue. By batching we can review our work and discover errors to avoid in the next batch.

We've also discovered that, no matter how hard we try, we get off schedule. It's terrible to have "talent" who volunteered (or were paid) for a particular scene standing around waiting because we're running late. If our time schedule gets really skewed, they may have to leave and we may have to reschedule the entire scene. Far better to deal with batches than to try to do too much.

But, let's get back to the chart. If people are involved in audio and video (talking on camera) or just audio (talking off camera), it is necessary for them to have a script well in advance. We've also found it helpful to highlight their part so they see sequence and cues. Even people involved only in the video part, doing something but not talking, need to have a script to see how they fit. It is possible to provide only the part of the script with their scene, but they still need to know, in advance, what we're expecting and how they fit in.

Practice Makes Perfect

We've also discovered that a conversation, even a brief one, is necessary with each person before any rehearsal and definitely before a final shoot. We talk about what to do, what to wear, how to talk, hand gestures, and what we are trying to communicate in their scene. It shows what we want, it makes people feel involved, it speeds up shooting at the final run-through, and, since we're acting as director, it's our job.

Rehearsals are a good idea, especially if they can be done in advance. Sometimes advance work is not possible and a rehearsal will have to be right before the shoot. Walk through it, then do it. Shooting without practice creates problems, so it is a good idea to videotape the rehearsal. The videotape doesn't have to be perfect since it is just for reference. It helps to identify problems: too-long pauses, an awkward angle for someone to perform a task the audience can see, a plant that's in the way, a light that glares, a window that reflects.

Another organizational aspect is to scout every scene. Analyze the lighting with the camera so you can gage its reaction. Another advantage of many VHS-produced programs is that they have low light capabilities. The scouting also gives us time to look for busy, distracting backgrounds, to decide where we'll place the talent, the camera, and the microphones.

These preparations often take time. Taking up people's volunteer time to check out camera angles and lighting is a disregard of the individual's importance. They'll be far more willing to help again if you seem professional and organized. The scouting lets you avoid arriving for a shoot at night without compensating for the light that was there in the daytime when you first considered the site. Always scout at the same time of day you anticipate shooting.

More Charting the Course

Once we've checked out everyone and everything and every setting involved, we develop a shooting schedule (see figure 12.6).

The day before the shoot, we recheck the charts to be sure all is ready. The day of the shoot, we check off each segment as we complete it. We schedule our "audio only" segments for voice over the same way because we shoot them on videotape. We can then edit a videotape rather than audiotape.

This constant checking and listing makes everyone involved aware of the effort. It helps things to go smoothly the day of the shoot and avoids unnecessary delays because someone forgot a prop. We also schedule a make-up shoot day, a reserve day in the event something doesn't come out. Everything and everyone is on hold because they knew in advance this would be make-up time, if needed. However, reshoots are tricky. We have to be certain the scenes match. If a main character is in every scene and we need to reshoot one, we must be sure clothing, jewelry, hairstyles, and background all match. Therefore, it is a good idea to schedule all scenes involving the same character on the same day, if at all possible. Then that unexpected haircut doesn't create havoc.

SHOOT DATE: May 25

Scene #	Location	Time	Progress/Notes
3	Burckle lmc	10 a.m.	✓ – 3 boys, 2 girls
5	Dunn's classroom	8:15 a.m.	✓
6	Burckle lmc	10:15 a.m.	✓ - mix ages
7	Burckle lmc	10:30 a.m.	✓
8	Burckle lmc	10:45 a.m.	✓- check her office for mess
9	Burckle lmc	11:00 a.m.	✓- note what they're wearing

SHOOT DATE: June 1

Scene #	Location	Time	Progress/Notes
4	studio	9 a.m.	✓

SHOOT DATE: June 2

Scene #	Location	Time	Progress/Notes
1	studio	1 p.m.	

SHOOT DATE: June 3

Scene #	Location	Time	Progress/Notes
2	Burckle Elem.	8:45 a.m.	

Fig. 12.6. Shooting schedule.

Once the entire shoot is complete, it is time to edit. Editing is as simple or as complex as your equipment allows. If your equipment is elementary, you'll just basically cut and paste electronically, feeding the original scenes from one recorder to a master tape on a second machine and pausing the master unit whenever you wish to cut out something. With this system, you cannot fade or create special effects, nor can you easily insert audio and video elements (unless your machine has these latter two features).

If your equipment is more sophisticated or is an editing system, you can do all kinds of character-generated titles, credits, music, wipes, fades, and special effects. Sometimes there are places, perhaps even the local cable station, which will rent editing equipment or arrange for community groups, like you, to learn to use the equipment which is then available for your use at no cost at a mutually convenient time.

If you have never edited before, remember *editing properly is time consuming*. It takes *time* to learn to use the equipment, and it takes *time* to practice to hit the edit right on the mark. If you separate audio and video tracks, it takes extra time to practice to get it right.

Editing a video production, like editing a book, makes or breaks the final product. It adds sequence and sense; it polishes off the rough edges. We have spent over four hours editing a 29-second introduction, but the result was fantastic.

Before doing editing, however, you must view all tapes and all takes. Using the original script as a guide, try to juggle tapes so you view things in order. Viewing as you complete shooting is essential to see if you got what you wanted, but you also need to review again at a later time for final edit.

In Sequence, Please

If you view in the proper order, you're more alert to transitions from scene to scene. Be critical, but unless every scene is an absolute mess, work with what you have. Reshooting is in order only when video or audio is of such poor quality that you cannot salvage it.

Look at every scene. Take detailed notes. We usually write down the last action or the last few words before a cut—followed by a slash mark. Then we write a cue to note where to pick up the scene and splice it in. We are especially sensitive to "jump cuts." A jump cut occurs when you edit out errors but the camera angle doesn't change. For example, the person is standing next to a desk on a medium shot. In the next edited scene the camera is at the same angle, the same focal distance but the person is turned, seated or his head has jumped from looking straight at you to being at an angle. For some "magical" effects, that's good, but jumps from one position to another, especially if they're close together, can look sloppy and be distracting to a viewer.

Jump cuts can be eliminated if you remember to change camera angles after mistakes. Say we're taping that medium shot we mentioned, and the talent fluffs his final line. We stop, focus in tight, and have him repeat the faulty line. Then our edit looks like a second camera took a different view, and we don't have to reshoot the entire scene. Actually, it's nice to stop action and change angles on a one-camera shoot just to add variety.

It is also important to pay attention to your audio track. Your jump here can be a sentence with parts left out. Or you can get an "echo" effect if you overlap your audio track when editing.

Once you've been through every scene and taken detailed notes on where to cut, it's time to do it. If you are not editing yourself, be sure you view with the person who will edit. Discuss scenes and create notes together so you both know the desired results. Here again, you could hire a professional, a patron familiar with video, or someone from another library who has this expertise. If you're the editor, choose a time when you won't be interrupted. Editing takes concentration. You cannot be accessible to staff and still edit well.

Once you have your full edit done, complete the opening title sequence, and be sure to add credits. People like recognition for their efforts. Credits are especially nice with background music and maybe interesting video footage under them. Practice first with different colors for the lettering so the credits will show up on the background footage. If you're just shooting letters on colored background, again shoot the different color combinations first to see what works best.

Credits should be given to everyone who helped: to talent, to scriptwriters, to prop-finders, to scene-creators, to those who donated anything. These visible thank-yous are a good PR gimmick. Be sure to include a credit and copyright for your library. Should you wish to formally pursue copyright, do so. But, remember, if you have used popular music without permission or shot copyrighted art work, you cannot consider copyright. One way to avoid this difficulty is to purchase copyright free music from companies which specialize in its production.

When your final tape is done, plan an occasion to preview it. Then make a copy to use for showing, saving the original as a backup. Organize a gala premier for all those involved, if for no one else. Or make it a crowning moment for a special program, perhaps after those involved have had a private showing. Make your first public showing a significant event, enjoy it, reap the glory and rewards, and then start planning the next one.

Last Things Last
Conclusion

By now our philosophy is quite obvious to our readers: we believe in effective public relations. We are convinced that the interaction between us and our publics—whether it is the general community, students, parents, faculty, or employees of a major company, is vital to our continued existence and well-being.

We believe this concept so thoroughly that we identified nine general characteristics of effective library public relations projects, as evidenced in John Cotton Dana award winners. To remind us all, these winners:

- develop a wide variety of approaches
- form partnerships with other groups
- offer strong programs featuring services and resources
- capture attention with imaginative, creative ideas
- spotlight special events
- use eye-catching graphics
- demonstrate a concern for people, both patrons and staff
- create an appealing "we care" environment
- find ideas to adapt creatively

While we recognize that not all nine elements will be present at all times in all public relations projects, we know that those which are appropriate to the project at hand will be evident. In addition, we believe at some point during a year-long PR program, all nine will come into play as they are needed to support the designated objectives.

The practical examples we offered in part I will help practicing librarians understand how to implement these nine basic characteristics for the improvement of their PR efforts. But we also recognize that these characteristics frequently need to be "married" to appropriate skills so that they can be translated into effective action. Therefore, we offered four chapters devoted to those skill areas which may not be in the repertoire of every librarian. While these nitty-gritty chapters will not make you an expert in the area, will not answer every question and solve every problem, they will give you an idea of what is involved in each skill and they will give you a point at which to start.

THE SUBTLE PROCESS

It is our hope that as you observed the intertwining of characteristics and skills, you also were conscious of a distinct and consistent process. In nearly every chapter we encouraged you, sometimes subtly, sometimes stridently, to approach each project, each program, each plan with full consideration of some basic questions. These are the same questions we have learned to answer in journalistic pursuits: who, what, where, why, when, and how. It is somewhat ironic that they are so appropriate to any plan.

These questions are similar to those used in the National School Public Relations Association's (NSPRA) model for planning. NSPRA suggests that the who and the what are, in reality, a brief statement of the project, which indicates what you want to do and to whom you wish to do it. But, we feel there's another who to consider, as in who's to do it? Whether staff members, volunteers, or friends will actually work on the project is immaterial for planning purposes. But a clear understanding of who is going to do what is important.

The where aspect of the project is sometimes a foregone conclusion; most libraries assume they will be the site for any endeavor. But, there are other possible locations, especially if the library is involved in partnerships. And these other locations are sometimes an excellent idea because they place the library in a spot where it is not expected to be, thus giving it an opportunity to meet individuals who have, perhaps, never used its services.

Why we do anything is a question we should constantly ask ourselves. If we don't have a reason, maybe we should do nothing. Purpose gives direction to our efforts and acts as a guidepost to help us get someplace we feel we should go. It is a rallying point for our brains.

When is also an issue we must consider in our planning. When we intend to have a project culminate is critical, for that effects all the other whens in the seemingly endless set of steps we must undertake to accomplish our task. And, finally, the how is our chance to become truly creative. This is the question we ask which unleashes our creative power, power to try something different, to approach a problem in a fashion that's never been used before, or to tackle the unusual.

When we ask ourselves each of these questions and honestly and realistically seek the answers, we find we are establishing a process for tackling any and all public relations endeavors. The sequence in which we consider these questions frequently varies with the exact project being planned, but all the questions should be answered, or the project is doomed to difficulty and even failure.

YOUR OWN BEST AWARD

While we have focused on the Dana award winners, we are not suggesting that these are the only PR efforts worth emulating. Many libraries have won Dana awards for projects other than those we profiled. Many others have never entered the Dana contest but have achieved other recognition.

Some libraries do not seek recognition outside their community. Most of us realize that the best award we can get is the gratification of a job well done. There is no substitute for someone from your community or your public telling you that your library is important, that what you do has meaning or that your service is appreciated and needed. We hear from libraries of all types all over the United States, and even overseas. Consistently, the happiness they have with their efforts is expressed in terms of what someone they serve has said to them, written to them, or told to others about them. That "pride in being" cannot be replaced by any certificate, trophy, or award.

But, we shall continue to review winners of the Dana awards since they are the only national library PR awards for both year-long efforts and special projects. And we shall continue to analyze these award winners, to evaluate their components, and to help librarians adapt their ideas to a local situation.

The importance of public relations to all of us, regardless of library situation or type, cannot be underrated. In 1979 one recommendation of the White House Conference on Libraries was that libraries need to increase their visibility. National concern was expressed about public ignorance of the services and values of the libraries in their communities.

The intervening years have not lessened that concern. In several states action has been undertaken to assist libraries in public relations planning and implementation. Some of this concern has been apparent in the state campaigns which won Dana recognition. Some of the concern is evidenced in guidelines for PR established by the state library agency or the state library association.

For example, in our home state of Illinois, the Public Library Section of the Illinois Library Association, in conjunction with the State Library of Illinois, has created a document entitled *Avenues to Excellence*. The preface clearly indicates that the developers recognize the differences between communities but also are cognizant that the provision of information access and the means necessary to inform the citizenry of that access are common to all libraries.

One section is devoted to evaluation of PR efforts. We believe the introductory statement to this section is noteworthy in that it stresses PR as a by-product of everyone's attitude and activities:

> Public relations refers to many things—but primarily to the communication of a positive image, starting with the first impression people get when they walk in the door. All library staff and board contribute to this image, from the maintenance staff who directly affect that first impression, to the technical services staff, whose cataloging practices can easily give patrons the message that the library is not concerned about the difficulty they have in using the card catalog. Public service staff make the most long lasting impression, however. Studies have shown that even when patrons do not get information they have asked for, they are generally satisfied if the staff are pleasant and try to be helpful. Library policies, from meeting room policies to collection development policies, affect public relations; so does the physical layout of the building, the type of furniture, etc. All of these elements can give one of two messages: "We don't care." or "We do care ... about your information needs, your comfort, your feelings, your convenience."
>
> Publicity is a subset of public relations. It refers to the means used to increase people's awareness of the library and library services.
>
> Poor public relations are as much a deterrent to people's ability and willingness to make use of the world of information available through the library, as are limited hours and physical barriers. In order to fulfill its purpose, as defined in this document, a public library must have an active, ongoing, planned, and coordinated approach to public relations.*

**Avenues to Excellence* is available at no charge from the Publications Unit, Illinois State Library, Springfield, IL 62756.

The document then lists four items required to meet standards in PR. Inservice training, designated staff for PR efforts, a budget for PR, and evaluation of policies on basis of their effect on public relations. Publicity techniques which "are generally accepted as effective" include:

- Television and/or radio exposure (PSAs, talk shows, etc.)
- Newspaper articles, columns, or ads
- Library newsletters
- Talks to community groups and organizations
- Posters, flyers, brochures, bookmarks, etc., advertising library services
- Annual reports attractively packaged and made available to the public
- Encouragement of staff and board involvement in community organizations and activities
- A staff and board "walk through" the library to assess the image it projects
- Attractive and frequently changed exhibits, displays, and bulletin boards

The document grades the library by indicating that three of these activities are worth a "C," five merit a "B" and seven or more deserve an "A." (We find it interesting that all of these activities have been mentioned in the pages of this book, and a few merited special attention in our skills chapters.) We don't mean to imply the Illinois document is better than any other, nor that it is more usable. However, we do think it is evidence of the growing state level interest in good public relations.

One final point should be noted: public relations cannot be a mask for poor library services. Glitz, flash, and gimmicks may catch the public's eye, but they will not substitute for a library program that has been carefully planned and effectively executed. Perhaps these few words best describe what's necessary for great PR: do the right thing; let others know.

Appendix
Libraries Cited

The year cited for each John Cotton Dana award winner is the year the award was presented at the American Library Association annual conference.

INTRODUCTION

Illinois Valley Library System
845 Brenkman Dr.
Pekin, IL 61554

John Cotton Dana Award Winner: 1982

Valerie Wilford
Executive Director
(309) 353-4110

CHAPTER 1

Council for Florida Libraries
1700 E. Las Olas Blvd.
Ft. Lauderdale, FL 33301

John Cotton Dana Award Winner: 1983

Rosemary Jones
(305) 525-6899

Health Science Center Library
University of Texas
7703 Floyd Curl Dr.
San Antonio, TX 78284

John Cotton Dana Award Winner: 1984

Evelyn Olivier
(512) 691-6271

Houston Public Library
500 McKinney Ave.
Houston, TX 77002

John Cotton Dana Award Winner: 1979

Joyce Claypool
Public Information Officer
(713) 236-6964

Salt Lake City Public Library
209 E. Fifth South
Salt Lake City, UT 84111

John Cotton Dana Award Winner: 1983

Sally M. Patrick
Community Relations Director
(801) 363-5733

Somers Public Library
Purdys Rd., Rte. 116
Somers, NY 10589

John Cotton Dana Award Winner: 1980

(914) 232-5717

State Library of Pennsylvania
Box 1601
Harrisburg, PA 17105

John Cotton Dana Award Winner: 1983

Annette McAlister
(717) 783-5746

Tucson Public Library
111 E. Pennington, Box 27470
Tucson, AZ 85726

John Cotton Dana Award Winner: 1981

Kathy Dannreuther
(602) 791-4391

Union Public Schools
Library Media Department
5656 S. 129th East Ave.
Tulsa, OK 74134

John Cotton Dana Award Winner: 1983

Barbara Rather
Media Director
(918) 252-3561

CHAPTER 2

Broward County Main Library
100 S. Andrews Ave.
Ft. Lauderdale, FL 33301

John Cotton Dana Award Winner: 1985

Donna Grubman
(305) 357-7464

Brown County Library
515 Pine St.
Green Bay, WI 54301

John Cotton Dana Award Winner: 1982

Pat LaViolette
(414) 497-6222

Columbus & Franklin County Library
28 S. Hamilton Rd.
Columbus, OH 43213

John Cotton Dana Award Winner: 1983

Pat Groseck
Communications Director
(614) 864-8050

Council for Florida Libraries
1700 E. Las Olas Blvd.
Ft. Lauderdale, FL 33301

John Cotton Dana Award Winner: 1984

Rosemary Jones
(305) 525-6899

Duluth Public Library
Children's Services
520 W. Superior St.
Duluth, MN 55802

John Cotton Dana Award Winner: 1986

Karen W. Richgruber
Librarian
(218) 723-3818

Handley Public Library
Braddock & Piccadilly, Box 58
Winchester, VA 22601

John Cotton Dana Award Winner: 1981

Richard A. Miller
Director
(703) 662-9041

Illinois Valley Library System
845 Brenkman Dr.
Pekin, IL 61554

John Cotton Dana Award Winner: 1982

Valerie Wilford
Executive Director
(309) 353-4110

Kentucky Department for Libraries & Archives
300 Coffeetree Rd., Box 537
Frankfort, KY 40602-0537

John Cotton Dana Award Winner: 1986

Pyddney Jones and Sarah Kelley
(502) 875-7000

Lincoln Library
326 S. 7th
Springfield, IL 62701

John Cotton Dana Award Winner: 1982

Corrine Frisch
Public Relations Director
(217) 753-4900

Los Angeles County Public Library
7400 E. Imperial Highway
Downey, CA 90241

John Cotton Dana Award Winner: 1985

Linda Katsouleas
Volunteer Programs Director
(213) 922-8345

Louisiana State Library
P.O. Box 131
Baton Rouge, LA 70821-0131

John Cotton Dana Award Winner: 1985

Ben Brady
Associate State Librarian
(504) 342-4931

Louisville Free Public Library
4th and York Sts.
Louisville, KY 40203

John Cotton Dana Award Winner: 1982

(502) 584-4154

Mercer County Public Library
109 W. Lexington
Harrodsburg, KY 40330

John Cotton Dana Award Winner: 1983

Mary Jo Thomas
Librarian
(606) 734-3680

Milwaukee Public Library
814 W. Wisconsin Ave.
Milwaukee, WI 53233

John Cotton Dana Award Winner: 1979

R. Gerald Peters
Communications Coordinator
(414) 278-3572

Prince George Public Library
887 Dominion St.
Prince George, BC V2L 5L1
Canada

John Cotton Dana Award Winner: 1985

Joan Jarman
Public Relations Coordinator
(604) 563-9251

Ralph Ellison Library
2000 Northeast 23rd
Oklahoma City, OK 73111

John Cotton Dana Award Winner: 1986

Denyvetta Davis
(405) 424-1437

Reading Public Library
64 Middlesex Ave.
Reading, MA 01867

John Cotton Dana Award Winner: 1985

Susan Flannery
Director
(617) 944-0840

St. Paul Public Library
90 W. Fourth St.
St. Paul, MN 55102

John Cotton Dana Award Winner: 1986

Mark L. Reidell
Public Information Officer
(612) 292-6332

Tucson Public Library
111 E. Pennington, Box 27470
Tucson, AZ 85726

John Cotton Dana Award Winner: 1981

(602) 791-4391

Westbank Community Library
2224 Walsh Tarlton Ln.
Austin, TX 78746

John Cotton Dana Award Winner: 1986

Beth Fox
Director
(512) 327-3045

York County Library System
118 Pleasant Acres Rd.
York, PA 17402

John Cotton Dana Award Winner: 1985

Roberta Greene
(717) 757-9685

CHAPTER 3

Albany Public Library
161 Washington Ave.
Albany, NY 12210

John Cotton Dana Award Winner: 1985

Fran Lewis
Public Relations Director
(518) 449-3380

DeKalb Library System
3560 Kensington Rd.
Decatur, GA 30032

John Cotton Dana Award Winner: 1983

Barbara Loar
Director
(404) 294-6641

Houston Public Library
500 McKinney Ave.
Houston, TX 77002

John Cotton Dana Award Winner: 1984

Joyce Claypool
Public Information Officer
(713) 236-6964

Lincoln Library
326 S. 7th
Springfield, IL 62701

John Cotton Dana Award Winner: 1982

Corrine Frisch
Public Relations Director
(217) 753-4900

Milwaukee Public Library
814 W. Wisconsin Ave.
Milwaukee, WI 53233

John Cotton Dana Award Winner: 1979

R. Gerald Peters
Communications Coordinator
(414) 278-3000

New Hampshire State Library
Library Development
20 Park St.
Concord, NH 03301

John Cotton Dana Award Winner: 1986

Judith A. Kimball
Administrator
(603) 271-2425

Oklahoma Department of Libraries
200 NE 18th St.
Oklahoma City, OK 73105

John Cotton Dana Award Winner: 1985

Marilyn Vesely
Public Information Officer
(405) 521-2502

Prince Georges County Memorial Library System
6532 Adelphi Rd.
Hyattsville, MD 20782

(301) 699-3500

Providence Public Library
150 Empire St.
Providence, RI 02903

John Cotton Dana Award Winner: 1983

Annalee M. Bundy
Director
(401) 521-7722

Riverside-Brookfield High School
Media Services
Ridgewood and Golf Rds.
Riverside, IL 60546

National School Library Media Program of the Year: 1984

Dawn Heller
Media Services Coordinator
(312) 442-7500

Spokane Public Library
W. 906 Main Ave.
Spokane, WA 99201

John Cotton Dana Award Winner: 1985

Lisa Wolfe
Public Information Coordinator
(509) 838-6757

Tucson Public Library
111 E. Pennington, Box 27470
Tucson, AZ 85726

John Cotton Dana Award Winner: 1981

Kathy Dannreuther
(602) 791-4391

CHAPTER 4

Alabama Public Library Service
6030 Monticello Dr.
Montgomery, AL 36130

John Cotton Dana Award Winner: 1981

Blane K. Dessy
Director
(205) 277-7330

Bad Axe Public Library
200 S. Hanselman
Bad Axe, MI 48413

John Cotton Dana Award Winner: 1980, 1982

Marilyn Berry
(517) 269-8538

Brooklyn Public Library
Grand Army Plaza
Brooklyn, NY 11238

John Cotton Dana Award Winner: 1983

Ellen Rudley
Director of Public Information
(212) 780-7758

Chicago Metropolitan Library System
425 N. Michigan Ave.
Chicago, IL 60611

John Cotton Dana Award Winner: 1981

Eva Brown
(312) 269-2900

Clark Air Force Base
FL5251 3rd Combat Support Group
APO San Francisco, CA 96274

John Cotton Dana Award Winner: 1981, 1982

Eleanor Ballou
Librarian

Cornell University
Albert R. Mann Library
Ithaca, NY 14853

John Cotton Dana Award Winner: 1984

Samuel Demas
Head, Collection Development
(607) 255-6919

Dauphin County Library System
101 Walnut St.
Harrisburg, PA 17101

John Cotton Dana Award Winner: 1984

Sarah Ann Long
Director
(717) 234-4961

Eufaula Memorial Library
232 Broadway
Eufaula, OK 74432

John Cotton Dana Award Winner: 1984

Marguerite Bridges Schmitt
Community Librarian
(918) 689-2291

High Street Christian Church
H. A. Valentine Memorial Library
131 S. High St.
Akron, OH 44308

John Cotton Dana Award Winner: 1982

Evelyn Ling
Librarian
(216) 434-1039

Illinois Valley Library System
845 Brenkman Dr.
Pekin, IL 61554

John Cotton Dana Award Winner: 1982

Valerie Wilford
Executive Director
(309) 353-4110

John McIntyre Public Library
220 N. Fifth St.
Zanesville, OH 43701

John Cotton Dana Award Winner: 1984

Peg Harmon
(614) 453-0391

Lutheran Church Library Association
122 W. Franklin Ave.
Minneapolis, MN 55404

John Cotton Dana Award Winner: 1984

Wilma W. Jensen
Executive Director
(612) 870-3623

Nellis Air Force Base
554 CSG/SSL
Nellis Air Force Base, NV 89191

John Cotton Dana Award Winner: 1984

Dorothy Hart
Base Librarian
(702) 643-2280

North Carolina State Library
109 E. Jones St.
Raleigh, NC 27611

John Cotton Dana Award Winner: 1983

Diana Young
(919) 733-2570

Plaza Junior High School
Library
3080 South Lynnhaven Rd.
Virginia Beach, VA 23452

John Cotton Dana Award Winner: 1984

Dorothy Jones
Librarian
(804) 486-1971

St. Louis County Library
1640 S. Lindbergh Blvd.
St. Louis, MO 63131

John Cotton Dana Award Winner: 1984

Jo Ann Rogers
Public Relations Director
(314) 994-3300

Tacoma Public Library
1102 Tacoma Ave., South
Tacoma, WA 98402

John Cotton Dana Award Winner: 1982

Terri Franklin
Community Relations Officer
(206) 591-5688

Ventura County Library Services Agency
Box 771
Ventura, CA 93002

John Cotton Dana Award Winner: 1984

Susan Peterson
Children's Coordinator
(805) 654-2626

CHAPTER 5

Alameda County Library System
3121 Diablo Ave.
Hayward, CA 94545

John Cotton Dana Award Winner: 1986

Bruce Vogel
Coordinator, Children's Services
(415) 670-6270

Broward County Main Library
100 S. Andrews Ave.
Ft. Lauderdale, FL 33301

John Cotton Dana Award Winner: 1985

Donna Grubman
Public Information Officer
(305) 357-7464

Dauphin County Library System
101 Walnut St.
Harrisburg, PA 17101

John Cotton Dana Award Winner: 1985

Sarah Ann Long
Director
(717) 234-4961

Kentucky Department for Libraries & Archives
300 Coffeetree Rd., Box 537
Frankfort, KY 40602-0537

John Cotton Dana Award Winner: 1986

Pyddney Jones and Sarah Kelley
(502) 875-7000

Las Vegas-Clark County Library District
1401 E. Flamingo Rd.
Las Vegas, NV 89119

John Cotton Dana Award Winner: 1984

Iris Fieldman
Community Relations Coordinator
(702) 733-3620

Louisiana State Library
P.O. Box 131
Baton Rouge, LA 70821-0131

John Cotton Dana Award Winner: 1982

Michael McKann
Deputy State Librarian
(504) 342-4922

Martinsburg-Berkeley County Public Library
On the Square
Martinsburg, WV 25401

John Cotton Dana Award Winner: 1982

(304) 267-8933

Needham Free Public Library
1139 Highland Ave.
Needham, MA 02194

John Cotton Dana Award Winner: 1982

(617) 444-0087

Osceola High School
Library Media Center
9751 98th St. North
Seminole, FL 33543

John Cotton Dana Award Winner: 1985

Carlene M. Aborn
Media Specialist
(813) 393-8734

Salt Lake City Public Library
209 E. Fifth South
Salt Lake City, UT 84111

John Cotton Dana Award Winner: 1985

Sally M. Patrick
Community Relations Director
(801) 363-5733

Salt Lake City School District
1575 S. State St.
Salt Lake City, UT 84115

John Cotton Dana Award Winner: 1985

Marian E. Karpisek
(801) 328-7279

Sheridan County Fulmer Public Library
320 N. Brooks
Sheridan, WY 82801

John Cotton Dana Award Winner: 1981

Betty E. Patterson
Branch Librarian
(307) 674-8585

Spokane Public Library
W. 906 Main Ave.
Spokane, WA 99201

John Cotton Dana Award Winner: 1985

Lisa Wolfe
Public Information Coordinator
(509) 838-6757

Tacoma Public Library
1102 Tacoma Ave., South
Tacoma, WA 98402

John Cotton Dana Award Winner: 1982

Terri Franklin
Community Relations Officer
(206) 591-5688

Tucson Public Library
111 E. Pennington, Box 27470
Tucson, AZ 85726

John Cotton Dana Award Winner: 1984

(602) 791-4391

CHAPTER 6

Akron-Summit County Public Library
55 S. Main St.
Akron, OH 44326

John Cotton Dana Award Winner: 1983

Patricia H. Latshaw
Community Relations Director
(216) 762-7621

Alameda County Library System
3121 Diablo Ave.
Hayward, CA 94545

John Cotton Dana Award Winner: 1986

Bruce Vogel
Coordinator, Children's Services
(415) 670-6270

Carlsbad City Library
1250 Elm Ave.
Carlsbad, CA 92008

John Cotton Dana Award Winner: 1986

Pat Hansen
Public Relations Coordinator
(619) 438-5614

Elmer Holmes Bobst Library
New York University
70 Washington Sq. South
New York, NY 10012

John Cotton Dana Award Winner: 1984

Nancy Kramich
(212) 598-2140

Health Science Center Library
University of Texas
7703 Floyd Curl Dr.
San Antonio, TX 78284

John Cotton Dana Award Winner: 1984, 1986

Evelyn Olivier
(512) 691-6271

Houston Public Library
500 McKinney Ave.
Houston, TX 77002

John Cotton Dana Award Winner: 1984

Joyce Claypool
Public Information Officer
(713) 236-6964

King County Library System
300 8th Ave., North
Seattle, WA 98109

John Cotton Dana Award Winner: 1982

Jeanne Thorsen
Public Information Coordinator
(206) 684-6606

J. Paul Leonard Library
San Francisco State University
1630 Holloway Ave.
San Francisco, CA 94132

John Cotton Dana Award Winner: 1982

Victoria Scarlett
Exhibits/Graphics Specialist
(415) 469-1198

Lincoln Library
326 S. 7th
Springfield, IL 62701

John Cotton Dana Award Winner: 1981, 1982

Corrine Frisch
Public Relations Director
(217) 753-4900

McBride Library
3380 ABG/SSL
Keesler Air Force Base, MS 39534

John Cotton Dana Award Winner: 1984

Elizabeth A. DeCoux
Administrative Librarian
(601) 377-2604

Mid-Hudson Library System
103 Market St.
Poughkeepsie, NY 12601

John Cotton Dana Award Winner: 1979

Paul Sanker
Public Relations Director
(914) 471-6060

Reeves Memorial Library
Seton Hill College
Greensburg, PA 15601

John Cotton Dana Award Winner: 1986

Deborah Pawlik
Director
(412) 834-2200

Richmond Public Schools
301 N. 9th St.
Richmond, VA 23219

John Cotton Dana Award Winner: 1982

Beverly Bagan
Media Services Administrator
(804) 780-7691

Santa Ana Public Library
26 Civic Center Plaza
Santa Ana, CA 92702

John Cotton Dana Award Winner: 1983

Rosalind Morris
Public Information Officer
(714) 647-5291

St. Louis Public Library
1301 Olive St.
St. Louis, MO 63103

John Cotton Dana Award Winner: 1982

Marta Hawthorne
Public Relations Officer
(314) 241-2288

State Library of Pennsylvania
Box 1601
Harrisburg, PA 17105

John Cotton Dana Award Winner: 1983

Judith M. Foust
Library Development Director
(717) 787-8007

Timberland Regional Library
415 Airdustrial Way, Southwest
Olympia, WA 98501

John Cotton Dana Award Winner: 1979

Louise Morrison
Director
(206) 943-5001

Travis Air Force Base
Library
60 ABG/SSL
Travis Air Force Base, CA 94535

John Cotton Dana Award Winner: 1983

Nina Jacobs
Librarian
(707) 438-5254

University of California, Irvine Library
Library Publications
Box 19557
Irvine, CA 92713

John Cotton Dana Award Winner: 1985

Joan Ariel
(714) 856-4970

CHAPTER 7

Alabama Public Library Service
6030 Monticello Dr.
Montgomery, AL 36130

John Cotton Dana Award Winner: 1981

Blane K. Dessy
(205) 277-7330

Alameda County Library System
3121 Diablo Ave.
Hayward, CA 94545

John Cotton Dana Award Winner: 1985

Judy Flum
Coordinator of Public Relations
(415) 670-6270

Bad Axe Public Library
200 S. Hanselman
Bad Axe, MI 48413

John Cotton Dana Award Winner: 1982

Marilyn Berry
(517) 269-8538

Brown County Library
515 Pine St.
Green Bay, WI 54301

John Cotton Dana Award Winner: 1980, 1986

Pat LaViolette
(414) 497-6222

Clark Air Force Base
FL5251 3rd Combat Support Group
APO San Francisco, CA 96274

John Cotton Dana Award Winner: 1981

Eleanor Ballou
Librarian

Dauphin County Library System
101 Walnut St.
Harrisburg, PA 17101

John Cotton Dana Award Winner: 1984

Sarah Ann Long
Director
(717) 234-4961

Genesee District Library
G-4195 W. Pasadena Ave.
Flint, MI 48504

John Cotton Dana Award Winner: 1983

Marian Gamble
Director
(313) 732-0110

Health Science Center Library
University of Texas
7703 Floyd Curl Dr.
San Antonio, TX 78284

John Cotton Dana Award Winner: 1984

Evelyn Olivier
(512) 691-6271

Houston Public Library
500 McKinney Ave.
Houston, TX 77002

John Cotton Dana Award Winner: 1979, 1984

Joyce Claypool
Public Information Officer
(713) 236-6964

Laurel Bay School Libraries
Marine Corps Dependents' School
Laurel Bay, SC 29902

John Cotton Dana Award Winner: 1981

Cecile Dorr
Program Developer
(803) 846-6112

Louisville Free Public Library
Community Relations
4th and York Sts.
Louisville, KY 40203

John Cotton Dana Award Winner: 1983

Robert Gottlieb
(502) 584-4154

Milwaukee Public Library
814 W. Wisconsin Ave.
Milwaukee, WI 53233

John Cotton Dana Award Winner: 1979

R. Gerald Peters
Communications Coordinator
(414) 278-3572

Nellis Air Force Base
554 CSG/SSL
Nellis Air Force Base, NV 89191

John Cotton Dana Award Winner: 1984

Dorothy Hart
Base Librarian
(702) 643-2280

Oklahoma Department of Libraries
200 NE 18th St.
Oklahoma City, OK 73105

John Cotton Dana Award Winner: 1984

Marilyn Vesely
Public Information Officer
(405) 521-2502

Travis Air Force Base
Library
60 ABG/SSL
Travis Air Force Base, CA 94535

John Cotton Dana Award Winner: 1983

Nina Jacobs
Librarian
(707) 438-5254

Ventura County Library Services Agency
Box 771
Ventura, CA 93002

John Cotton Dana Award Winner: 1984

Susan Peterson
Children's Coordinator
(805) 654-2626

Westfield High School
550 Dorian Rd.
Westfield, NJ 07090

John Cotton Dana Award Winner: 1980

Dawn S. Ganss
Head Librarian
(201) 789-4522

CHAPTER 8

Chicago Public Library
425 N. Michigan Ave.
Chicago, IL 60611

John Cotton Dana Award Winner: 1981

Liz Huntoon
Director of Children's Services
(312) 269-2885

Columbus & Franklin County Library
28 S. Hamilton Rd.
Columbus, OH 43213

John Cotton Dana Award Winner: 1983

Pat Groseck
Communications Director
(614) 864-8050

Council for Florida Libraries
1700 E. Las Olas Blvd.
Ft. Lauderdale, FL 33301

John Cotton Dana Award Winner: 1983

Rosemary Jones
(305) 525-6899

Elk Grove Village Public Library
1 Morrison Blvd.
Elk Grove Village, IL 60007

John Cotton Dana Award Winner: 1983

Jill E. Derkits
Art Director
(312) 439-0447

Handley Public Library
Braddock & Piccadilly, Box 58
Winchester, VA 22601

John Cotton Dana Award Winner: 1981

Richard A. Miller
Director
(703) 662-9041

Martinsburg-Berkeley County Public Library
On the Square
Martinsburg, WV 25401

John Cotton Dana Award Winner: 1982

Diana S. Abshire
(304) 267-8933

Mobile Public Library
701 Government St.
Mobile, AL 36602

John Cotton Dana Award Winner: 1979

Christina Bowersox
Information Services Officer
(205) 438-7097

National Geographic Society Library
17th & M Sts., Northwest
Washington, DC 20036

John Cotton Dana Award Winner: 1985

Susan Canby
(202) 857-7787

Nicholson Memorial Library System
625 Austin St.
Garland, TX 75040

John Cotton Dana Award Winner: 1983

Kathryn S. Connell
Associate Director
(214) 494-7187

Tacoma Public Library
1102 Tacoma Ave., South
Tacoma, WA 98402

John Cotton Dana Award Winner: 1982

Terri Franklin
Community Relations Officer
(206) 591-5688

Travis Air Force Base
Library
60 ABG/SSL
Travis Air Force Base, CA 94535

John Cotton Dana Award Winner: 1983

Nina Jacobs
Librarian
(707) 438-5254

(**Note:** No libraries are cited in chapters 9 and 10.)

CHAPTER 11

Denver Public Library
1357 Broadway
Denver, CO 80203

Suzanne Walters
Director of Marketing
(303) 571-2366

Edmonton Public Library
7 Sir Winston Churchill Sq.
Edmonton, AB, T5J 2V4
Canada

(403) 423-2331

Elk Grove Village Public Library
1 Morrison Blvd.
Elk Grove Village, IL 60007

Jill E. Derkits
Art Director
(312) 439-0447

Fairfax County Library
5502 Port Royal Rd.
Springfield, VA 22151

Sam Clay
Director
(703) 321-9810

Memphis-Shelby County Library & Information Center
Media Relations Department
1850 Peabody Ave.
Memphis, TN 38104

Ellen H. Baer
Public Relations Officer
(901) 725-8800

Prince Georges County Memorial Library System
6532 Adelphi Rd.
Hyattsville, MD 20782

Julia Losinski
(301) 699-3500

Providence Public Library
150 Empire St.
Providence, RI 02903

Annalee M. Bundy
Director
(401) 521-7722

Tulsa City-County Library
400 Civic Center
Tulsa, OK 74103

Cathy Audley
Head of Public Relations
(918) 592-7897

Washington Middle School
Alschuler & Winifred
Aurora, IL 60506

Mary Hauge
Librarian
(312) 844-4483

(**Note:** No libraries are cited in chapter 12.)

Index